LIBRARY
BOOK
Writers on Libraries

 Publication of *Library Book* funded by
Friends of the Santa Barbara Public Library
in support of the Santa Barbara Public Library

Library Book

Writers on Libraries:

A Celebration of the 100th Anniversary of the Santa Barbara Central Library

Edited by Steven Gilbar

Foreword by T. C. Boyle

Prefaces by Jessica Cadiente and Milton Hess

Afterword by Katie Szopa

Library Director, Mrs. Frances Burns Linn, breaks ground in 1916 to build the Central Library, which is still a vibrant part of our community one hundred years later.

Contents

Foreword
T. C. Boyle

I WAS raised in a working-class household in Peekskill, New York. My father spent his teenage years in an orphanage and was educated to the eighth grade only. My mother graduated high school as salutatorian of her class, but did not have the financial means to go to college, a lifelong regret of hers. Books were expensive and we did not have a library at home, though I remember my mother making the sacrifice to buy me a set of Children's Classics and to read aloud to me out of love and the desire for me to have what she couldn't, but essentially my education—and love of books—would not have been possible without the Peekskill Public Library and the school libraries at Toddville Elementary and Lakeland High. I was a hyperactive kid, outdoors most of the time, playing sports, running wild, but for me the libraries were where I could get cozy, where I could be my own boss, read anything I liked, stay as long as I liked, get comfortable, feel comfortable, and mold my own kind of church out of the experience. For this—and for the civic pride and deep appreciation of the foundational necessity of educating our citizens that our libraries represented and continue to represent—I am eternally grateful. Needless to say, I would not have had the chance to go on to higher education and to become a writer and professor if it were otherwise.

In my adult life, I have made extensive use of the libraries of both USC and UCSB as well as our own public library system here in Santa Barbara. Many of my twenty-seven books have historical settings and require research, both on-line and in the tried-and-true (and never-to-be-superseded) form of the book-in-hand. I like the book-in-hand. I like to feel it, hold it, make notes from it, keep it beside me to refer to as I spin off into the delirium of the cascading stories I am creating. Which is why this anthology is so very appealing to me. What strikes me most about the narratives Steve Gilbar has collected here is the affirmative notion that so many writers and readers share this same passion for the public libraries that are the very essence of our democracy. Each writer has a story and each writer's story begins with a book. We are so very different and yet so very much alike. Common humanity. Literature. Words on a page. They are my passion and my life, and as you will see in the following selections, they are equally the lives of the writers we have all learned so much from. Truly, we are blessed.

Prefaces
Jessica Cadiente
Director, Santa Barbara Public Library System

ON AUGUST 27, 1917, the Santa Barbara Public Library opened its doors with the mission of providing free access to information, cultural activities, and educational and recreational reading materials to the community. This was a time of information scarcity; today's connected world is one of information overload. The spread of new technologies has touched every aspect of our lives, creating new opportunities and challenges. The internet is now the gateway for accessing informational, career, financial, educational, healthcare, and government resources. This new world requires essential skills. Access to digital resources and digital literacy skills are now required for full participation in today's society. In 2016, Santa Barbara libraries provided nearly 300,000 computer sessions and over 1,000 one-to-one computer coaching sessions. The library also started loaning personal Wi-Fi hotspots so library users can check out the internet. Economic, educational, civic, and social opportunities are tied to a whole new set of knowledge and skills, skills that were nonexistent even a generation ago. People who do not have access to this information or do not have these skills are often left behind. The new economy is driven by knowledge and innovation and technology, and education in these areas is central to performance and prosperity.

Our public libraries will be at the center of these changes. We are one of the most trusted institutions—a platform for education, creation, and innovation—and a conduit for connecting the needs of our users to the community. Every day we are tackling social inequalities by providing access to online information and supporting all forms of literacy. The library is a safe place for our children after school, and as a key strand in the social safety net, we provide a lifeline to jobs, educational opportunities, and community resources. The 21st century public library reflects a shift away from building collections to building communities. The community is at the center of our mission and the library is working to strengthen our community by inspiring and cultivating learning.

Today the library is the anchor to economic development, provides a connecting place, champions all literacies, serves as a civic resource, and is the community learning platform. Over the course of the next one hundred years, the world will continue to change, and technology will continue to drive these changes, but the library's mission to educate, captivate, and connect will remain.

Milton Hess
Chair, Santa Barbara Library Board

FOR MOST of the last one hundred years the Central Library has existed as a traditional book repository. When I applied to City Council for appointment to the Library Board, my goal was to participate in the evolution of the Library from its traditional function to something else. But what else? I have fond memories of the library in my hometown of Baltimore as a place where I became an avid reader. It was, however, very much just a place to check out books and, in high school, do research for papers. Later in life I continued to view the library as a storehouse for books.

In January 2010 that started to change. I became a volunteer computer coach at the Santa Barbara Public Library and started to see the library from a different perspective—from the inside. Although I didn't think of it in those terms, I already was seeing evolution happening.

Certainly, online technology was becoming a prominent element of the library's offerings. This trend manifested in the reduced demand for reference help, in the increased demand for computer workstations, and in the variety of online delivery tools for books, magazines and other resources.

But something else was happening. The library was increasingly becoming the public square for the community, a place where residents of all ages can come together for social, literary, musical, artistic, political and related pursuits.

Library Director Jessica Cadiente has spearheaded enhancements to the interior of the Central Library that make it a brighter, more inviting space for residents while preserving the historic character of the building. The space is being revitalized for the anticipated future we wish and hope for. What it will be when the bicentennial is celebrated is almost impossible to imagine.

Whereas these initiatives represent physical elements of the public square, the concept envisions far more in terms of outreach to the community. This outreach has been accelerated with diverse, rich programs that draw residents to the library for events and activities.

Technology and realigned responsibilities have been introduced to enable the librarians to provide more personal support to the public. As a result the library now offers a variety of programs for adults and children of all ages to encourage reading, teach new skills, and create a direct, positive effect on people's lives.

The Library is no longer simply a building where people go to borrow books. It is evolving to a place where children and adults of all ages can experience, enjoy and learn from a variety of programs. It is becoming the public square for our community

Editor's Introduction
Steven Gilbar

THIS ANTHOLOGY could not have come into being without the support of the Friends of the Santa Barbara Public Library which enthusiastically volunteered to underwrite the costs of the book and the many writers who took the time to write original pieces out of the goodness of their hearts and their appreciation of the role libraries have played in their lives. Most writers were at one time serious library consumers. That stereotype of the bookish kid who grows up to be an author holds some truth. Thus many of the pieces here are about the future writer as a shy child enchanted by the magic of the public library. This is illustrated in Ray Bradbury's short story, "Exchange," the only work of fiction in the anthology. The childhood library remembrances by Fannie Flagg, Betty Fussell, and Sue Grafton are three further examples of the theme

Almost all of the contributors have some Santa Barbara connection: they were raised there, they live or did live there, the city has a special place in their heart, or their books are much loved by Santa Barbara readers. Those that spent their childhood there include Gretel Ehrlich, Leon Litwack, and Dean Stewart. Others, such as Brian Fagan, Shirley Geok-Lin Lim, and John Ridland, had come there to teach at UC Santa Barbara. All five of the living Santa Barbara Poets Laureate contributed pieces. Not to be too parochial, I have included previously published pieces by non-Santa Barbara writers who have interesting things to say about libraries. Among these are Neil Gaiman, Eva Hoffman, and Ursula K. LeGuin, to whom I am grateful for their permission to include their essays.

On a personal note, I am deeply indebted to the resources, both paper and human, of the Central Library. The first book I did, *The Book Book*, published in 1981, acknowledges at the very beginning: "I wish to thank the patient and helpful staff of the Santa Barbara Public Library for their assistance." In the ensuing thirty-five years I have continued to be grateful to the staff for its professionalism and courtesy. For this anthology I am particularly indebted to Beverly Schwartzberg, Library Services Coordinator and Local Hero; for her scrutinous copyediting; to Susan Gulbransen for her assistance in rounding up contributing authors and encouragement for this project; and to T. C. Boyle for generously agreeing to write the Foreword.

Original Anacapa Street entrance

Kathryn J. Abajian
A Quiet Privacy

A California native, the author moved to Santa Barbara from the Bay Area in 2016, after teaching writing and literature at the high school and college levels for thirty years. Her book, First Sight of the Desert, *is about discovering the art of the early feminist artist Ella Peacock. Abajian leads writing workshops in Santa Barbara and Italy. To learn more about her see www.HeartofMemoir.com.*

IN CLOSE to a dream state, I walk through the stacks, running my finger along the spines of books shelved for eight year olds. I read only the titles at my eye level, occasionally stopping if a word catches my interest. I find my nickname in a title, *Kathy's Trip to New York*, and add it to my small armful of books, each chosen by chance. My mother and I will return to our branch library the same day two weeks later to replenish our allotments—five books for her and three for me.

I regret that I didn't keep a running list of every book I'd read from the time I began reading—along with other lists, journals and collections of ephemera that I've treasured solely in my head for seventy years. I recognized when I was nine that cartoons of men (always men) stranded on deserted islands were a cartoon trope I could anticipate. I didn't know the word "trope," but sensed the concept. And every time I encountered a cartoon in that setting, I felt the need to preserve the cartoon and at the same time felt it was already too late to start. I'd love to have such a scrapbook now—bursting with revelatory details of cultural shifts over decades reflected by lonely, wistful men stranded in oceans of solitude.

The city bus stopped in front of the Alhambra Public Library in our suburb just east of Los Angeles. The main library intimidated me with its looming Ionic columns and grand entrance—wide and shallow marble stairs descending to a solemn interior with the librarian's desk at the base of the steps. She glanced over her glasses this particular Saturday and, as usual, frightened me. I was there to get a particular book, one that a classmate had "reported" on in my fourth grade classroom. She had told the class about a poor boy who dreamed of being a prince and schemed a way to disguise himself to get what he wanted. I was intrigued and, figured that book by Mark Twain had to be in the big library. As it turned out, I went to the library weekly for a month; every time, the librarian reported, "No it's already taken out!" I have no idea now whether or not there was a system to reserve books then; if there was I had no knowledge of such a thing, no encouragement to use it. I'm dismayed now at my passivity at that age, at how little I expected from others, and for myself.

A few years later I was alone, wandering deep in the stacks of the main library's lower floor when I found *Forever Amber*. It was reportedly, this time in whispers among some of the eighth grade girls, a book that held secrets of how romance, and more, worked. I read a few pages but soon lost interest in its 17th century language and setting. Much later I learned the book, written the year I was born, had been banned for its sexual content that contained "at least ten descriptions of women undressing in front of men." (Nothing in the review commented on the number of men seducing the women into disrobing.)

So I read on—indiscriminately, without any advice, lists, or considered recommendations. I came across *The Harder They Fall* in the library stacks, and, intrigued by the title (and its meaning), acquired an unlikely fascination with prize fighting. That interest earned me two tickets to see Ingemar Johansson fight Floyd Patterson, a gift from my father after he saw me devouring my brother's *Sports Illustrated* photo spread featuring the Swedish fighter's swimsuit style.

So I grew up finding my own reading way in an era without library reading circles, book clubs or online reading forums, and despite the current accessibility, I've never felt the draw. I think my mind and reading habits are too random and unruly to contain the organization that sort of commitment requires. Either that, or it's too much like a busman's holiday after years in the managing classroom literature discussions.

It's no secret that people drawn to reading are often fond of solitude. I can find it publicly in quiet libraries or those noisy with coffee shops, in actual coffee shops where silent readers and writers line up in rows behind their laptops, in parks and on buses and sitting most consolingly on a low chair close to the Pacific's warm breezes and rhythmic waves.

As I'm drawn to broad swaths of solitude and greedy for the indulgence of quiet privacy, I have to remind myself of the value of in-person social connection, an important chiaroscuro of balance within that juxtaposition.

Cynthia Anderson
A Home for Poetry

In 1982 Cynthia Anderson moved to Santa Barbara, where she resided for over twenty-five years and was active in the local poetry scene, serving as co-ordinator of a reading series at the Santa Barbara Botanic Gardens and as an organizer of the Santa Barbara Poetry Festival. She co-founded (with David Oliveira) the Mille Grazie Press. She is the author of six poetry collections. In 2008 she moved to the high desert near Joshua Tree National Park.

THROUGHOUT MY Connecticut childhood, thanks to my book-loving parents, visiting the library was as natural as breathing. My first card was from the Avon Public Library—a tiny cottage straight out of a fairytale—followed by the Simsbury Free Library, a yellow, two-story Colonial Revival edifice next to a historic graveyard brimming with centuries-dead Puritans. To me these libraries were wondrous worlds both inside and out, imbued with the presence of the past. I immersed myself in everything they had to offer and emerged a lifelong bookworm.

During my first year in college, at the University of Pennsylvania in Philadelphia, my refuge and favorite place to study was the art library—a serene, modernist structure that offered absolute quiet in the midst of the bustling campus and city. And when I moved to Ojai, California, the Carleton Winslow-designed, Spanish hacienda-style library became my refuge, as well as the place where I gave my first poetry reading.

So it seemed inevitable that when I arrived in Santa Barbara in 1982, to study poetry at UCSB's College of Creative Studies, the commodious main branch of the Santa Barbara Public Library—another lovely Carleton Winslow building—became one of my favorite haunts, and remained so for years to come.

The poetry section exerted a magnetic pull. I spent untold hours in that far corner of the second floor, browsing the shelves to find names I didn't know before, and then reading, reading, and reading some more. My education was

rounded, furthered, and honed by those hours of discovery. Apparently some-
one had gone to great trouble to ensure that the poetry section was exceptional.
From Neruda to Pound, Akhmatova to Levertov, I harvested that bounty and
reaped the rewards.

Then there were the reference librarians. Gods and goddesses of the age be-
fore Google! Whatever questions I had on any subject, I went to them eagerly,
standing in line to await my audience with the oracle. They always delivered,
cheerfully and skillfully diving into their treasure troves to bring up pearls of
wisdom. Most people I knew had no idea their services existed, so I sang their
praises to anyone who would listen. And while it was possible to talk to them
by phone, I found it much more satisfying to visit them in person. The human
connection—for me, that's what the library was about.

Finally, there was the Faulkner Gallery and the important role it played in
the local poetry community. Many readings took place there in the 1980s and
early 1990s. Some were connected with poetry festivals, and others were unique
events for special occasions. Invariably, these readings would run overtime—
suddenly, it would be 5 pm, and the stalwart librarians would stay late once
more so that the last readers could finish and we could get the chairs put away.

One flyer I still have is especially worth noting—an event titled "Portrait of
a Woman in Poetry," held May 21, 1989 and sponsored by the Women's Com-
munity Center. Over 30 women poets read that day in the Faulkner Gallery.
Organizers included Kate Silsbury, Annabel Abbott Wilson, and Mary Lou
Robinson. Four *grande dames* of the poetry community were dubbed laureates
and honored: Julia Bates, Julia Cunningham, Katy Peake, and Kit Tremaine. If
those women were here now, I can only imagine that they would be speaking
truth to power.

I recall the Santa Barbara poetry community back then as being large,
open-hearted, and welcoming to poets of all levels of ability. I owe a debt of
gratitude to a number of poets for supporting and encouraging me on my
path—among them, Abdal-Hayy Moore, Sojourner Kincaid Rolle, Perie Longo,
Abigail Albrecht (Brandt), Katharine J. Ingram, Maia, Carla Martinez (Riedel),
Bettina Barrett, Lee Davis, Edwin Shaw, Idee Levitan, and Randolph Maxted.
I made close and valued friendships during those years, with poets who remain
my friends today. The library helped nurture us all.

Though I moved away from Santa Barbara in 2008, my connection with the library was destined to continue. In a nod to the ghosts of poetry readings past, Enid Osborn and I chose the Faulkner Gallery in 2011 for the launch of an anthology we co-edited—*A Bird Black as the Sun:* California Poets on Crows and Ravens. As in the days of old, the gallery was packed with poets and poetry lovers. That energy is what I will always remember about the Santa Barbara Public Library—a place designed, cared for, and cherished so that the entire community, including poets, might thrive.

Reading before the fireplace, 1950s

Ellen K. Anderson
Library Lover

Author of twelve full-length and six one-act produced plays, Anderson has been an integral part of Santa Barbara's arts scene for decades, not just writing plays, but helping found Access Theatre, leading the art collaborative I.V. Arts and heading Dramatic Women.

I HAVE a lover in Greenwich Village. She's histrionically Gothic, yet undeniably gorgeous, and has known too many women before me. She adorns the corner of West Tenth and Sixth Avenue, and although solidly built, her jeweled spires rise to pierce the heaven over lower Manhattan.

I didn't realize I was in an unfathomable relationship with NYC's Jefferson Market Library until a friend, who lives in the Village, snuck in and took a picture of eight workers at eight laptops plugged into a long, electrified library table. They sat in the Adult Reading Room, a chamber that began its stained-glass life as the main courtroom of the Jefferson Market magistrate. But, why was she sending me a photo of a jumble of cords and computers bathed in ethereal light? She knew I loved her neighborhood library, everyone loves a beauty, but why this photo? Then I recognized my tense, hunched, chubby—yet ecstatic self. *National Geographic* could not have published a more believable shot of a writer in her natural habitat. Sometimes, making something out of nothing (writing) feels like it will hunt you down and kill you, but this little picture seemed proof that no harm could come to me in this library. After all, I was camouflaged by architecture that conjured fairytale castles!

Although I'd worked on several plays in the magical "Old Jeff," our affair became complicated while researching the 1911 Triangle Shirtwaist Fire for "Shirtwaist: A musical ghost story." Discovering that I was writing in the former courtroom where garment workers who struck for better working conditions, prior to the fire, had been tried and sentenced drew me closer to the stories of the women who would eventually perish in the disaster. In an attempt to shame the strikers and their middle-class supporters, they were hauled into Night Court, widely known for trying accused prostitutes. Sadly, my favorite arched brick alcoves in the basement Reference Room turned out to be holding cells for strikers awaiting trial. My sanctuary had a sad past, as many old lovers do. The play opened at the Lower East Side Tenement Museum one wickedly cold winter. Every March 25th, the date of the tragedy, a memorial is held on the sidewalk at the site of the fire. Today, NYU houses their chemistry department in the very same building. On the day of the memorial the NYC Fire Department brings a ladder truck and solemnly raises it to the sixth floor demonstrating that in 1911 the ladders were too short to reach girls stranded on the higher factory floors. Modern labor unions gather, civic leaders speak, and during this particular year our actresses, who were currently portraying victims from the fire, were asked to read the names of those who had actually perished. A bell tolls, a name is read, a bell tolls, a name is read. Total dead 146—most young immigrant women. Our actresses were not too cold to cry.

I made it to the end of the ceremony, but was dizzy from looking up at the 8th-floor window ledges where the girls had fled the fire, fled to the windows because they had no other choice, and jumped. One newspaper called it, "The day girls fell like rain." I imagined my sister, my daughter, my niece on that ledge and knew I was going to be sick. I ran for the "Old Jeff" just a few blocks away, entered the overheated vestibule and remembered that this library was lacking one critical item. There were no public restrooms. So, instead of puking, I put my head down on a library table and sobbed. No one looked up. No librarian approached. It was no secret that this pile of Victoriana had seen pain more wrenching than my own.

Before I collapsed in sleep seated between a gentlemanly street person sketching in the margins of the *Science Times* and a woman reading from a braille manuscript, I wondered—was I in the arms of my lover, or my mother? Mother to many writers. Mother to many stories. Mother of all libraries.

Isaac Babel
The Public Library

This character sketch, one of the Russian writer's earliest works, first appeared in a St. Petersburg newspaper in 1916, the year that construction was started on the Santa Barbara Central Library, a world away. Babel (1894-1940) is widely acknowledged to be one of the great masters of twentieth-century literature.

ONE FEELS right away that this is the kingdom of books. People working at the library commune with books, with the life reflected in them, and so become almost reflections of real-life human beings. Even the cloakroom attendants— not brown-haired, not blond, but something in between—are mysteriously quiet, filled with contemplative composure.

In the reading room are the more elevated staff members, the librarians. Some, the "conspicuous ones," possess some starkly pronounced physical defect. One has twisted fingers, another has a head that lolled to the side and stayed there. They are badly dressed, and emaciated in the extreme. They look as if they are fanatically possessed by an idea unknown to the world. Gogol would have described them well!

The "inconspicuous" librarians show the beginnings of bald patches, wear clean gray suits, have a certain candor in their eyes, and a painful slowness in their movements. They are forever chewing something, moving their jaws, even though they have nothing in their mouths. They talk in a practiced whisper. In short, they have been ruined by books, by being forbidden from enjoying a throaty yawn.

Now that our country is at war, the public has changed. There are fewer students. There are very few students. Once in a blue moon you might see a student painlessly perishing in a corner. He's a "white-ticketer," exempt from the service.

He wears a pince-nez and has a delicate limp. But then there is also the student on state scholarship. This student is pudgy, with a drooping mustache, tired of life, a man prone to contemplation: he reads a bit, thinks about something a bit, studies the patterns on the lampshades, and nods off over a book. He has to finish his studies, join the army, but—why hurry? Everything in good time.

Near the librarians' desk sits a large, broad-chested woman in a gray blouse reading with rapturous interest. She is one of those people who suddenly speaks with unexpected loudness in the library, candidly and ecstatically overwhelmed by a passage in a book, and who, filled with delight, begins discussing it with her neighbors. She is reading because she is trying to find out how to make soap at home. She is about forty-five years old. Is she sane? Quite a few people have asked themselves that.

There is one more typical library habitué: the thin little colonel in a loose jacket, wide pants, and extremely well-polished boots. He has tiny feet. His whiskers are the color of cigar ash. He smears them with a wax that gives them a whole spectrum of dark gray shades. In his day he was so devoid of talent that he didn't manage to work his way up to the rank of colonel so that he could retire a major general. Since his retirement he ceaselessly pesters the gardener, the maid, and his grandson. At the age of seventy-three he has taken it into his head to write a history of his regiment.

He writes. He is surrounded by piles of books. He is the librarians' favorite. He greets them with exquisite civility. He no longer gets on his family's nerves. The maid gladly polishes his boots to a maximal shine.

Many more people of every kind come to the public library. More than one could describe. There is also the tattered reader who does nothing but write a luxuriant monograph on ballet. His face: a tragic edition of Hauptmann's. His body: insignificant.

There are, of course, also bureaucrats riffling through piles of *The Russian Invalid* and the *Government Herald*. There are the young provincials, ablaze as they read.

It is evening. The reading room grows dark. The immobile figures sitting at the tables are a mix of fatigue, thirst for knowledge, ambition.

Outside the wide windows soft snow is drifting. Nearby, on the Nevsky Prospekt, life is blossoming. Far away, in the Carpathian Mountains, blood is flowing.

Bob Bason
I Always Wanted to Be a Librarian

Bob Bason was variously a Methodist minister, a missionary in Africa, an assistant chancellor at UCSB, a vice president for national Planned Parenthood in New York, a book publisher and a consultant to almost 200 charities. But, he never got to be a real librarian

SHE WAS an important person in my life, so I wish I could remember exactly what she looked like. She may have been young and gracious and beautiful, or she may have been old and doughty, with a hair bun. It was so long ago, at that little branch library on Hull Avenue in Des Moines, Iowa, that I just can't remember. So, all I can do is bless her—that beautiful, old, gracious, dowdy, young librarian with a hair bun—for she started me on a life with books. She also started me wanting to be a librarian.

My parents had not had access to much education in their early lives. My mother in South Dakota was allowed to go through fourth grade, and my dad in rural Iowa had made it through eighth. In any case, there were no books in our house. It strikes me now that they were probably so financially strapped that buying books would have been beyond imagination. But my mother, especially, had been bitten by that mid-twentieth century bug of improvement. Her kids were not only going to *read*; they were going to go to college. They were going to have a better life.

So, in those earliest days, my mother would walk with me to the library and I was allowed three books for the week. I suppose they were picture books, for I think I can remember a rabbit and a kangaroo and a sailing ship. Later, when I was allowed to walk by myself to Jonathan Cattell Elementary School, I could alter my path home and go by the library to pick up more books. It was always an agony to select the five I wanted, the maximum allowable by then. I would take them up to the desk and the librarian (oh, why can't I remember what she looked like?) would take my library card out of the file and check out the books for me, stamping the little card with the date stamp and putting it in the pocket at the back. I thought that it seemed like the best job in the world. I wanted to be a librarian.

It's hackneyed and trite to say that it opened the world to me. But it did. As a little red-headed, "four-eyed" (I wore glasses from age 9 on), skinny boy in Iowa, I still got to climb the ladder to that wonderful treehouse in the South Seas with the Swiss Family Robinson. I rode a camel in the Arabian desert with my pal, T. E. Lawrence. I fought the British in Concord and panned for gold in Sacramento. Ah, the traveling I did.

When I got to graduate school, books took ahold of me in a different way. One of my professors had a personal library of 10,000 books. I was stunned at the concept. You could get your own books—and keep them. Amazing. I wrote away to Blackwell's in London and made my first order. When they arrived, I was overwhelmed at first with their beauty, the new-book smell, an almost un-believable realization that these were mine—and then I immediately arranged them carefully, in alphabetical order by the author's last name. I was off and running. Cataloguing was my first small step toward being a librarian.

At a long-gone used bookstore in Santa Barbara, I purchased for $3 my first book signed by the author, Christopher Morley. That purchase—and the whole new idea of owning SIGNED books—took me off on what became a life-long search and passion. I haunted used bookstores across the country and even throughout England, always trying to get them to let me into the back room where all the good stuff was kept, the unidentified T. S. Eliot and the misfiled C. S. Lewis. When the selling of used books was taken over by computerized sites, I voraciously surfed the web for the missing volume to fill out my signed John Updike collection or the first edition of T. C. Boyle's first book. My own library was growing with lightning speed, but it was also causing a significant space problem.

My nearly complete collection of the works of Christopher Morley was the first to go—to Special Collections at the UCSB Library. Soon after, I had to give up on collecting signed first editions of Santa Barbara authors. It turned out that everyone in Santa Barbara was writing a book and there was no way I was going to get ahead of that game. But, in the process of doing that collection, I stumbled across some beautifully printed works by Capra Press, a small publishing company right in Santa Barbara, still owned by the founder Noel Young. Because of Noel's ill health, the press was for sale. There was no question what I had to do—and the day that I held the first book that I had published in my hands, I was absolutely the happiest man in the world. I had become a book publisher. I was not yet a librarian, but I was getting closer.

As I write these lines of remembrance at age 78, I am surrounded by four walls of precious books, all signed by the author, all in fine condition in dust jacket, all catalogued in my computer, all shelved in absolute order from floor to ceiling. There are well over 10,000 now. I may be having trouble remembering my cousin's name in Oskaloosa, but I know where every single book is. I also know the bookstore where I bought it and how much it cost.

And, suddenly, I am struck by the fact that, at this end of my life, I have realized my boyhood dream. I am a librarian—and I am happy.

Mashey Bernstein
Stand to Attention and Tell Me What You Read:
Why We Need Public Libraries

Recently retired from UCSB where he taught in the Writing Program since 1991, Bernstein holds a PhD from UCSB for his work on Norman Mailer. He holds a Simon Rockower Award for Excellence in Jewish Journalism.

IN 2006, I attended with a friend, Stephen, the world premiere of the play *Nothing But the Truth* at the Mark Taper Forum in downtown Los Angeles. Written by South African playwright and author John Kani, it told the story of two brothers and their different reactions to apartheid. The play starred Kani himself in one of the leading roles. After the performance Stephen and I stayed downtown to have a meal and as we strolled back to our car, I noticed Kani on the curb waiting for the lights to change. I immediately went over to him and told him how much I had enjoyed the play and learned from it and then in a moment of inspiration, I said, "It seems some of this must have been based on real life." "Indeed," he answered, and proceeded to tell us the germ of the play.

Many years before, during apartheid, young Black South African children were not allowed access to public libraries. Being poor, they also could not afford to buy books. However, the janitor of one of the libraries would take the torn or ratty books thrown away by the authorities and bring them to the children. "But," said Kani, "he had several rules before you could get a book: first, you could not mark the book and had to return it in the shape you got it in. Secondly," and here Kani stood to attention—he was an actor after all—and told us the *pièce de résistance*. "As you handed back the book, you had to tell the janitor the plot of the novel and only then would you get another book to read." It was a compelling performance and one seared into my memory.

The next day, Stephen, who was also, as it turns out, a librarian, came to me with a book that he had bought years before and had originally, it seemed, come from a library. "When I was down South I went to a book seller and found this." And he opened the flap to show me what was stamped there: "For Coloreds Only." I am not sure what this meant. Did it mean that only certain books were acceptable for Black readers? Or that no White person would touch a book handled by a Black? Or that simply Whites and Blacks could not share the same facilities? When we think of segregation, we think of sitting at the back of the bus or separate water fountains but I doubt that many of us realize the depths of this separation and the harm that seeps into one's soul from such treatment.

The lessons of these two stories affected me deeply: As someone who grew up with access to libraries and whose home was always filled with books and for whom reading was as natural as having corn flakes for breakfast, the image that these stories raised struck me worse than any Edgar Allan Poe horror story. At the time I was teaching writing at UCSB and one of the most difficult tasks I faced was to get my students to read: Read not just their class textbooks which are often not written in crystalline prose but to read novels. None of them were English majors, and from what they told me, they dreaded reading literature for a variety of reasons. So, when I told my students these stories, I admonished them. "Here are young children eager to read and learn but who find their paths to enlightenment bestrewn with thorns and obstacles that prevent them from achieving their goal." And then comes the kicker: "And here I am having to twist your arms to read a book not on the class list. Think about your privileges and how you can so easily access books." I reminded them that if they did not read they will miss out on so much human experience. They could learn to empathize with women in the nineteenth-century looking for husbands or prisoners in the Gulag trying to make it through the day or people of color facing lives of deprivation and loss of internal identity. "Reading gives you so much." I put it another way: "You are not going to wake up at forty with a mortgage and your 2.7 kids and suddenly decide you are going to read Jane Austen. Those habits have to be nurtured now. Your lives will be all the richer for it." And so I had them select a book to read: Anything from *One Hundred Years of Solitude* to *The Plague* to *Wuthering Heights* or *The World According to Garp* and while they never had to stand to attention and tell me the plot I tracked their progress and asked them what they had learned. I can only hope that my plan worked and that in years to come they will continue this practice and pass it on.

Laure-Anne Bosselaar
Discovering Rhyme

The Belgian-born poet moved to the United States in 1987 where she has taught poetry workshops around the country. Her poetry has been widely published. Her third collection, A New Hunger, was selected as an ALA Notable Book in 2008. She and her late husband, the poet Kurt Brown, moved to Santa Barbara in 2010 after teaching many years at Sarah Lawrence College in New York. They both briefly taught at UCSB, then retired. She is a member of the Founding Faculty at the Low Residency MFA Program at Pine Manor College in Boston. For more about the poet visit her website at www.laureannebosselaar.com.

They came cheap, the "Petites Punitions"
nuns flung at us for lesser sins: dyslexic
signs of the cross, skipped

confessions, whispers during Silence —
and sentences followed: copy two, ten, twenty
Lord's Prayers or Hail Marys

on calligraphy paper, cursives
correctly curled, capitals clinging to margins,
black ink for consonants, vowels in red.

The wars I waged in those French
syllables—wanting love-red vowels to win
over habit-black consonants!

I hated hailing Mary, for anything
full of grace shamed me: I was homely,
clumsy, and had never been baptized—

three reasons for perpetual doom:
no sips of our Savior's red liquor for me,
or tastes of His wan

flesh on my tongue. Banished,
I spent mass in the chapel's back pews,
bored, counting red stained-

glass pieces over blue, gold
versus green in the west window
where Mary Magdalene

held Christ's foot to her breast
so tenderly. On drizzly days, slow
raindrops sobbed down

Christ's flank unto her longing
face—I loved watching how nothing
distracted her from looking up at Him,

how she let Him quench His gaze
into hers. It was on one of those days
that novices sang a new hymn.

Its melody was rueful, flowed
with long "ooo" sounds: two words,
amour and toujours

swooned in harmony—it was
new to me: music inside a song, words
poured melody into a tune—

swooned in harmony like Christ
and Mary Magdalene. I hadn't heard this
as achingly before.

After that day, I slipped rhymes
in each line of my small punishments:

Hail frail Mary,
blessed art *thou now...*

my sounds crimson with *amour*, rhyme's songs
always *pour toujours*.

THIS POEM describes one of my memories of growing up in Belgian convents from 1947 to 1963. Sixty years later, I still clearly remember listening to the young novices singing hymns, and hearing, consciously and for the first time, the musicality and wonder of the rhyme. I was about eight or nine. I recall this "discovery" made me want to read "things that rhymed," but it was strictly forbidden to read anything else than a few religious books that were available in the nunnery. So it is only when I escaped the nunnery—I was almost eighteen—that I learned about the existence of public libraries. I didn't know such things existed—and that they housed thousands and thousands of books filled with "things that rhymed"!

After that exhilarating discovery, I spent almost all the free time I had catching up on all those years I felt had been lost, taking the tramway back and forth to the National Library in Brussels, with my precious piles of books, most of them poetry. It's then I read the French poets, the Italians, the German, the English: Verlaine, Montale, Rilke, Dylan Thomas. I read and read, and the more I read, the more I knew I wanted to be a poet. I owe this all to that first public library, with its honeyed tables, soft lights, and high windows behind which mourning doves sang their complaints all afternoon. Since then, I have spent the most deeply inspiring, peaceful and elating hours in libraries in Brussels and London, in New York, Boston, and, now, in Santa Barbara.

Ray Bradbury
Exchange

This short story by Ray Bradbury (1920-2012) about a boy, now grown, who finds the one place where you can go home again, is set in a public library that probably resembles the one in Waukegan, Illinois where Bradbury grew up and cut his literary teeth. He wrote that libraries formed his "complete education. I didn't go to college, but when I graduated from high school I went down to the local library and I spent ten years there, two or three days a week, and I got a better education than most people get from universities. So I graduated from the library when I was twenty-eight years old." Bradbury was a favorite of Santa Barbarans—for over twenty years he delivered the opening address at the Santa Barbara Writers Conference and in 2009 spoke as part of the Santa Barbara Public Library Big Read *programming on* Fahrenheit 451. *The official website for his work is www.raybradbury.com.*

THERE WERE too many cards in the file, too many books on the shelves, too many children laughing in the children's room, too many newspapers to fold and stash on the racks . . .

All in all too much. Miss Adams pushed her gray hair back over her lined brow, adjusted her gold-rimmed pince-nez, and rang the small silver bell on the library desk, at the same time switching off and on all the lights. The exodus of adults and children was exhausting. Miss Ingraham, the assistant librarian, had gone home early because her father was sick, so it left the burden of stamping, filing, and checking books squarely on Miss Adams' shoulders.

Finally the last book was stamped, the last child fed through the great brass doors, the doors locked, and with immense weariness, Miss Adams moved back up through a silence of forty years of books and being keeper of the books, stood for a long moment by the main desk.

She laid her glasses down on the green blotter, and pressed the bridge of her small-boned nose between thumb and forefinger and held it, eyes shut. What a racket! Children who finger-painted or cartooned frontispieces or rattled their roller skates. High school student arriving with laughter, departing with mindless songs!

Taking up her rubber stamp, she probed the files, weeding out errors, her fingers whispering between Dante and Darwin.

A moment later she heard the rapping on the front-door glass and saw a man's shadow outside, wanting in. She shook her head. The figure pleaded silently, making gestures.

Sighing, Miss Adams opened the door, saw a young man in uniform, and said, "It's late. We're closed." She glanced at his insignia and added, "Captain."

"Hold on!" said the captain. "Remember me?"

And repeated it, as she hesitated.

"Remember?"

She studied his face, trying to bring light out of shadow. "Yes, I think I do," she said at last. "You once borrowed books here."

"Right."

"Many years ago," she added. "Now I almost have you placed."

As she stood waiting she tried to see him in those other years, but his younger face did not come clear or a name with it, and his hand reached out now to take hers.

"May I come in?"

"Well." She hesitated. "Yes."

She led the way up the steps into the immense twilight of books. The young officer looked around and let his breath out slowly, then reached to take a book and hold it to his nose, inhaling, then almost laughing.

"Don't mind me, Miss Adams. You ever smell new books? Binding, pages, print. Like fresh bread when you're hungry." He glanced around. "I'm hungry now, but don't even know what for."

There was a moment of silence, so she asked him how long he might stay.

"Just a few hours. I'm on the train from New York to L.A., so I came up from Chicago to see old places, old friends." His eyes were troubled and he fretted his cap, turning it in his long slender fingers.

She said gently, "Is anything wrong? Anything I can help you with?"

He glanced out the window at the dark town, with just a few lights in the windows of the small houses across the way.

"I was surprised," he said.

"By what?"

"I don't know what I expected. Pretty damn dumb," he said, looking from her to the windows, "to expect that when I went away, everyone froze in place waiting for me to come home. That when I stepped off the train, all my old pals would unfreeze, run down, meet me at the station. Silly."

"No," she said, more easily now. "I think we all imagine that. I visited Paris as a young girl, went back to France when I was forty, and was outraged that no one had waited, buildings had vanished, and all the hotel staff where I had once lived had died, retired, or traveled."

He nodded at this, but could not seem to go on.

"Did anyone know you were coming?" she asked.

"I wrote a few, but no answers. I figured, hell, they're busy, but they'll be *there*. " They weren't."

She felt the next words come off her lips and was faintly surprised. "I'm still here," she said.

"You are," he said with a quick smile. "And I can't tell you how glad I am."

He was gazing at her now with such intensity that she had to look away. "You know," she sad, "I must confess you look familiar, but I don't quite fit your face with the boy who came here—"

"Twenty years ago! And as for what he looked like, that other one, me, well—"

He brought out a smallish wallet which held a dozen pictures and handed over a photograph of a boy perhaps twelve years old, with an impish smile and wild blond hair, looking as if he might catapult out of the frame.

"Ah, yes." Miss Adams adjusted her pince-nez and closed her eyes to remember. "That one, Spaulding. William Henry Spaulding?"

He nodded and peered at the picture in her hands anxiously.

"Was I lot of trouble?"

"Yes." She nodded and held the picture closer and glanced up at him. "A fiend." She handed the picture back. "But I loved you."

"Did you?" he said and smiled more broadly.

"In spite of you, yes."

He waited a moment and then said, "Do you still love me?"

She looked to left and right as if the dark stacks held the answer.

"It's a little early to know, isn't it?"

"Forgive."

"No, no, a good question. Time will tell. Let's not stand like your frozen friends who didn't move. Come along. I've just had some late-night coffee. There may be some left. Give me your cap. Take off that coat. The file index is there. Go look up your old library cards for the hell—heck—of it."

"Are they still there?" he said in amazement.

"Librarians save everything. You never know who's coming in on the next train. Go."

When she came back with the coffee, he stood staring down into the index file like a bird fixing its gaze on a half-empty nest. He handed her one of the old purple-stamped cards.

"Migawd," he said, "I took out a lot of books."

"Ten at a time. I said no, but you took them. And," she added, "read them! Here." She put his cup on top of the file and waited while he drew out canceled card after card and laughed quietly.

"I can't believe. I must not have lived anywhere else but here. May I take this with me, to sit?" He showed the cards. She nodded. "Can you show me around? I mean, maybe I've forgotten something."

She shook her head and took his elbow. "I doubt that. Come on. Over here, of course, is the adult section."

"I begged you to let me cross over when I was thirteen. 'You're not ready,' you said. But—"

"I let you cross over anyway?"

"You did. And much thanks."

Another thought came to him as he looked down at her.

"You used to be taller than me," he said.

She looked up at him, amused.

"I've noticed that happens quite often in my life, but I can still do this."

Before he could move, she grabbed his chin in her thumb and forefinger and held tight. His eyes rolled.

He said: "I remember. When I was really bad you'd hold on and put your face down close and scowl. The scowl did it. After ten seconds of your holding my chin very tight, I behaved for days."

She nodded, released his chin. He rubbed it and as they moved on he ducked his head, not looking at her.

"Forgive, I hope you won't be upset, but when I was a boy I used to look up and see you behind your desk, so near but far away, and, how can I say this, I used to think that you were Mrs. God, and that the library was a whole world, and that no matter what part of the world or what people or thing I wanted to see and read, you'd find and give it to me." He stopped, his face coloring. "You did, too. You had the world ready for me every time I asked. There was always a place I hadn't seen, a country I hadn't visited where you took me. I've never forgotten."

She looked around, slowly, at the thousands of books. She felt her heart move quietly. "Did you really call me what you just said?

"Mrs. God? Oh, yes. Often. Always."

"Come along," she said at last.

They walked around the rooms, together, and then downstairs to the newspaper files, and coming back up, he suddenly leaned against the banister, holding tight.

"Miss Adams," he said.

"What is it, Captain?"

He exhaled. "I'm scared. I don't want to leave. I'm afraid."

Her hand, all by itself, took his arm and she finally said, there in the shadows, "Sometimes—I'm afraid, too. What frightens *you*?"

I don't want to go away without saying good bye. If I never return, I want to see all my friends, shake hands, slap them on the back. I don't know, make jokes." He stopped and waited, then went on. "But I walk around town and nobody knows me. Everyone's gone."

The pendulum on the wall clock slid back and forth, shining, with the merest of sounds.

Hardly knowing where she was going, Miss Adams took his arm and guided him up the last steps, away from the marble vaults below, to a final, brightly decorated room, where he glanced around and shook his head.

"There's no one here, either."

"Do you believe that?"

"Well, where are they? Do any of my old pals ever come visit, borrow books, bring them back late?"

"Not often," she said. "But listen. Do you realize Thomas Wolfe was wrong?:

"Wolfe? The great literary beast? Wrong?"

"The *title* of one of his books."

"You Can't Go Home Again?" he guessed.

"That's it. He was wrong. *This* is home. our friends are still here. This was your summer place."

"Yes. Myths. Legends. Mummies. Aztec kings. Wicked sisters who spat toads. Where I really lived. But I don't see my people."

"Well."

And before he could speak, she switched on a green-shaded lamp that shed a private light on a small table.

"Isn't this nice?" she said. "Most libraries today, too much light. There should be shadows, don't you think? Some mystery, yes? So that late nights the beasts can prowl out of the stacks and crouch by this jungle light to turn the pages with their breath. Am I crazy?"

"Not that I noticed."

"Good. Sit. Now that I know who you are, it all comes back."

"It couldn't possibly."

"No? You'll see."

She vanished into the stacks and came out with ten books that she placed upright, their pages a trifle spread so they could stand and he could read the titles.

"The summer of 1930, when you were, what? ten, you read all of these in one week."

"Oz? Dorothy? The Wizard? Oh, yes."

She placed still others nearby. *"Alice in Wonderland. Through the Looking-Glass.* A month later you reborrowed both. 'But,' I said, 'you've already *read* them!' 'But,' you said, 'not enough so I can speak. I want to be able to *tell* them out *loud.'"*

"My God," he said quietly, "did I say that?"

"You did. Here's more you read a dozen times. Greek myths, Roman, Egyptian, Norse myths, Chinese. You were *ravenous.*"

"King Tut arrived from the tomb when I was three. His picture in the rotogravure started me. What else have you there?"

"*Tarzan of the Apes*. You borrowed it . . ."

"Three dozen times! *John Carter, Warlord of Mars*, four dozen. My God, dear lady, how come you remember all this?"

"You never left. Summertimes you were here when I unlocked the doors. You went home for lunch but sometimes brought sandwiches and sat out by the stone lion at noon. Your father pulled you home by your ear some nights when you stayed late. How could I forget a boy like that?"

"But still—"

"You never played, never ran out in baseball weather, or football, I imagine. Why?

He glanced toward the front door. "They were waiting for me."

"They?"

"You know. The ones who never borrowed books, never read. They. Them. *Those*."

She looked and remembered. "Ah, yes. The bullies. Why did they chase you?"

"Because they knew I loved books and didn't much care for them."

"It's a wonder you survived. I used to watch you getting, reading hunch-backed, late afternoons. You looked so lonely."

"No. I had *these*. Company."

"Here's more."

She put down *Ivanhoe, Robin Hood,* and *Treasure Island*.

"Oh," he said, "and dear and strange Mr. Poe. How I loved his Red Death."

"You took it so often I told you to keep it on permanent loan unless someone else asked. Someone did, six months later, and when you brought it I could see it was a terrible blow. A few days later I let you have Poe for another year. I don't recall, did you ever—?"

"It's out in California. Shall I—"

"No, no. Please. Well, here are your books. Let me bring others."

She came out not carrying many books but one at a time, as if each one were, indeed, special.

She began to make a circle inside the other Stonehenge circle and as she placed the books, in lonely splendor, he said their names and then the names of the authors who had written them and the names of those who had sat across from him so many years ago and read the books quietly or sometimes whispered

25

the finest parts aloud, so beautifully that no one said Quiet or Silence or even *Shh*!

She placed the first book and there was a wild field of broom and wind blowing a young woman across that field as it began to snow and someone, far away, called "Kathy" and as the snows fell he saw a girl he had walked to school in the sixth grade seated across the table, her eyes fixed to the windblown field and the snow and the lost woman in another time of winter.

A second book was set in place and a black and beauteous horse raced across a summer field of green and on that horse was another girl, who hid behind the book and dared to pass him notes when he was twelve.

And then there was the far ghost with a snow-maiden face whose hair was a long golden harp played by the summer airs; she who was always sailing to Byzantium where Emperors were drowsed by gold birds that sang in clockwork cages at sunset and dawn. She who always skirted the outer rim of school and went to swim in the deep lake ten thousand afternoons ago and never came out, who was never found, but suddenly now she made landfall here in the green-shaded light and opened Yeats to a last sail from Byzantium.

And on her right: John Huff, whose name came clearer than the rest, who claimed to have climbed every tree in town and fallen from none, who had raced through watermelon patches treading melons, never touching earth, to knock down rainfalls of chestnuts with one blow, who yodeled at your sun-up window and wrote the same Mark Twain book report in four different grades before the teachers caught on, at which he said, vanishing, "Just call me Huck."

And to *his* right, the pale son of the town hotel owner who looked as if he had gone sleepless forever, who swore every empty house was haunted and took us there to prove it, with a juicy tongue, compressed nose, and throat gargling that sounded the long October demise, the terrible and unutterable fall of the House of Usher.

And next to him was yet another girl.

And next to her . . .

And just beyond . . .

Miss Adams placed a final book and he recalled the fair creature, long ago, when such things were left unsaid, glancing up at him one day when he was an unknowing twelve and she was a wise thirteen to quietly say: "I am Beauty. And you, are you the Beast?"

Now, late in time, he wanted to answer that small and wondrous ghost: "No. He hides in the stacks and when the clock strikes three, will prowl forth to drink."

And it was finished, all the books were placed, the outer ring of his selves and the inner ring of remembered faces, deathless, with summer and autumn names.

He sat for a long moment and then another long moment and then, one by one, reached for and took all of the books that had been his, and still were, and opened them and read and shut them and took another until he reached the end of the outer circle and then went to touch and turn and find the raft on the river, the field of broom where the storms lived, and the pasture with the black and beauteous horse and its lovely rider. Behind him, he heard the lady librarian quietly back away to leave him with words. . .

A long while later he sat back, rubbed his eyes, and looked around at the fortress, the encirclement, the Roman encampment of books, and nodded, her eyes wet.

"Yes."

He heard her move behind him.

"Yes, *what?*"

"What you said, Thomas Wolfe, the title of that book of his. Wrong. Every-thing's *here*. Nothing's changed."

"Nothing will as long as I can help it," she said.

"Don't ever go away."

"I won't if you'll come back more often."

Just then, from below the town, not so very far off, a train whistle blew. She said: "Is that *yours?*"

"No, but the one soon after," he said and got up and moved around the small monuments that stood very tall and, one by one, shut the covers, his lips moving to sound the old titles and old, dear names.

"Do we *have* to put them back on the shelves?" he said. She looked at him and at the double circle and after a long moment said, "Tomorrow will do. Why?"

"Maybe," he said, "during the night, because of the color of those lamps, green, the jungle, maybe those creatures you mentioned will come out and turn the pages with their breath. And maybe—"

"What else?"

"Maybe my friends, who've hid in the stacks all these years, will come out, too."

"They're already here," she said quietly.

"Yes." He nodded. "They are."

And still he could not move.

She backed off across the room without making any sound and when she reached her desk she called back, the last call of the night.

"Closing time. Closing time, children."

And turned the lights quietly off and then on and then halfway between: a library twilight.

He moved from the table with the double circle of books and came to her and said, "I can go now."

"Yes," she said. "William Henry Spaulding. You can." They walked together as she turned out the lights, one by one. She helped him into his coat and then, hardly thinking to do so, he took her hand and kissed her fingers.

It was so abrupt, she almost laughed, but then she said, "Remember what Edith Wharton said when Henry James did what you just did?"

"What?"

"'The flavor starts at the elbow.'"

They broke into laughter together and he turned and went down the marble steps toward the stained-glass entry. At the bottom of the stairs he looked up at her and said:

"Tonight, when you're going to sleep, remember what I called you when I was twelve, and say it out loud."

"I don't remember," she said.

"Yes, you do."

Below the town, a train whistle blew again.

He opened the front door, stepped out, and he was gone.

Her hand on the last light switch, looking in at the double circle of books on the far table, she thought: "What was it he called me?"

"Oh, yes," she said a moment later.

And switched off the light.

Ashleigh Brilliant
On the Retirement of Shirley Morrison as Santa Barbara Children's Librarian

The English-born author and syndicated cartoonist has lived in Santa Barbara since 1973. He is best known for his Pot-Shots, single-panel illustrations with one-line humorous remarks, which began syndication in the United States in 1975, though he prefers to think of himself as a "philosopher-prophet-poet rather than a cartoonist." His wife and business partner, Dorothy, served as president of the Friends of the Library, 1986-1989. Shirley Morrison served as Children's Librarian for almost twenty years, and after her retirement, was a member of the Board of the Friends of the Library. Brilliant's personal website is www.ashleighbrilliant.com.

IT ISN'T a law, and it's not a requirement,
But one thing I know about what's called retirement
Is that it's an occasion, as here now with us,
For giving good wishes and making a fuss.
So Shirley, I'll start with the wishes—they're easy—
May the rest of your life be as sunny and breezy
As the best of your life (if the dates will allow),
Has, all things considered, been up until now.
And of your useful years, though this seems the ninth inning,
May it not be the end, but a whole new beginning,
So you'll say decades hence "I was not yet alive
That day I retired back in 2005!"

OK, enough wishing, and it's not for me
To say all you've done for this great Library.
For all of the children you've helped and inspired,
For all the parents too glad you were hired,

For all other folks whom our labors connected,
Making you loved and admired and respected.

No, honestly, what I feel I'm really here for,
What I represent and can now raise a cheer for,
Are all the authors who've sat on your shelves,
I wish they could all shake your hand for themselves.
You've done what society almost forbids—
You've opened the minds up of thousands of kids.
Librarians rarely reap big dividends,
But there's no way to know where their influence ends.

But let's not forget—and I have them beside me—
These copious notes that our Sol has supplied me—
How proudly he's watched you through many a year,
Climbing the heights of a splendid career,
Creating the crafts that made children adore you,
refusing to "HUSH!" like your mother before you.
Puppeting parties with glove and with glue,
Acquainting your husband with Winnie the Pooh,
But most of all, doing that what's most needing,
Helping young people to really love READING.

Your library saga began in L.A.
And has ranged up the coast, till we find you today,
After posts and positions too many to list them,
Children's Big Cheese of the whole S.B. system.
Nearly how many years? Put a 2, then a zero,
(And you're now, more than ever, a true Local Hero!)

If I don't finish soon someone's going to start cussing,
So this is the end of my wishing and fussing,
And if I may do so without impropriety,
I'd like to conclude on a nice note of piety:

Tradition on this day demands
A gold watch, for our golden hands;
But I'm apologetically confessing
I've nothin but this Brilliant blessing:

For all that thou hast been and meant,
For all the effort thou has spent,
Retiring from the hurly-burly

WELL DONE, THOU GOOD AND FAITHFUL SHIRLEY!

Frances Burns Linn Children's Room, 1964

Christopher Buckley
Libraries & Books

*Christopher Buckley has lived in Santa Barbara since 1952. He has pub-
lished three memoirs about growing up there:* Cruising State, Sleep Walk,
and Holy Days of Obligation. *His most recent poetry collections are* Star
Journal: Selected Poems *and* Spanish Notebook.

MY FIRST library was a small child's trunk in which my books and a few toys
were kept. My mother read to me from a collection of Golden Books each
night, and often I'd look at the pictures and turn each page again in the morn-
ings even though I could not read the black ribbons of text running along the
bottom. I knew by heart all the images of Pecos Bill and his cowboys, the camp-
fires and dry Texas landscape; and one I remember as *Bill and the Steamroller*,
was about a nice man who owned a steamroller and came around to smooth
out the bumps in the childrens' playground and on their neighborhood streets.
But I was not initially recognized as a scholar or someone likely to become a
writer. In first grade at Marymount, I was the last student in the room judged
to read proficiently and thus the last to receive my own red-covered *Dick and
Jane Reader*, replete with dog Spot. I think my slowness was more due to the
overbearing manner of the nun than lack of interest. This would not change in
my educational experience for several years.

In the fourth grade at Our Lady of Mt. Carmel School I was captivated by a
large illustrated edition of *The Iliad* and *The Odyssey* in a Giant Golden Book
De Luxe Edition—a bright red book with Greek warriors on their very strange
looking horses on the cover. It took both hands to open and hold it or lay it out
on top of the desk. Most of the pages were illustrations, but still I managed to
read the script at the bottom and absorb the names of the warriors and princi-
pals and follow the very condensed plot of the war. That book was available for
loan/use on our free time and never left the classroom. It always seemed to be

there resting on top of the sets of shelves filled with books that ran the whole length of the room beneath the large transom windows looking out onto Montecito; it was the only library we had for many years.

I didn't regularly ride my bike down to the big Santa Barbara Public Library to borrow books much until I was in high school at Bishop Garcia Diego High School. But I was aware this was possible via a schoolmate, Loren Van Wyk, one of the brightest students in our class, introspective and exceptionally well read for a lad of sixteen. Loren spent plenty of time at the main library and he had books on philosophy checked out which he brought to Religion Class to quote from and reference, not the least of which was Teilhard de Chardin's *The Phenomenon of Man*. Loren had worked out the faults in logic in the priest's position while the rest of us were day-dreaming fast-breaks and twenty-foot set shots on the basketball court. Loren rose to his feet to dispute traditional orthodox claptrap served up about creation and the "prime mover" and sent poor neurotic Fr. Geary into an apoplectic fit when he quoted from de Chardin regarding the unfolding of the material cosmos and the unification of consciousness. Loren had a stack of four or five library books on his desk which had provided his collateral reading for the class and picked up one with a blue cover to read a relevant passage to the priest. I had no idea who de Chardin was but I took notice when I heard his name as it sounded like baseball players Cookie Lavagetto, Zoilo Versalles, and Gino Cimoli who I liked just for the mellifluousness of their names. Language interested me for its music if not its sense; for me then, the Four Horsemen were the backfield of Notre Dame's 1924 football team under Knute Rockne, not Death, Destruction, Pestilence, and Famine from the Apocalypse.

In any event, we all could tell Fr. Geary had had a couple nervous breakdowns by the way he stuttered and repeated details from the life of Saint Ubaldus, Bishop of Gubbio; he was only given a couple religion classes to teach and wandered around the school grounds mumbling into his breviary most of the day. Before Loren could read the passage from the reference book, Geary began waving his arms over his head and rushed down the row of desks toward Loren saying he could be excommunicated and cast forever into perdition for reading books proscribed by the church and on "The Index" of forbidden books! Loren seemed a little confused that Fr. Geary could not see the lines of reason in his argument and finally sat down, looking to me a bit embarrassed for the old priest as he closed his book.

My real forays into libraries came in my junior and senior years in history and civics classes taught by Fr. Bernard, a Franciscan who held an M.A. and who, though he assigned a text for the class, never referred to it. Instead he lectured the entire hour expecting us to take notes, very like a college course. Midterm and final tests consisted of one or two questions written on the board about which we were expected to write an essay responding to the questions, without use of our notes. Bernard did regularly suggest and list supplemental reading he expected us to do, saying we should go off to the libraries to find the books. He especially encouraged us to use the library at UCSB. I went out there a time or two with other students but it was huge and even if we found the texts, we could not take them out. I went instead to the Santa Barbara Library and asked for help from the librarian and copied out my notes—on economic systems and theories mainly—a research skill that would serve me well at St. Mary's College as an English major.

How exactly I made it from there to here, is a long story, part of which is covered in *Holy Days of Obligation*. The short explanation is Books! As a graduate student at San Diego State and UC Irvine, I relied weekly on the libraries for critical exposition and backup as well as for editions of poetry I could not begin to afford. As a writer, I have become a book collector, closets re-worked and turned into bookshelves, bookcases everywhere in the house. For a while living in Lompoc we had a big two-story house and when we managed to move back home to Santa Barbara, I disposed of fifteen cases of books, similarly when moving back to California from Pennsylvania I had to pare down to hundreds of essentials and collectibles.

It seems I use the main public library more and more these days as I have very little room in our house for more books and my wife and I like to read, and return, of course, current novels and mysteries that we read for simple enjoyment before turning in to sleep each night.

Carolyn Butcher
The People's Library

Carolyn Butcher, who was the President of the Board of Directors of Speaking of Stories in Santa Barbara for eight years, has been a writer since landing her first job on a local newspaper near London when she was 18 years old. She has a PhD in English from UCSB. After more than a decade writing academic papers, she returned to her first love: writing. Currently teaching Critical Thinking Through Literature at Santa Barbara City College, she has published personal essays in several print and online journals.

AS I write this, I am supported by the presence of about four thousand books in my home, three thousand of which are the "gentleman's library" I inherited from my late father-in-law. I'm lucky enough to have the room, and the bookcases, to store them.

'Twas not always so.

Growing up in post-war England in the mid-1950s, commodities were still scarce and I was taught that to waste anything was shameful. My grandmother unpicked sweaters and re-knitted the wool into "new" sweaters, cut down out-of-fashion jackets and sewed them into "play clothes" for my brother and me, and when bed sheets became thin in the center (as they do) she cut them in half lengthwise and seamed the sides together so that the worn areas got tucked between the mattress and boxspring when the bed was made. Nobody got more wear out of sheets than Grandma.

So what good is a book once it has been read? Who would waste money buying one when you could get it from the library for free? And so it was that one of my mother's regular errands was to go into town on the bus and return with a shopping bag full of library books for herself and her mother. She loved Graham Greene novels, John Betjeman's poetry and travel books, and she chose novels by women authors such as Frances Parkinson Keyes and Daphne du Maurier for my grandmother who read in bed every morning for the rest of her life (in the latter years nourished by her first gin and tonic of the day). Sometimes I would go with my mother as a "special outing" and make a beeline for any Bobbsey Twins books in which I could immerse myself in America where there were beaches with warm sand and exotic food such as milkshakes and hotdogs.

What seems odd now is that I always associated the public library with entertainment and pastime opportunities, but never information resources. Even in high school, where my father spent a very large chunk of his salary so I could attend "the best" independent schools, no one ever told me to use the public library to conduct research for English and history papers. I knew I needed to consult books, but the only ones we had at home were shelved in a small bookcase that contained all my father's textbooks for his training as a Fleet Air Arm observer, a three-book set of *The Reader's Digest Great Encyclopaedic* [sic] *Dictionary*, a copy of *Roget's Thesaurus* and an etymological dictionary. I swear no teacher ever explained that my sources were inadequate. Perhaps the other girls had gentleman's libraries at home, but my parents did not know any better. My mother had left school at the age of 14 to go to work in an office until she was old enough to join the Women's Land Army, and my father had enlisted in the Royal Navy immediately after his 18th birthday in 1942, having studied only mathematics and accounting during his final two years in school.

Fast forward to the late 1980s when I wondered what to do with myself now that both of my children were in school. Someone suggested I take a class at Santa Monica College. Having thought of myself as "not college material" for the first 37 years of my life, I was suddenly thrust into the world of academe and I couldn't stop until I had earned a Ph.D in English from UCSB twenty years later. All libraries became delightful spaces of information that was perpetually finger-tip available. The library at SMC was where I first learned to do research. UCSB's Davidson Library offered tireless librarians who helped me search for sources as my area of interest grew more vast in inverse proportion to its narrowing. And when I travel now, it is libraries that blow my mind as much as any other architecture: The British Library, second only to the Library of Congress in size, where Virginia Woolf and Karl Marx found space to write; the Cotsen Children's Library where I felt I had walked through the looking glass into a fairy tale; and the Special Collections Library at Princeton, where my son and I nerdishly poured over Sylvia Beach's papers—thrilled to touch the early galleys of James Joyce's *Finnegans Wake* on which she had written suggestions.

However, as delightful as these famous and important libraries are, it is the public libraries in cities and towns all over the world that service individual and communal knowledge. They are one of the great social equalizers. That is why we have supported and protected Santa Barbara Central Library for a century and will continue to do so. Just as the light streams in through those magnificent windows, our library illuminates the lives of all of us whether we have a gentleman's library at home or not. It is our People's Library.

Reflecting pool - 1950s

Elias Chiacos
Public Libraries Are Essential

Longtime local resident Elias "Lee" Chiacos is a writer and tour guide. He is the author of Mountain Drive: Santa Barbara's Pioneer Bohemian Community *and numerous articles in local periodicals. He leads tours of the historic neighborhoods of Santa Barbara.*

FREE SPEECH and open discussion by informed citizens is essential in a democratic society. Our public libraries provide access to the information citizens need in order to become wise decision makers. We cultivate the critical thinking necessary to discern truth from opinion and fiction. Education is essential to the discipline of civil discourse.

The dissemination of information that leads to knowledge presents unique challenges in this era of "fake news," internet-posted opinions presented as truth, and "alternate facts." The public library provides a path to the citizen's goal of acquiring knowledge, which leads to wisdom. This can happen when diverse points of view based on facts provide a matrix from which we make good decisions.

Knowledge gained by reading, listening, and discussing issues helps us to be vigilant and to protect our republic from tyranny. The antidote to tyranny is an informed and participatory populace. The tyrant's strategy of creating a spectacle of confusion and propaganda when society is not thinking clearly, obscures the best interests of society as a whole. Social afflictions such as gender inequality, racism, apartheid, slavery, and genocide depend on ignorance in order to facilitate control by a tyrant. This is why slaves in the American South were punished for learning to read, and why tyrants destroy and burn books and libraries that threaten totalitarian control.

In our country, with profit-driven media presenting propaganda as news, and a constant barrage of fragmented images, we need access to the unbiased information that can be found in our public libraries. Whether it comes from non-fiction sources or novels, or the wide variety of media our libraries hold, wisdom and wise decisions develop in an atmosphere of tolerance, compassion, and empathy. The library provides a quiet environment conducive to thought and contemplation.

The sensory experiences of holding and reading books, as well as the craft of writing, have always been essential components of civilization, and these are especially important today. Additionally, our Santa Barbara public libraries and their auxiliary galleries provide an environment that nurtures the arts and builds community. Free concerts, art shows, lectures and films, and programs for children are a few of the many opportunities for enrichment offered by our libraries. It is our great good fortune to have such an institution in our city.

Susan Chiavelli
How to Fall in Love with your Library

Susan Chiavelli is the recipient of the Chattahoochee Review's *Lamar York Nonfiction Prize for "Death, Another Country," also named a notable essay in 2008 by* Best American Essays. *Her fiction, nonfiction and poetry have appeared in* The Los Angeles Review, The Louisville Review, New Millennium Writings, Minnetonka Review, Miramar, bosque, *and elsewhere.*

WHEN YOU'RE in the third grade, step over the threshold of your public library for the first time. Breathe in the hushed air, the weighty scent of knowledge. See how many more books they have than your school library? Don't be intimidated by the mysteries of the Dewey Decimal System. Find a kindly librarian who will be happy to teach you the secret code, and suggest reading a biography of Melvil Dewey while you're at it. Laugh a relieved laugh when she says she's only kidding.

Be prepared to tell her what you have already read: *Nancy & Plum* by Betty MacDonald, because the orphaned sisters are brave and escape evil Mrs. Monday's boarding home all on their own. And all of *Grimms' Fairy Tales*, of course. Assure her you will never go into the woods alone—that you know how to watch out for the wolf. Follow her through the maze of shelves as tall as trees as she guides you through the forest of books. She knows exactly the perfect book for you. Watch her pluck it from the shelf and place it in your hands:

Little House in the Big Woods.

Here, she says. You will not be going into these woods alone. Open the book and discover the magic—the alchemy it takes to travel through time and space. See the frost paint patterns on the windowpane of the Ingalls' log cabin? Your eyes are Laura's eyes, your heart, her heart. Travel across the prairie in a covered wagon to the banks of Plum Creek and the shores of Silver Lake. Read the entire series. Learn that pioneer life is hard, but also full of love. Move on to *The Last of the Mohicans* and Willa Cather's Prairie Trilogy. Never stop reading. Learn to be brave and resourceful. When adults ask what you want to be when you grow up, tell them, a pioneer.

Years later, when your parents forbid you to date on school nights, tell them you're going to the library with your girlfriends to study. It won't be a lie. Let the revolving glass door spit you into the library one by one—Patty, Penny, Kristy, Denny, and you. Make a grand entrance in your mini skirts and knee highs. Drop off your library books and check out a few new ones. That will only take five minutes. What a coincidence that the boys are there to study, too! There is so much to learn in this world!

Take your boyfriend's arm and step into the night. Be sure to avoid eye contact with the librarian. After all, she knows you have learned to be brave and resourceful. She knows you are no longer afraid of the woods.

Louise Currey
The Library Was My Sanctuary

Since retiring in 2001 after over thirty years as a nurse with the Santa Barbara County Mental Health Department, Curry has been writing. A couple of stories from the memoir of her remarkable life have been published to date.

THE HOME in which I grew up had only three books initially: the telephone book, a family address book, with phone numbers, and an old Bible—King James Version. We were poor, and books, as possessions, were seen by my parents as "frills." "If you want to read, get a library card or read the newspaper," I was told. I was in the second grade, already an avid reader and reading at a seventh grade level, having learned "my letters" at the age of three with the help of my grandmother.

When relatives gifted me a beautiful copy of *Peter Pan* with color plates it was taken down only two or three times a year, as it was "too good" to be used regularly. It was stored on a very high closet shelf where I could only look at it longingly.

When I was six, I got my own library card. The rule was you could get one as soon as you could print your full name on the three-inch line on the card that was provided. I carefully practiced until I could do this.

In summer, I would walk the six blocks each way to the library every other day, checking out the maximum ten books each time. When I had read the entire content of the children's library by age eight, I would sneak down the stairs to the adult books when the children's librarian was not looking. Though I could not check out adult books, I could, and often did, read them undisturbed until the library closed. The library, especially in the summertime, was my sanctuary.

Neglect was part of our upbringing. I could see once I started school, and finally had playmates, that other kids wore clean clothes or didn't wear the same clothes all week. When I told my mother my socks were dirty, she said "Turn them inside out" and I had often already done that.

Once when my little sister Patsy and I were coming back from the library we were met on the sidewalk by the library steps by a girl from my elementary classroom, Lucille. She said she lived near the library and I could come to her apartment and meet her mother. I was puzzled by this, since Lucille and I were not friends in class.

"You are both terribly dirty—your hair, faces and hands and clothes—and my mother could help," she explained.

This embarrassed me to the point of speechlessness and I numbly took my sister's hands and went to Lucille's apartment. Her mother shook her head and drew her lips together in a mix of anger and sadness. She then took us into the bathroom and preceded to scrub away several weeks worth of dirt from hands, face and legs. She gently untangled our hair snarls and redid my braids and combed my sister's. She wrote a note to our mother. At our house, Lucille knocked on the door, reported her mother's shock at our appearance, and handed her the letter, turned and left to go.

Mother took the letter, pulled us inside, shut the door and that was that. I had wished mightily that the humiliating experience would make a difference in our lives, in our cleanliness, in Mama being a good and proper mother. It did not.

Through reading the *Washington Post*, I found out that people who neglected or abused their children could be arrested, and their children could be taken from them. It had actually happened. The message I got from this reading was that this was very wrong and even a crime. One set of parents went to jail.

The neglect in our home continued, and it got worse. On one occasion, mother had been in bed for a week, wearing the same filthy housedress, unwashed, sleeping around the clock. When I approached her bed, the strong stench made me sway.

"What is the matter, Mama? Are you sick?"

No answer. She rolled over wrapping tighter into the covers moaning, "Leave me alone!"

"Mama, this is not right. You've been in bed for a week. Papa works six days a week and takes care of his mom. He doesn't come home till 7 or 8 PM. I can't run the house or take care of my sister. I have to call the police. They will know what to do. If you are sick they will bring the doctor." Her eyes opened and she turned her head. "If you are not sick and are not taking care of us, it's a crime. They will take us away and put us in foster care. You could go to jail."

I had calculated this, hoping it would work, knowing that mother "feared the authorities" from being raised in occupied Latvia before World War I. I had no choice.

Mother looked startled. She could see I meant what I said. She got up, drew a bath for herself, washed and put on a clean housedress. Then she went into the kitchen, washed a week's worth of dishes, made supper and put in a load of laundry.

Had I not been such an avid reader of library books and newspapers, who knows what would have happened to me and my sister. The library and books opened up the world to me, in more ways than one. For this, I am forever grateful.

John Daniel
Remembrance des Temps de la Recherché Perdu

Not only is John Daniel the founder (with his wife, Susan) of Daniel & Daniel Publishers, which is the home of three different publishing imprints as well as a wide range of publication and literary services, he is also a novelist in his own right. The imprint of John Daniel & Company, a small-press publisher of belle-lettres, was founded in 1985 in Santa Barbara. After almost twenty years there, the Daniels pulled up stakes and moved themselves and their publishing company to a small town in Humboldt County, California. More about Daniel can be found at www.danielpublishing.com.

DURING THE summer of 1961 I worked for an antiquarian bookstore in Dallas. While I was there the store acquired a *Book of Common Prayer* inscribed by Caroline of Brunswick to her ward, William Austin, dated Christmas 1805, Montague House, Blackheath. The store manager sent me downtown to the public library to research these people, in order to put a price on this book. What I uncovered allowed us to charge $100, which was cheap, I thought. A hundred bucks bought a lot of book back then, but this one had a royal signature and included a special prayer for the King's health, which was touch and go at the time, to the grief of his adoring subjects and the annoyance of his heir, who was impatient for the old man to get on with the business of dying. Who were these people? The King was George III, who had lost his American colonies in 1776 and who was now mad as a hatter. The heir was George, Prince of Wales, the promiscuous, over-eating scoundrel who would eventually become Prince Regent and finally King George IV. Caroline Amelia Elizabeth of Brunswick was the Prince's first cousin as well as his wife, and the person he hated most in all the world. William Austin was Caroline's darling child, whom she adopted in 1802, when he was three months old. Little "Willikins" lived and traveled with Princess Caroline until she died in 1821. I learned all this information in a couple of hours at the Dallas Public Library.

I typed up a one-page paper relating these facts, and it was displayed in a glass case next to the book. That one page was the first of hundreds of pages I wrote about Caroline and Willikins, off and on over the next twenty years. It turned into a novel of love and hatred, insanity and cunning intrigue, manners and scandal. Fortunately for my career, my novel, *Willikins Rex*, never got published. I had no business attempting a historical novel, but I enjoyed all the writing and—especially—all the research.

That's the main thing I got from that trip to the public library in downtown Dallas. Discovering the joys of research.

In the 1970s I worked as a freelance editor, a part-time gig that often took me to the Menlo Park, California, Public Library to do fact-checking on a number of college textbooks being published by Wadsworth Publishing Company. In addition to routine copy-editing (wouldn't you think authors of textbooks, who are college professors, after all, would know how to spell and punctuate? Think again), I had the great pleasure of finding gross errors in books about the histories and workings of Public Relations, Mass Media, Data Processing, and Popular Music back in the era when AM Radio meant Top 40 tunes.

I loved that work so much it was almost like something other than work. Most of all I loved getting sidetracked, finding myself wandering into areas of information off the subject for which I was hired and for which I was billing by the hour. I've forgotten all that information by now, which is just as well because the information on those up-to-date subjects has long gone obsolete. And what a pleasure it was to claim a table in that quiet room and stack it high with reference tomes! To ask for help and receive it served to me by smiling librarians. And to know I was straightening out a messy manuscript and getting the facts right. I was appreciated, and I appreciated that in return.

In the 1980s I moved to Santa Barbara and became a publisher, along with Susan, with whom I teamed up in business and in life. The best choices I ever made were moving to Santa Barbara, teaming up with Susan, and becoming a publisher.

That's also when I met the best library of my life. The Santa Barbara Public Library was, and I presume still is, a gem. I didn't have much fact-checking to do for the books we were publishing, which were mainly fiction, poetry, and memoir; but I did get great pleasure doing research in the picture file upstairs, looking for images to adorn the covers of our books. And getting lost again, led astray to wander through such a treasure trove of unrelated pictures.

Susan, who was (and still is) the business, sales, and marketing maven of our company, spent many an hour doing research in the Santa Barbara Public Library, compiling lists of media to whom we sent review copies. She also made good use of important reference books, like *Literary Market Place, Publishers' Trade List Annual, American Book Trade Directory, Readers' Guide to Periodical Literature*, and *Ulrich's Periodical Directory*. (Susan loves libraries. She did graduate work in Library Science at Cal State Fullerton back in the 1970s, and now she spends her Wednesday afternoons as a volunteer at the Arcata Public Library.)

In 2003, Susan and I relocated to McKinleyville, in Humboldt County, California, where, in addition to publishing books, I am now once again a freelance editor, and much of my work involves serious fact-checking. I am sorry to report that it's not the same game anymore. I do my editing in my office at home, and I do all my fact-checking online. Google. Wikipedia. I use iStock Photo for picture research. Instead of enjoying sidetracks and byways, I'm careful not to surf the Web. It's all business now.

It's faster. It's more informative. It's thorough. But it's nowhere near as fun as getting lost in research projects at a quietly busy public library. I wistfully remember when my research was full of surprise, a hands-on book adventure that took place in shared, friendly, hushed rooms.

I miss the public library.

Fran Davis
The Bookmobile

Writer and editor Frances Pettey Davis lives in Summerland, California and is a columnist for Coastal View News. *She has written for the* Santa Barbara News-Press, *the* Santa Barbara Independent *and the* Carpinteria Herald. *Her stories, essays and poems regularly appear in magazines and print and online journals, many of which can be found at her website, francespetteydavis.com.*

Nine years old shifting foot to foot
 in the dusty schoolyard
waiting for the bookmobile
 books on wheels, ambulatory books
loaf of a truck bearing promises
 books for running, leaping, flying
dancing, brown oxfords take the long step up
 smell of paper, paste and motor oil
bindings red, green, black
 printed road signs for the journey
fingers slide along the spines
 press tiny canals down each hard side
a tactile trip before the plunge within
 the dive to words

Depository of paper riches
 the bookmobile, shelves of words
and worlds, warrior queens and flying carpets
 jewels and open sesame, which book

to choose in this rare surround
    time's a wedge, narrowed to four walls
which one, just one, one spoke
    from the wheel of books, books on wheels
look with a question at the librarian
    chauffeur, captain of books and engines
which one before all roll away
    which is the book that will sing me
into the journey, a startlement into time
    and space as big as all tomorrows

Santa Barbara Bookmobile, 1950s

Pamela Davis
My Librarian, Myself

Pamela Davis's first book, Lunette, *won the ABZ Poetry Award. Her poems have appeared in more than seventy publications. She lives in Santa Barbara with her husband and two Labrador retrievers. For more about Davis and her poetry visit www.pamela-davis.com.*

THE ONLY reason I wanted a bike was to ride to the library. I didn't care about color, but it had to have a basket. Every Saturday, I'd pedal twelve long blocks to the Henry Dana Branch Library, a single story mid-century building painted the same blue as a Ford Edsel. Returning my books, the librarian sighed at my selection. I was indifferent to her recommendations of Nancy Drew and *Little House on the Prairie*. When she suggested *Little Women*, despite the "little" attached to women, I said yes, not knowing it would introduce me to my first literary role model, Jo March.

My librarian—how can I not remember her name? A spinster with black dyed hair and peep-toe shoes, she was the first person to encourage my writing, introducing me to books beyond my years, *Jane Eyre*, the poems of Emily Dickinson. In my teens I fell asleep with *Les Misérables* propped heavy as a sultan on my bed. When I went to college, she gave me *Webster's New Collegiate Dictionary*, still on my desk, spine splayed, gold lettering broken.

A certain humility overtakes me entering our library, overwhelmed by stacks of books bearing all the knowledge of civilization. Entrée to worlds upon worlds—the past, the future, the imagined. In its book sale, I once found a first edition copy of *The Lost Son*, long out of print. Signed by poet Theodore Roethke, the fine poems typeset on vellum rich as loam. Its provenance was his hometown library in Saginaw, Michigan, and on the flyleaf, the poet's flowing signature in faded blue ink.

Some books have secret hearts beating in their pages—phrases that arrest a reader like a bell. Books—catalogued, shelved, taken down by readers locked in an impossible love affair. We say *yes* to Fitzgerald's green lights beckoning Gatsby from a dock, to Anna Karenina at the train station standing too close to the rail. Yes to an earlier reader whose tear warped its shape on the page Anna jumped. To this library that transports us anywhere we wish to go, we whisper *thank you* and say Yes.

Carol DeCanio
Library

Carol DeCanio, recipient of The Santa Barbara Arts Fund Individual Award in Poetry and published poet for 30 years, is poetry columnist for Voice Magazine. *She organizes local poetry events and has had art shows of her poetry paired with her photography*

You take the #1 California
transfer to the #55 Sacramento

and after a bumpy ride
watching what's outside

you get off
right across, from

the Library.

Up the stairs
designed for tribute

is a path away
from ordinary

and all those
telling you what to do.

A little dim
a lot quiet

books on shelves
orderly and different

all wanting you
to find them.

Not at the big table
with the wooden chairs

not next
to the grown-ups there

but right on the floor
flat carpeted and gray

you plop down,
it's the Children's Section

while Time
waits.

The big book you like
has pictures

and you ask nothing because
the title alone, is

The Wizard of Oz.

And after a while, when
light shows up slow

it's time to pick a few,
to show

the empress
of nobility

show her your card
because you belong,

on card alone
she will take your word

you'll be back in 2 weeks
books returned.

On the #55 Sacramento
transferring to the #1 California

these arms are full of books

Leslie Dinaberg
Don't Lock the Libraries

With over twenty years of professional experience as a writer and editor, Leslie Dinaberg is currently plying her considerable talents as the managing editor of Santa Barbara Seasons *magazine. She has lived in Santa Barbara since age five, and other than a decade of infatuation with the world of entertainment in Los Angeles, has continued to live and work in her hometown. More about her professional career can be found at www.LeslieDinaberg.com.*

"Libraries are not safe places, and the reason for that is there are ideas to be found." —*John Bookman*

"You know the republic will survive when there is new money for libraries."—*Denis Hamill*

A LOT of the people I grew up with were surf rats or skate rats or gym rats. I was a library rat. From the first time I signed my name on a card at the public library downtown, I was addicted to being around all those books. But my obsession with libraries really began when I was nine years old, I had just transferred to Harding School. Sherry Thompson was the librarian.

"Where are the books about the CIA?" I asked her. "I want to learn about them because I think I might make a good spy when I get older."

And her magic answer. "Let me show you how to find them yourself."

She led me to the card catalog—for you youngsters who have never heard of such a thing, the cards were like Pokemon cards, only with less information on attack points and more information on how find a book, and she showed me how it worked. Not only did I learn about the CIA, the FBI and James Bond that day, I finally solved the mystery of who that Sarah Bernhardt lady was that my grandma was always comparing me to when I'd get a bit dramatic.

All of those cliches about libraries opening doors came true for me that day. I was hooked. It wasn't about falling in love with reading. I had caught that bug years before. My mom was a teacher, so I certainly didn't need a librarian to encourage me to read. But Mrs. Thompson introduced me to research, and I dove right in with vigor, the beginning of a new life-long love.

Learning how to find information, to answer questions all by myself, gave me such a sense of sovereignty over my world. Learning to explore the world of information was just as important to me as learning how to flirt with boys or learning how to swim. I felt like I had harnessed the powers of Wonder Woman, Nancy Drew and Batgirl (a librarian in disguise). I could solve just about any mystery in the world by wielding my magical powers over the Dewey Decimal System. What could be better than that?

Mrs. Thompson became my concierge into the world of information. She was always encouraging me to try to find out the answers by myself, but keeping an eye on my progress—and always right there when I needed help. For me she was the perfect kind of teacher.

I keep thinking about Mrs. Thompson when I read about all the budget cuts in the elementary schools. Our libraries have already been hit hard, and they're threatened with being hit even harder. I can't imagine what my elementary school years would have been like without the library—and the librarian—to rely on.

Mrs. Thompson noticed my preference for fiction and promised me a lunch at the Yacht Club if I could read every biography in the school library. To this day, that was still the best burger I've ever had.

Mrs. Thompson was the first person I ever knew that died. I was thirteen and knew enough to do some research about cancer, thanks to her.

I know the public schools are in a budget crisis, but asking a school, "an institution of learning," to cut its library programs seems absurd to me, like asking someone whether they'd rather have an arm cut off or a leg. Cutting off our kids from such an important resource seems just as awful. There has got to be a better way.

"A library that is not accessible out of business hours is of as little value as gold hoarded in a vault and withdrawn from circulation," said Alexander Graham Bell. Looked it up—at the library.

Sharon Dirlam
Books Bound for Russia

Sharon Dirlam was a reporter, assistant city editor and city editor at the Santa Barbara News-Press *(1971-1978). She was a staff writer for the* Los Angeles Times, *in the View, Real Estate and Travel sections (1979-1989), as well as penning book reviews. She was a foreign expert for the* China Daily *(1989-1990); a Peace Corps volunteer (1996-1998)—the subject of her memoir,* Beyond Siberia: Two Years in a Forgotten Place—*and a Peace Corps trainer (1998-2002). She returned to Santa Barbara in 1990, and except for travels has lived here ever since, writing for pleasure and occasional profit, and editing for friends.*

IN THE depth of winter, layers of frost built up inside our windows creating thick icy tapestries with designs remarkably similar to twisted vines in a tropical jungle.

Never before or since have we read as many books as we did during our two years as Peace Corps volunteers in the Russian Far East. I treasured the books we brought with us, and one by one as I finished one, I eagerly traded it for another volunteer's book, even if mine was a short story collection by Alice Munro and theirs was a bestseller by Danielle Steele.

It's impossible to overestimate the value of books when the supply is scarce.

I doubt there is a Peace Corps office anywhere in the world that doesn't have a makeshift library consisting of books brought into the country, read, traded, and left behind by Americans, to the joy of those who follow them.

Our assignment in Russia was to teach English-language skills to college students being educated as English teachers. Most of their professors were Russians who had never heard a native English speaker. Their reading and writing skills were advanced, but their speaking and listening skills were rudimentary. Their course materials were astonishingly sparse. The only complete classroom set of an English-language novel was *The Great Gatsby* by F. Scott Fitzgerald, selected no doubt as a forum for discussing decadent American values.

There were books that contained dozens of parts of stories, mostly by British authors. These were used for reading practice, but they were frustrating because they were edited, apparently, for the purpose of avoiding any discussion of values or philosophies that might engender critical thinking.

When students began to visit us in our apartment, their eyes soon traveled to the shelf full of books, their gaze full of curiosity and longing. We decided to start a book-lending service, keeping a ledger of their names and the date we expected the book to return. It made some of the students nervous to commit to paper these extracurricular readings; others signed their names with a flourish, emboldened by those years of Perestroika.

Friends from Santa Barbara wrote and asked what we needed, and it didn't take us any time at all to reply that our most pressing need was for books! More books! What kind of books? Well, what do you have?

A friend at Sana Barbara City College gave us a classroom set of an American poetry anthology. A Santa Barbara school principal confided that used textbooks aren't recycled there because parents would notice and complain about the cost of texts being constantly updated. But since the books we wanted would be leaving the country, he happily donated four boxes of outdated textbooks for mathematics, chemistry and physics. In Russia, faculty members volunteered to translate these texts for their students.

Peace Corps friends passed along to us books by their favorite mystery writers, such as Robert B. Parker and Ross Macdonald, their literary choices, such as Naguib Mahfouz, Margaret Atwood and Vladimir Nabokov, as well as Russian writers including the poet Anna Akhmatova and the memoirist Eugenia Ginzburg who wrote about her years in the Gulag.

As sad as I was about parting with some of these books, it seemed more important to pass them along than to keep them for myself. To be a librarian, not a collector.

I have loved libraries since childhood when my father would take us every other Saturday to discover new books and return the books we'd already read. Sometimes I found it so difficult to give back a wonderful book that I would hide it under my bed for another two weeks, just to enjoy reading it for a little while longer. Only when my father decided to take the overdue fine out of my allowance did I learn the value of sharing.

When we left Russia, after our two years there, we donated to our college some eight hundred English-language books. Peace Corps volunteers who followed us expanded our library to three thousand books. In 2002, the Peace Corps Russia branch was closed down. But at least our little library is still there, and every once in awhile, one of our Russian friends emails us about having read another treasured book.

Periodicals room, 1958

Gretel Ehrlich
Going Miles for Books

The Santa Barbara-raised, award-winning author has written more than a dozen books, including three books of narrative essays, a novel, a memoir, three books of poetry, a biography, a book of ethnology/travel, and a children's book, among others. She has spent much of the last two decades traveling in Greenland and the Arctic. She lives in Wyoming.

TAPED TO the wall by my writing table is a photograph of a donkey carrying panniers full of books. I later learned it was a part of Biblioteca Equina, in this case, Biblioburro in the South American country of Colombia. I sent the photo around to my rancher friends in northern Wyoming, many of whom live in remote areas but are avid readers, as are many in the world who live in places where winters are long and severe.

The image of an animal carrying books brought together the two most salient parts of my life: I've always been horseback; I've always been a voracious reader with very high standards, and somehow needed to get my hands on those books while living in what has become a rural, isolated, outdoor life for the last forty-three years.

I attribute my love of reading, of inked words on paper, to a basic sense of loneliness. My visual hunger—I loved the way poems looked on the page coincided with my intellectual appetite. I spoke little as a child, but had things on my mind, and my forays to the Central Library in downtown Santa Barbara satiated a hunger I couldn't explain.

My mother once reminded me that as a child I wrote books, plays and music, and bound them with kitchen string, then presented them to her, never imagining that actual books I had written would someday be bought by libraries everywhere. I was often taken to see the huge Heidelberg printing press at Noel Young's studio, where he was printing up party invitations to make a living, and chapbooks of poems for the love of it. Eventually, he printed my first small volume of poetry. I watched the pages come off the press, watched the binding of them, and drank wine with local writers and poets from up the coast at the hot tub party to celebrate the book's publication.

That small book was the carrot that urged me to fulfill my dream of being both a rancher and a writer. I dove back into the local libraries, the Montecito public library, the Central Library downtown, and later the capacious UCSB open stacks where my interests in Asian poetry, arctic culture, Japanese theatre, theoretical physics, and the art of the novel were more than satisfied.

I was sent off to boarding school when I was twelve. Deeply unhappy there, and despairing about living without animals, I again resorted to reading books. "Lights out" at 10 PM meant my life was about to begin. Using a small flashlight under blankets, I attempted to read a book a night, or maybe two nights, and by my final year, at age 16, I'd gone through the works of Octavio Paz, Camus, Gide, Rimbaud, Verlaine, Thomas Hardy, Henry James, Virginia Woolf, Eliot, Wordsworth, Hemingway, Shakespeare, Kawabata, Joyce, Tolstoy, Turgenev, Melville, Conrad, Dostoevsky, Chekhov, Wallace Stevens, and many others.

The school library, the local public library, and the independent bookstore down the street all fed into one another to keep the stack of books by my bed robust and fresh. I had no interest in a formal education in literature, but rather sought out books as windows into the lives and consciousness of others. In boarding school as in no other place, no matter how remote (and I've spent many years a few hundred miles south of the north pole) life gets small. Books allowed me to travel in the deepest and most profound way to Japanese villages, Russian farms and cities, whaling boats, French hideouts, Mexican landscapes, Lake District sheep farms, the Florida Keys, and the places inside us that emanate from the font of the natural world, the urban world, and the verbal ways the conscious mind unravels.

My own 7,000-volume library is testimony to those early inspirations. But libraries still play an important part in my life. When I began going to northwestern Greenland and traveled with subsistence Inuit hunters by dogsled on ice—when there was ice—I used my "Friend of UCSB Library" card to educate myself about Inuit culture. Each time I went to Greenland I took one of the thick AMS Press volumes of Knud Rasmussen's ethnographic notes, and carried it on the dogsled. Later, when I confessed to the librarian what I had done—and of course, after returning the books in perfect condition, she was thrilled. She said, "You took Rasmussen home."

During my ranching days, my own cache of books became a lending library for others. In the winter months when we fed cattle with a team of horses and a wagon, then retreated to the house to stoke the wood-burning stoves, we read. There was no NPR, no PBS, no internet, no Kindle. I'd make up a stack of books for each of my friends in the area—which they read and returned. Marquez, Flaubert, Shakespeare, Singer, Flannery O'Connor, Updike, and Maugham went out, and when returned were replaced with others. As a result, one winter I was urged to give a weekly writing class in a community of a few hundred souls. About six attended. When one hardcore Texas cowboy showed up, I asked why he had come, and he said, "My ballet class was cancelled." He wrote the best story of them all.

Books beget books. I still mourn the loss of the great Alexandria library with its scrolls, gardens, and scholars' rooms. On the other hand, my favorite Wyoming library—now gone—was in Daniel: one side was the bar, where you can still order a "slaw dog" or a slice of previously frozen pizza. The other side was the library where you could borrow anything from Faulkner to Zane Grey. And interlibrary loans in states like Wyoming and Montana make it possible to research any subject deeply while never leaving home.

I continue to read out in "the sticks." I'm a bookworm "hick," and made sure my saddle bags were big enough to hold a paperback. In the old days I found ways to do ranch work—irrigating fifty acres of grass hay and alfalfa, moving cattle every three days, riding colts, practicing roping, feeding animals, and growing food for the winter—with books scattered about. One in the outhouse, one to read sitting on a stool in the huge vegetable garden when weeding became too boring, one in my saddlebag. I made cotton sleeves for books of various sizes and inserted those in waterproof plastic bags.

Now I'm a cabin-dweller, still growing food and riding, and it gladdens my heart to think of all the mobile libraries in the world: the Camel Library Service in Kenya, donkey-drawn library carts in Zimbabwe, the library ship—*Epos*—that plies the rough coast of Norway, the two book-bearing donkeys in South America named "Alfa" and "Beto," and I frequently look down my dirt road to see if a few boxes of books by equine express might be coming my way.

Brian Fagan
On Homer, Ashurbanipal,
and My Love Affair with Libraries

A Santa Barbara resident since 1967, Brian Fagan is Distinguished Emeritus Professor of Anthropology at the University of California, Santa Barbara, and one of the world's leading archaeological writers. He has written or edited forty-six books, including seven widely used undergraduate college texts; a bibliography can be found at his website, www.brianfagan.com.

I FELL in love with libraries—and Homer—in high school. We studied the *Odyssey* in a library-turned-classroom, surrounded by shelves of leather-bound Victorian tomes, which beckoned one seductively with their delicious obscurity. Not that we had much time to peruse them, for our elderly teacher was a tiger. His great passion was Homer. He could recite the great bard effortlessly for hours in the original tongue. We had to read forty lines a day in Greek, then translate them. A quiet voice often stopped you in mid-sentence, correcting pronunciation or grammar. At first, he was intimidating, but he gave me a love of Homer which remains with me still. To him, the hexameters were like chants, to be performed like music, with triumph and pathos, bravado and sheer poetic description. Three hundred of his former students attended his funeral. The Regius Professor of Greek at Oxford, who learned ancient Greek from him, recited Helen's lament over Hector from the *Iliad*. There was not a dry eye in the congregation.

I was a mediocre student, but for some reason our teacher liked me. He would bark, but was a kind man. One rainy afternoon, he took me through the library books, some in Greek or Latin, others in English, French, and German. He made a seemingly arid literary journey fascinating. We were surrounded by learning every day as we immersed ourselves in the *Odyssey*, but I also learned much of the atmosphere of libraries, and about how to use them. "Don't just look for one book, look at the entire shelf," he told me once. I've done this ever since.

Sixty-five years later, I can still recite some Homer and revel in verses that originated as chants and stories recited by bards and storytellers. We often forget that, until about five thousand years ago, all knowledge passed down the generations by word of mouth, through chant and recitation, fable, legend, and oration. Many traditional societies still value their oral traditions, which define the cosmos, celebrate legendary creators, and celebrate the endless cycles of human life. In the past, libraries were in the mind, preserved in human memory and by carefully rehearsed mnemonics. Until the past century, Polynesian navigators traversed the remote Pacific using sailing directions passed from generation to generation by rigorous chant and oral recitation. All this began to change when writing, originally a device for commercial transactions, came along, first in Egypt and Mesopotamia. By 2000 BC, written records extended far beyond business and ritual into literature and epic, correspondence, and dynastic histories. Most commoners were illiterate, but many people would have known a few hieroglyphs inscribed on a temple wall or some wedge-shaped cuneiform symbols stamped on clay tablets. Full literacy was a specialized trade for scribes, such as the ubiquitous petty officials who recorded Egyptian harvests and offerings, or gifts to temples by the Euphrates. Libraries came into being because someone had to create order out of literary chaos.

King Ashurbanipal (668-627 BC) was the last great Assyrian monarch. He apparently had a bookish mind, which caused him to assemble a magnificent royal library of cuneiform-inscribed clay tablets at Nineveh in what is now northern Iraq. Ashurbanipal was a literary collector. He sent agents the length and breadth of his domains to collect rare documents: "Search them out and bring them to me." Ashurbanipal's library became the richest repository of cuneiform tablets ever assembled under one roof. But when Nineveh fell to foreign conquerors in 612 BC, the library was forgotten. Austen Henry Layard, a Victorian archaeologist and adventurer, who later became a politician and diplomat, unearthed the king's priceless archive by chance in 1850. He shoveled thousands of tablets into baskets and shipped them to the British Museum. There they remain to this day, the remnants of what was one of the earliest libraries in the world.

Ashurbanipal's more than 180,000-tablet library could have sunk into academic obscurity. But, in 1872, a shy bank engraver-turned-epigrapher named George Smith deciphered a Babylonian account of a flood that had a close resemblance to Noah's inundation in Genesis. Ashurbanipal's library became famous overnight. A handful of experts—and their qualifications are daunting—are still working their way through the king's repository. Visiting a tablet library is a fascinating experience. I once spent an enthralling afternoon in the Sumerian archives at the University of Pennsylvania Museum, another major collection of cuneiform tablets from nineteenth-century excavations. You peer through magnifying glasses and microscopes, trying to fit incomplete and worn tablets into single documents. You need the patience of Job, brilliant linguistic skills, and a passion for the puzzling and obscure. Like almost everyone, I don't have the patience. But such records were the ancestors of the Santa Barbara Public Library, and libraries everywhere.

Archaeologists dig sites and survey landscapes in search of the past. The British humorist P.G. Wodehouse once wrote of spectators at a London building site. "A mere hole in the ground, which of all sights is perhaps the least vivid and dramatic, is enough to grip their attention for hours at a time." The same can be said of archaeologists, who do indeed spend a great deal of time contemplating the nuances of trenches large and small. I spent my early career doing just that, but time and chance took me onto the far wider stage of public outreach, communicating archaeology to the public. Today, I spend my time visiting sites and poring over museum collections, but above all, in libraries, both academic and public. The debt I owe Santa Barbara's libraries is enormous. You can talk at length about the World Wide Web and instant access to the most arcane data, but there is nothing like the book and the printed page. This is especially true when you're an author with specialized training writing about much broader issues. Then you need books, imaginative, thoughtful volumes that range over major topics, in my case like climate change, Egyptology, or water. You need to flip back and forth, to consult indexes and explore bibliographies for days on end. Only books make this possible.

Even half a century ago, archaeology was about artifacts and sites, occasionally about people. Back then, we archaeologists often tended to think of such things as museum specimens and inanimate objects rather than the work of living beings. Fortunately, we have moved on to a new era that relies heavily on multidisciplinary science to study people, on data drawn from literally dozens of scientific disciplines. Some of them are positively esoteric, such as the study of the climatic adaptations of 20,000-year-old fossil beetles brought up from the sea bed of the Bering Strait, once dry land. But all these seemingly minor fragments of knowledge are part of the complex jigsaw puzzles of the past. These days, my researches range broadly and involve hours in the quiet stacks of academic and non-academic libraries.

The absurd and anachronistic "publish or perish" system has manifested itself in a deluge of edited volumes and monographs of very limited distribution. Relatively few of them become e-books. They can only be found on the shelves of museums and universities. I find myself tunneling into edited volumes having read of one relevant paper on the web. When I settle down in the library and read the table of contents, almost invariably I end up consulting two or three papers, which I would otherwise never have read, unless I found them by chance in the ever-expanding bibliographies of such volumes. If I can, and if I'm lucky, I may be able to find the reference in yet another edited volume in the stacks. Otherwise, I must get them from elsewhere, which can take days, even weeks. Periodicals are no problem these days, for they are almost invariably accessible on the web from my office at home.

Many of the subjects I research are dauntingly obscure, like, for example, the graffiti inscribed on the walls of Roman brothels and taverns at Pompeii. I found one monograph, which was crushingly dull, then scanned the neighboring shelves, just as my high school teacher had advised. Bingo! Two or three much more informative and sexually explicit volumes told me all I needed to know—and far more. I'm very lucky to have taught at the University of California, which has one of the finest library systems in the world. In over forty years, I have never defeated it, thanks to the efficient interlibrary loan system, which has obtained books for me from as far away as Oxford.

The greatest challenge I, and other authors, face is the tidal wave of books that descends on us day after day—over 305,000 in the US alone in 2013, and that was four years ago. Here the Public Library comes into its own, for the librarians, and the publications they consult, winnow down titles across a broad spectrum of non-fiction topics. I find myself reading books on fly-fish tying and gin, consulting weighty tomes on California history, Indian birch bark canoes, and bicycling, subjects I never imagined I would explore. Exploring like this is truly a joyous experience, far more fun in an eclectic public library than in a more specialized academic setting. It's amazing just how often I find something relevant to the research I have in progress, as I did when exploring ancient and modern horse training and the realities of travel by camel across the Sahara Desert. I also learn what my readers are thinking about, how even obscure topics like donkey packing have deep roots in the past, and, above all, a great deal about human nature. My writings would be truly lost without the shelves of the public library and its enthusiastic librarians.

Most of my reading is, inevitably, very serious non-fiction, and arid non-fiction at that. The public library is where I turn for relief, for good fiction and bad, for thrillers, war books, humor, and detective stories—to mention only a few. Again, I scan the shelves and often discover a new author, whose writings delight and take me far away from the sober world of more academic non-fiction. I cannot live without good fiction and frequently borrow older works from the library, just for the pleasure of reading truly evocative, old-fashioned description. Fiction provides me with welcome "snorts between the solid orgies," as the immortal Wodehouse memorably remarked.

We live in times of profound change, assailed by prophets of doom who bloviate about the death of the printed book in the face of cyberspace. Nonsense! The book will always be alive and well, for the delights of a glass of wine, a comfortable chair, and a nice read still charm, and they always will. And public libraries like ours are wonderful arbiters of quality and good writing in a world where self-publishing provides us with an endless torrent of, let's be frank, literary garbage. The challenge is not finding a book about something, it's unearthing quality among the plethora of just plain lousy writing.

Long live our beloved public library! I wish I could be here for the second centenary.

Karin Finell
Of Books and Libraries and Peace.

Karin Finell's book, Good-bye to the Mermaids: A Childhood Lost in Hitler's Berlin, *was published in 2006 by University of Missouri Press. It conveys the horrors of war as seen through the eyes of a child. It tells of a convoluted world where children searched for truth and were torn between fear and hope. The essay below recounts her return to her homeland after the war. Finell taught five years of* Writing Your Pain: Grief and Transformation, *at Adult Education at Santa Barbara City College. For more about her life and her work, visit www.karinfinell.com.*

WHEN I returned to Berlin in 1945, no libraries existed. The war ended May 7, and in the autumn of 1945 we moved into the first floor of a relative's villa in the suburbs.

When school started in the fall, I heard that a private lending library would soon open nearby. I walked past the address and found a dark, three-storied mansion, reminding me of the one Mrs. Havisham had lived in. Two Fräulein Hubert, elderly spinster-sisters, had inherited the house from their bibliophile father. I filled out a card at school, and became a member of this impromptu library. For 5 Pfennig I could check out a book for two weeks.

On my first visit I opened the garden gate and heard its rusty moaning, and I thrilled to the shiver of the unknown, coupled to a delicious curiosity, wondering what I might find inside this house. It felt spooky, as if I'd slipped into a bygone century. One of the sisters had heard the moaning gate, and opened the great mahogany entry door, I showed the lady my library card, and she waved me inside to the large foyer, which led to the great salon. I passed the broad, curving staircase to the upper floors. I sniffed. Yes, the air held the musty smell of ancient books, of old leather, of paper that had absorbed human scents and transformed them into the odor of books.

In the salon, burgundy velvet curtains were held back by a braided rope, permitting light to enter. A Bluethner grand piano stood in one corner of the room, waiting for a musician to lift the cover and play. Maybe a Schumann sonata?

Floor to ceiling bookshelves covered the walls. On this floor mostly twentieth century publications were found. On several shelves were books in English and French. Books were censored during the Hitler years, and several copies I found of Hemingway and Steinbeck must have been hidden during that period. And there was Thomas Mann, formerly canonized as being the greatest of the new generation of German writers, but later ostracized by Hitler when Mann left Germany, ostensibly not wanting to share the same air with the "Great Fuehrer."

The second floor was dedicated mainly to writers of the nineteenth century, but there were a few books from the eighteenth and seventeenth, many in German, but some in French and English. And an entire bookshelf of Shakespeare stood there, in the original English and in the excellent German translation by Ludwig Tieck.

I read the German translations of the Russian writers: Pushkin, Dostoyevsky and Tolstoy, but my favorites were Anton Chekhov's plays. I hoped to be an actress and pictured myself on stage as Anya in *The Cherry Orchard*.

Volumes of philosophy and anthropology were located on the third floor and here were few visitors. I did not find much to read, but my curiosity made me pick up illustrated volumes of anthropology which showed various strange practices of aboriginal societies. When I left the third floor, one of the sisters followed me and her eyes told me she had watched me and disapproved of my excursions into aborigines' practices.

As autumn turned to winter, a black iron stove on each floor generated a pleasant warmth. Without the library, the sisters might have frozen to death during the extremely cold winters of 1945, 1946 and 1947. By having declared the mansion a library for the public's use, the city arranged for the coal burning stoves to be installed, and extra rations of coal were deposited in the cellar. To keep the many lights on when days shortened, the library was allowed to use more than the allocated units of electricity.

It was one of life's strange ironies. The wealthy home owners of this suburb, with the most up-to-date kitchens, bathrooms and the newest of central heating, depended on electricity, which was rationed, or gas, which by then was nonexistent. But the poor in other neighborhoods still used their old iron stoves, and new ones were being manufactured. Up was down and down stayed down, as always.

The two Fräulein Hubert were our book angels in many different ways. It was great to have such a varied choice of reading material, and it was a warm place, and having a library in our neighborhood felt as if things were slowly getting back to normal.

What would man be without books? Without the access to books? What would man be without understanding his own history, the intricate interweaving of various religions throughout time, the domination of one people by another and eventually freedom gained, the poetry and literature resounding to us through the ages?

Fannie Flagg
One Library Book

One of America's best-loved writers, she is the bestselling author of, among other novels, Daisy Fay and the Miracle Man; Fried Green Tomatoes at the Whistle Stop Cafe; Welcome to the World, Baby Girl; *and* The All-Girl Filling Station's Last Reunion. *Flagg's script for the movie Fried Green Tomatoes was nominated for an Academy Award. Flagg lives happily in Santa Barbara and her native home of Birmingham, Alabama. More about her life and books can be found at www.fannieflaggbooks.com.*

I GREW up in Alabama, a mighty far distance away from London, England. Even though I was only 11 years old at the time, thanks to the local library, I was able to travel across the sea to London (in my mind, of course) and learn about people I might never have ever heard of.

I don't know why, but from an early age people had always fascinated me so I was naturally drawn to the section entitled "Biography." The very first book I picked out of the shelf was an autobiography of the great English actress and musical comedy star, Miss Gertrude Lawrence, entitled *A Star Danced*. As I sat alone in my room and read it, I was immediately transported back in time to the 1920s and 1930s of London, the heyday of the English musical revues. I learned all about all the stars that appeared with her so my next book was a bio about Noel Coward. Then came another about Beatrice Lillie, the English comedienne, who was their friend and contemporary. What exciting lives they led, so glamorous, so much fun, or so it seemed to me at the time.

I can't say for sure, but I strongly suspect it was that book about Gertrude Lawrence and the others that followed that spurred me to announce to my mother a few weeks later, "When I grow up, I want to be an actress!"

Strangely enough, I did grow up and did become an actress. And stranger still, years later as a professional actress, I toured the country in the Noel Coward play, "Private Lives," playing the very role that Gertrude Lawrence had originated on the London stage. At one point on the tour we happened to be playing a theatre in Houston, Texas, the exact same time as the first landing on the moon. Unbeknownst to me, Noel Coward, the man himself, was in town to entertain at a party for the returning astronauts. A friend brought him to the theatre to see the play. As you can well imagine when he walked in my dressing room after the show, I almost fainted. He was as charming and delightful in person as he was on stage.

Several years later in New York, while leaving the ladies room at Sardi's, I literally ran into none other than Miss Beatrice Lillie, who was in town doing the musical version of another Noel Coward play, "Blithe Spirit."

Sadly I never did get to meet Gertrude Lawrence or see her on Broadway in her last great performance of "The King & I" playing Anna. She had died long before I got to New York and I never saw her on stage. However, years later, I was cast as the lead in a play that was touring the east coast. One of the venues was the Dennis Playhouse, in Dennis, Massachusetts, the same theatre that Gertrude Lawrence's husband had owned and where she had starred in so many productions.

The day I arrived at the theatre and sat down in the very dressing room that had been her dressing room, I saw the scarf she had worn in the "King & I" hanging in a place of honor. Seeing that and so many photos of her on the wall, some I recognized from the book, needless to say I burst into tears.

My life had come full cycle. From that little 11 year old girl who first picked up a book, to this moment sitting in her dressing room in the same chair where she had sat so many years ago.

So you can see how one library book changed my life and gave me a career that I might never have pursued. On that day that little girl could never have dreamed all the magical things that were to come in her future. Nor could she ever have guessed that one day she would write ten books of her own.

Betty Fussell
The Public Library of Riverside CA 1935

Fussell is the award-winning author of numerous books ranging from biography and memoir to cookbooks and food history; a winner of the James Beard Foundation's Journalism Award who was inducted into their "Who's Who of American Food and Beverage" in 2009; and whose fifty years' worth of essays on food, travel, and the arts have appeared in scholarly journals, popular magazines and newspapers as varied as The New York Times, The New Yorker, *and* Vogue. *A selection of these was published in 2016 as* Eat Live Love Die. *She has lived in Santa Barbara since 2012.*

IN 1935 when I was eight, my parents would drop me off on a Saturday morning at the Junior Branch of the Riverside Public Library on Seventh and Orange Streets to wait on the porch until the doors opened at 9:00. On Saturdays, as every day, it was open 9:00 AM to 5:00 PM. On Sundays, it was open only from 1:00 to 5:00, after morning church service and family dinner at noon.

The Junior Branch was junior size, made from the remodeled family house of a man named Humphrey, with a little roofed porch and bench by the front door. It was homey compared to the grand Main Library building down the street, which reared in Mission Revival majesty to make Andrew Carnegie, a Calvinist Presbyterian like us, as proud as we were of the passion for education of our Scottish forbears who emigrated to America.

My eighth birthday was significant to me because children eight and older could apply for their very own library cards and borrow books. If you didn't know how to read, you could learn at the public library. A nice lady would come weekly and read stories aloud to a circle of us kids from totlet to teenager.

As a totlet, I grew up in a house with no story books, only medical and scientific texts to supplement God's Book. So, for me, the town's public library was a place of vast adventure into unknown worlds matched only by the movies projected at Riverside Fox Theatre, a fantastical palace matched only by the Mission Inn.

But a matinee movie was different from a borrowed book. The book was yours for one whole week or whatever the date stamped inside. You could take the book home and open its closed covers under a sheet at night to read by flashlight. It was like opening the doors of a darkened movie house to see in the distance a fabulous world of black and white photos come to life on the screen.

Either way, movie or book, both freed me from the upright and uptight box of our house on Walnut and Twelfth Streets. Now I could go anywhere in the universe, at any time, by any means. I could go by foot, horseback, train, car, airplane, rocket. I could be other creatures—Peter Rabbit in Farmer MacGregor's garden. I could be other people—Pollyanna in Beldingsville, Vermont. I could be every heroine that ever was: Dorothy skipping down the Yellow Brick Road, Alice falling down the Rabbit Hole, Cinderella riding to the Ball in a pumpkin.

I could fly, I could swim, I could dance, I could sing. Words sang to me and danced in the projected movies on the screen of my head and heart. Library books were a trailer for the movies of my life to come. They were also an entrée into the real world when innocence falls into knowledge.

One Saturday morning when I was around ten, waiting on the library's porch bench, a scruffy man in a beard hobbled up the stairs and sat down beside me. When he asked what I was doing there, I said I was waiting for the library to open. He told me he had something to show me. I had nowhere to go, so I stayed still. He zipped open his trousers and took out a long ugly red thing that looked stiff and swollen. I knew this was not right. "Don't be afraid," he yelled as I ran down the steps toward the big Main Library. Luckily, it had just opened and I called my parents to come get me.

Books knew it all, everything that is and was and could be, real, fantastic, horrific, romantic, legendary, historic. When I was finally old enough to escape my small town and travel the world for real, with my own family or alone, I was always accompanied by books. How else would I know where I was or what I was doing there? They were as necessary to grown-up life as water to a camel.

The library opened an ongoing narrative bounded only by the limits of my body, eyes and ears, mind and imagination. And this initial introduction to the universe was FREE. The library was not in a club you had to join or a school you had to attend or a rich kid's mansion you had to be invited to. It was public, its door open to every race, color, creed. It was like the public schools I attended, like the public municipal auditorium, like the Greek Revival county courthouse. Like California's state beaches and parks. Like Riverside's Fairmount Park and Mount Rubidoux.

Eighty-one years later in Santa Barbara, after sixty years of life in the East Coast where my children harbored in Princeton's Public Library just as I had in Riverside's, I remain a card-carrying member of the American Public Library system, whose devotion to truth and the continuing adventure of knowledge created a thirst that continues to make America great.

Neil Gaiman
Why Our Future Depends on Libraries

Self-described as a "feral child who was raised in libraries," the English author (who now resides in the United States) Gaiman is credited with being one of the creators of modern comics, as well as an author whose work crosses genres and reaches audiences of all ages. He is listed in the Dictionary of Literary Biography *as one of the top ten living post-modern writers and is a prolific creator of works of prose, poetry, film journalism, graphic novels, song lyrics, and drama. This is an excerpt from the author's lecture for the UK's Reading Agency's annual lecture on the future of reading and libraries. See www.neilgaiman.com for more about the author.*

ONE WAY to destroy a child's love of reading, of course, is to make sure there are not books of any kind around. And to give them nowhere to read those books. I was lucky. I had an excellent local library growing up. I had the kind of parents who could be persuaded to drop me off in the library on their way to work on summer holidays, and the kind of librarians who did not mind a small, unaccompanied boy heading back into the children's library every morning and working his way through the card catalogue, looking for books with ghosts or magic or rockets in them, looking for vampires or detectives or witches or wonders. And when I had finished reading the children's library, I began on the adult books.

They were good librarians. They liked books and they liked the books being read. They taught me how to order books from other libraries on inter-library loans. Thy had no snobbery about anything I read. They just seemed to like that there was this wide-eyed little boy who loved to read, and would talk to me about the books I was reading, they would find me other books in series, they would help. They treated me as another reader—nothing less or more—which meant they treated me with respect. I was not used to being treated with respect as an eight-year-old.

But libraries are about freedom. Freedom to read, freedom of ideas, freedom of communication. They are about education (which is not a process that finishes the day we leave school or university), about entertainment, about making safe spaces, and about access to information.

I worry that here in the twentyfirst century people misunderstand what libraries are and the purpose of them. If you perceive a library as a shelf of books, it may seem antiquated or outdated in a world in which most, but not all, books in print exist digitally. But that is to miss the point fundamentally.

* * *

Libraries are places that people go to for information. Books are only the tip of the information iceberg; they are there, and libraries can provide you freely and legally with books. More children are borrowing books from libraries than ever before—books of all kinds; paper and digital and audio. But libraries are also, for example, places that people, who may not have computers, who may not have internet connections, can go online without paying anything; hugely important when the way you find out about jobs, apply for jobs or apply for benefits is increasingly migrating exclusively online. Librarians can help these people navigate that world.

I do not believe that all books will or should migrate onto screens. As Douglas Adams once pointed out to me, more than 20 years before the Kindle turned up, a physical book is like a shark. Sharks are old: there were sharks in the ocean before the dinosaurs. And the reason there are still sharks around is that sharks are better at being sharks than anything else is. Physical books are tough, hard to destroy, bath-resistant, solar-operated, feel good in you hand: they are good at being books, and there will always be a place for them. They belong in libraries, just as libraries have already become places you can go to gain access to ebooks, and audiobooks, and DVDs and web content.

A library is a place that is a repository of information and gives every citizen equal access to it. That includes health information. And mental health information. It's a community space. It's a place of safety, a haven from the world. It's a place with librarians in it. What the libraries of the future will be like is something we should be imagining now.

Literacy is more important than ever it was, in this world of text and email, a world of written information. We need to read and write, we need global citizens who can read comfortably, comprehend what they are reading, understand nuance, and make themselves understood.

Libraries really are the gates to the future. So it is unfortunate that, round the world, we observe local authorities seizing the opportunity to close libraries as an easy way to save money, without realizing that they are stealing from the future to pay for today. They are closing the gates that should be open.

* * *

We have an obligation to support libraries. To use libraries, to encourage others to use libraries, to prevent the closure of libraries. If you do not value libraries then you do not value information or culture or wisdom. You are silencing the voices of the past and you are damaging the future.

William Gass
Slices of Life in a Library

Novelist, critic, and one-time philosophy professor, winner of three National Book Critics Circle Award prizes, and post-modernist icon, Gass is one of America's most honored writers.

I LIVE in a library * * * While in graduate school at Cornell, I spent hours in the university library, as PhD drudges are required to do. I had a carrel—a small nick in the wall of the stacks that held a mean metal chair and a bulb, a sheet of steel to write or rest a book on, a rack in front of my face for volumes taken from the shelves (but on one's honor not to be removed from the building), and a jar of hard candy whose contents were dangerous when wet. To take notes, pencils-only was a rule I was willing to observe, since, unlike those of the navy, it made sense. The building resembled a ship in some ways and bore me off smoothly. Not only were the stacks made of metal, the floor was of steel mesh that let an already worn out light sink toward a basement as distant as a bilge. Steps naturally rang a little unless you were in sneakers, but there were areas so removed from human interest (nutrition, for instance . . . it was a different era) that the only sounds you were likely to hear were those of the watchmen, who were apparently heavy men in boots. Nevertheless, sitting there day after day in dusky light, Eden's image began to change. It had no location on a map, but was a destination determined by the Dewey Decimal System.

When I wasn't reading or falling asleep over a page of Lovejoy's *The Great Chain of Being*, I roamed. Up and down the metal steps. Up and down the metal aisles. I stalked like a hunter through a dim light deemed beneficial for any volume's long interment, but barely feasible if you desired to read one, my fingers sometimes slipping along the edges of the books as a kid passing a fence might run a stick, my gaze on spines and their titles, a gaze full of wonderment that there were so many, as dead to me as those rows and rows of skulls in the catacombs were unless I removed one from their ranks, and opened it, and read the way Hamlet examined the skull of Yorick: Jean Henri Fabre's *Book of Insects* or *The Worst Journey in the World* by Apsley Cherry-Garrard? Who could resist an author whose name was Apsley Cherry-Garrard? I would check out the Henri Fabre for a son of my theses director, Professor Max Black, since I had been asked to find worthwhile but entertaining texts for one of his boys. Unfortunately, the young man loved my selections and Professor Black prolonged my service. The Apsley Cherry-Gerrard too was a hit. Therein was one of the most harrowing accounts of Antarctic adventure ever penned, pages of cold and snow, pain and uncertainty, plus a stubborn unintended heroism that I would try to remember when I wrote *The Pedersen Kid*, a novella set in a snowdrift. Since I was a philosophy student I tried to make into a paradox the fact that *The Worst Journey* was really the best trip I'd ever taken.

The heavy-footed guys guarding the darkness didn't like readers to stay the night. You could nod over John Locke all afternoon, they wouldn't mind, but come ten o'clock they'd begin to sweep us out. First they came scouting to see who was in their carrels. They would mark you by your light. Since our little nooks were as open as a supermarket, if they didn't see you sitting there, they would turn off your lamp. Hiding at the right time by making yourself thin at the end of a aisle or fleeing to another level like an amused draft, we would wait to return only after closing.

Dodging the gestapo's heavy tread became a game, but our abilities (and I was certainly not alone in this practice) were put to serious use each year when the library had its book sale. I knew succession, secession, recession, possession, concession, depression, and now I was to enjoy deaccession. A room on one of the lower levels would be set aside and furnished with several large library tables. Upon them rows of books, spines up, would be packed. The humanities filled more tabletops than the sciences did, which was not a surprise, because the scientists didn't read; they tested. And reported their results in magazines that cost more than books. Rumors accused persons unknown of hiding overnight in the stacks in order to be first in line when the sale began the next morning. But that was not the worst these sneaks would sink to. They would actually take the books they wanted from one table (literature, philosophy, history) and hide them among economics or statistics, and one person I know was accused of taking volumes entirely away to another part of the building for the night, only bringing them back as if freshly chosen the following morning. Some tell-all told all once again.

The competition was fierce and friendship had no standing. Every book belonged to each of us, and often there were juicy prizes to be taken, since our teachers sometimes had the decency to die and their heirs, in ignorance or indifference, to dump the bulky part of the inheritance in the bins of the library. But these books would never reach the shelves. They'd be denied admittance ("we already have this edition of *The Maid of Orleans*). A writer once said about editors that out of refusal comes redemption, in this case because the sale books would not have been disfigured by the library's boastful black footprint (PROPERTY OF THE CORNELL UNIVERSITY LIBRARY), or pricked by the university's embossed seal, or pasted with a withdrawal and return record, or embarrassed by a tattoo inked on their spines as if they were headed for the boxcars. We busy buyers said we were rescuing the books that we were early pulling out of the pack from who knew what calamitous destiny. Not death. That was nothing. The bleakest fate was to be always available but never molested.

I have been to many library sales since, and can vouch for the fact that the duplicates are rarely examined, or their source respected, for out of them have fallen, as out of book-fair books, treasures that sometimes surpass even their pages—not just the debts readers normally leave behind to keep their place—paper clips, kitchen matches, rubber bands, foil, curls of hair, bookmarks, bills, sucker sticks, lists, letters of love, post cards, postage stamps, gum wrappers—but photographs and threatening notices, greenbacks, checks, and a draft of a telegram to be sent to the Allied High Command asking him to expedite the transport of Werner Heisenberg out of Germany, which fluttered to my floor when I riffled one of Arthur Holly Compton's books after purchasing it for fifty cents at a Washington University purge.

Collectors who do not care for books but only for their rarity prefer them in an unopened, pure, and virginal condition, but such volumes have had no life, and now even that one chance has been taken from them, so that, imprisoned by stifling plastic, priced to flatter the vanity of the parvenu who has made its purchase, it sits out of the light in a glass-enclosed humidor like wine too old to open, too expensive to enjoy.

This is how I learned to live in the library, what routes to take to the bathrooms, what provisions to smuggle in by briefcase, how to cushion a hard seat, the skill to size up swiftly what is on the reshelver's trolley or to find the books they put back out of place like a dime gone missing at the beach, how to mourn the loss of the card catalog, and where it is easiest to read, where it is safe to sleep.

Covered patio circa 1950s

Dagoberto Gilb
Thou Shalt Not Need to Steal Books

Born and raised in Los Angeles, Gilb now lives in Austin, Texas. His books have won the PEN/Hemingway Award and have been finalists for the PEN Faulkner *and* National Book Critics Circle Award. *He edited* Hecho en Tejas: An Anthology of Texas Mexican Literature, *the canonical volume of Texas Mexican literature, which won the Southwest Book Award for non-fiction. His fiction and nonfiction have appeared in many magazines, such as* Harper's, *and* The New Yorker. *Gilb is writer-in-residence at the University of Houston-Victoria and executive director of CentroVictoria, a center for Mexican American Literature and Culture.*

I WASN'T a book boy. I did have a child's picture book of *Moby Dick*. Probably twenty-five words a page, very colorful drawings, thirty big pages total? My favorite, and only. I loved it. I have no idea how it got in my possession. I didn't steal it, I say to assure you. Books weren't an item in my home. I remember I did like the glossy-cover encyclopedias they sold, I think it was weekly (could have been monthly), in the supermarkets way back then. I'd persuaded my mom to buy one or two or even three. I never really read them, just liked the idea of them and getting smart if you had them around. I might read a sports page. Mostly scores and stats of especially baseball. I played sports. Whatever was around, whatever anybody wanted to play. I was good at that.

Things changed right after high school. By that I mean for and in me. These were the Vietnam years. Hippies, weed, mushrooms, all as common as long hair (acid seemed to be for nerdy or loony whiteboys who didn't need jobs or come from where they mattered) and those drafted and going, or finally back but a touch wacko and scary. I'd read a book my senior year—by that I mean I tried to—because I was in this special two-hour flunky English class. I thought the teacher was a drunk. Nobody and not me either in this class cared and that's why we were in it. One day this man told those who were listening (or overhearing? I can't remember him talking like a teacher) that hippies read a book called *Stranger in a Strange Land*, that it was like the hippie bible. I don't know where I got it but I don't believe I stole it. I wanted to learn about hippies because I liked marijuana and music and...all that seemed pretty nice about their cute girls and easy life. I didn't get the book at all, what it was about, and I never heard the word "grok" with any of the peoples I encountered then or ever. But I did like that I'd read a book (even if I don't think I did it, really, at least most of it). It made me feel smarter and that seemed...well, good. In the land I'd come up in, it was stupid sucks (the worst of them big and pissed off for being ugly), into scamming or gaming something, and mostly drunk or getting there. I wanted smart.

And so it was either Vietnam or, to stall, junior college. I didn't grow up with my father, a WWII Marine sergeant, but even he, like many, wasn't sure it was a wise move to be a draftee and go there. I kept my full-time employment and went to community college. It was like discovering girls for me. And my world flipped. There wasn't a class I came in knowing anything. I was starving for it all. And I wanted to read the books for class cover to cover. Slow at first, word after word looked up, graph to page to chapter to one after another. There followed books that weren't assigned. Then books others told me about. Then ones I found out about. Books that led to more books.

By the time I transferred to UC Santa Barbara, I thought I was a full-fledged intellectual. I wanted a revolution. I wanted a few. And I stole books. That had nothing to do with a revolution, since I used to steal shit when I didn't know that word and it was candy or beer or gin or albums—those were the gentle things. But it did help to justify it that I was, uh, stealing for the revolution and not me me me. They weren't often even anything to do with revolution. Of course I read Marx, Hegel, Marcuse and Fanon, the Soledad Brothers, Wright, Cleaver. I would steal Camus, Rulfo, Hesse, Paz, Beckett, and Dostoyevsky. Once even Porter (I saw all the pretty English majors carrying around her best-selling collection). Mostly it became stranger books. Because real fast I started changing too. I found I liked all kinds of subjects and titles. Plato to Chuang Tzu to Garcia Marquez and so on. And I wanted everything I read. What is that? That want to own that book you read, like it's yours?

My favorite bookstore was the Isla Vista Bookstore. I preferred used books, and it had the best quality ones. I spent hours there learning its sections, trying ones in Spanish, trying ones in French. I got into mass westerns, my keeper favorites those when the lead character was an Indian and particularly a half-breed, my specialty. I was such a regular I'd often go there and find a new subject or book and read right there. Sometimes I didn't steal, though mostly that could be seen as strategy—buy one or two real cheap, pants an expensive one or two. And so it was that there was this one pleasant day I'd come in and was wandering around, checking spines and then back covers and a few interior pages. I don't remember where I was, what section, which books. It must have been in a more open area than I usually was. The bookstore had an upper floor that surrounded the main floor, like a gigantic, railed, overhead shelf, where we patrons never went. And maybe I'd been getting so comfortable in there, so used to doing what I did, that I forgot where I was and what I was doing wasn't good: two books down my pants and I looked up (was something said, or all non-verbal alarms?) and the owner was glaring at me. I felt like we knew each other, we approved of each other. I loved his bookstore. So much of my intimate time there. He couldn't help liking me too—he was a bookstore owner, I was the epitome of who and what they were for. Except the stealing part.

I always thought he was Japanese. I don't mean that to imply he was Zen, something as silly as that. Only a California type that did things well and thoughtfully and wasn't messed up as . . . people like me. He didn't start screaming or calling me names or yelling about police or arrest, didn't rush down to shake or lecture me and cause me to run like a fool. He just stared at me calmly and spoke in a normal voice. "Never come back here again," he said sternly.

I put the stolen books back on their shelf. I creeped off, eyes down, a sicko. I was truly ashamed. And devastated by the loss. I wasn't sure what to do next, where to hide (I couldn't even walk that block for years, pass by), where to be me. I was 50% books, both mind and body.

How many hours or days later I don't remember, but I was in downtown Santa Barbara. I didn't go there so often, just easy to drive to the "city" (I came up in the city of LA) and there was a Mexican restaurant with chilaquiles which always cheered me up. After, I was walking. Not a big town, Santa Barbara was a romantically beautiful one. And I got to what is probably its prettiest public space (as in a five-hundred years later antiquity, would be its monumental center), the courthouse, museum, library. You know how it is when you're walking in the remnants of ancient cities. You sense time and history, your own life in a larger perspective.

I'd never been a book boy young. Back then libraries to me were field trips, where teachers took you every so often and I had to go and, there, be told to shut up. I walked into Santa Barbara's library. There were kind people at desks offering to help me out. Like nurses, or Franciscans blessing this animal, who was me. These library places were still and calm because there was reading going on. People reading, learning, from books. Obvious, right? I know, that's simple unless you'd never paid close attention with your brain. For me it was as if I walked into a cathedral, and a sweet hum of wind light was in my ears and turned my eyes both upward and inward.

Okay, that last part didn't happen thus or at all or with sound effects or a light show. Nothing mystical. But I was cured. I mean, I didn't like that I stole books. I stopped. Never again. Like that part of my stupid life was done. Coincided, a little, with me needing to use libraries with stranger books than any bookstore would or could have. My love of books and bookstores and especially IV Bookstore (I'm still ashamed, my penance this) blew up—expanded— to libraries great and small. I've read in a lot of them now, too. Not just UCSB's or UCLA's, not just Santa Barbara's, but ones in El Paso, Austin, Albuquerque, New York, Stanford, the Library of Congress, all these hexagons (what Borges called them) an entrance to an embracing homeland, where I am both innocent and mature over and over, where, good day or bad, sure or confused, I can always imagine I am going to heaven.

Rhyk Gilbar
The Making (and Unmaking) of a Librarian
(in Three Parts)

Author of several children's picture books noted for their sly humor, Gilbar enjoyed a brief career as a reference librarian before being seduced by the astigmatic muse of optometry. He has been visiting Santa Barbara for most of his life after his parents moved there in 1971. In 2011 he and his family moved to Santa Barbara, where he continues to write.

I. Dr. Kildare and the Facts of Life; or

What Secrets Lie on the Librarian's Special Bookshelf. Adults Only

MY PARENTS will let me do anything that might sway me toward becoming a doctor. That is why—on a cold Detroit afternoon in 1962 at age nine—I am watching "Dr. Kildare," though, frankly, I'll watch anything.

So, this young lady is in the emergency room and in comes Richard Chamberlain (Dr. Kildare) with his clipboard. He says, more or less, "The reason you're feeling so strange is because you're pregnant!" (yay!)

The young lady says—and this is an exact quote, burned into my neurons "I can't be pregnant. I'm not married!" She is clearly not happy.

Curious lad that I was, I ask my mom, "Why do you have to be married to have a baby?" She tried to remain calm. I have three older siblings. She knows the drill.

TO THE LIBRARY!

IMMEDIATELY.

Into the snowsuit and silently we drive the half-mile to our branch library. We enter the quiet Frank Lloyd Wright-inspired vault of knowledge. My mother goes directly to the (honest-to-God) gray-haired, bun-wearing, librarian archetype. Mom whispers. The librarian studies me over her reading glasses and reaches under the desk and pulls out some books. She furtively stamps the due dates and slides them over to my mother.

Oooh! There are secret books in the library! I want to know more. What could they be?

Back home, I'm treated to potato chips and silence and sat down in the living room. The LIVING ROOM! What's going on here? The living room is for adults reading newspapers.

"Read these books," my mom says.

No problem. I like reading more than TV.

The first book is cute and cartoony—a baby developing in a balloon only to be expelled when the balloon pops. Ok.

Book two: more prolix and adolescent, with intimations of intimacies. There are seeds and eggs. Check. Got it.

Book three: Maybe a bit too much anatomy for my nine-year-old eyes, but, ok, I get it.

My mother creeps in and sits on the grown-up couch. She primly lays her hand on the books lying between us. "So, did you understand this?"

"Yeah," I shrug. "I just don't get why you have to be married to have a baby?"

On subsequent library visits I would from time to time attempt a glance at the secret shelf while the librarian was busy checking out books. Besides the few "sex" books there was Arthur Miller, Flaubert and Salinger. I get the vapors just thinking about them.

II. The Librarian Thinks I'm Reading Too Much

In the olden days, circa 1960-62, children had an actual Library Class every week. We file into the school library and take out our reading logs, select a book, sit at our assigned spots and like good little boys and girls shut the f*** up. You could get in actual trouble if you spoke in this library.

Between the two gigantic windows is where the history books are. We're supposed to be well-rounded and read from different sections. I grab a fat Young Adult book with a chariot on the front. We're not supposed to read YA—it's waaay to advanced for the likes of us fourth-graders. Nonetheless, I read . . . and read and read and read. I devour every book on ancient history and archaeology that they have.

Apparently, I should have paced myself. I have filled up the entire reading log. The authorities are suspicious. What is he up to?

This is how you know that it was the olden days: They call my parents.

BOTH of my parents escort me back to school. Wooo. I am in some kind of trouble.

The librarian crossly shows my parents my reading log. They look at it unaware of the transgression.

"There is no way that your son could have read this many books," the librarian says pointing at the three-foot pile on the desk. "One of these books is over two-hundred pages long!"

She slides the offending tome over to my parents. My dad picks it up and skims it.

"Tell me what the book is about?" the librarian asks acerbically and crosses her arms smugly. (Hey, this is my memory.)

I regale them with excavation techniques, uses of royal seals, how hieroglyphics were decrypted, what a midden was and why they were so important. Needless to say (but I'll say it anyway), the librarian was humiliated! Or possibly impressed. Regardless, they all agreed that I had just taught them more about archaeology than they ever wanted to know.

The next Library Class the librarian takes me aside and suggest that I read some fiction. I wander over to that side of the library and pick up a science fiction book called something like *The Spaceship Under the Apple Tree*. From then on all allowance money for the next decade will be spent on SF paperbacks.

My dormant interest in archaeology was excavated in my junior year of college. I changed from the parent-approved Pre-Med to Ancient Near Eastern Studies. Yeah, that degree really had legs. That's why I then decided to go to Library School—now called Information Science. (Read all day and pay the rent). I served as the hippy reference librarian at the University of Kansas for four years.

And for sure, I got in trouble for reading too much.

The stacks were real stacks—six stories of iron shelving with suspended slab-glass floors. There were three buildings and the levels didn't match. On the main floor the doorway between buildings was less than five feet high. One of my fellow librarians, Clint, was walking and reading with his pipe in his mouth. Let's just say that a handy "Low Clearance" sign would have been nice.

III. The Hippie Librarian Fights the Man

In 1976 if you wanted to know what the name of Dudley Do-Right's horse*
was, you would have to go to the library. If you had that annoying itch for some
factoid, you were out of luck if the library was closed. You would have to toss
and turn all night, distraught, annoyed, impatient.

There were over 40,000 books in the reference collection in Watson Library
at the University of Kansas. You had to know them. I spent months just getting
sucked into them—just like I do with web searches now. Did you know that
Hungary continued to print an annual statistics and facts book during WWII?
In English! Did you know that they apparently still sold sour apple syrup to the
US during the war? There's a story there. Interesting aside, sour apple syrup is an
ingredient in Coke. Try finding that with Google! I just tried. Bupkis.

Today there are only about 1000 actual books in the reference area. What's
happening!!?? Sad.

So, anyway. We had millions of books but we didn't have any signs. This
is a huge library with a century of "improvements" that were haphazard and
wonky—floors that didn't match up between sections, subterranean areas,
lofts—with all the usual major library departments dispersed into every strange
nook and cranny. There was one section with over a million uncatalogued
books. A gigantic windowless vault that looked like a scene from "The Matrix."

The actual vest-wearing cigar-chewing Dean of Libraries thought signage
was unnecessary. You can always ask someone, I guess. Not that he was an advo-
cate for human interaction, he was just cheap.

I found some money, like $150, for student labor and my own money for
materials. We produced very professional signs nicely matte-cut and printed
with large vinyl letters. I showed them to the boss. No go. Even after I explained
that 70% of our professional/patron time was simply pointing to where some-
thing was. Still, no go.

Carol, the other hippie librarian, and I hatched a plan: guerilla sign place-
ment. It was a two-fork operation. All the signs were laid out and attached with
transparent fishing line ready to be hung to the ceilings. Phase two was colored

*It was Steed. I was going to make you sweat until the end of the story, but I
am not cruel. Nobody understands the thirst for facts more than a librarian.

tape to be applied to the floor so we could say things like, "Follow the yellow line to the circulation desk" or "Follow the green line to Periodicals."

Midnight. All is even quieter in the library, only the buzz of the ranks of fluorescents. Our team assembles, a half-dozen staff volunteers. By 5 am, it is done. We retire and wait to return later to the expected adulations of library faculty, staff and patrons.

I learned something valuable that day. When the boss says, "no," he/she is not likely to be happy. The staff was literally thumbs-upping me and beaming at the coup. The Dean, not so much. I got a chewing out about tape on the floor, but the signs remained for at least as long as I worked there.

There are those who say, "You know, they sure could use a few signs in this place" and think it's only a utopian vision. And there are those who say, "You know, I'm sick of telling people where the restrooms are," and act, daring to oppose the status quo and the nabobs of negativity.

That was pretty much the end of the road for me in the library as a professional. I didn't take to hierarchy or poverty. I became an optometrist—still kind of a related field in a spiritual sense. While I was in optometry school I worked in the education school making media, which in those days meant pretty much making signs.

We lived in Seattle for a while and the King County Libraries are sleek, modern but somehow still retain the reverence for books and reading.

My old KU library despite retaining the Romanesque façade is a white box full of computer cubicles, again, kind of Matrix-y.

These days I really appreciate the cozy awesomeness of the Santa Barbara Central Library. Books are still appreciated and present and computers are discreet. It feels like a place where people are quietly attending to the needs of their souls. And of course it has great signage.

I hope the next generation does their best to keep our beautiful, inspiring libraries intact and not succumb to the bleak info-terias that are replacing them.

Resist! All you hippie readers, Unite! Save the soul of the Library.

Nikki Giovanni
A Poem for My Librarian, Mrs. Long
(You never know what troubled little girl needs a book)

Renowned poet, activist for civil rights, Virginia Tech professor, and record-ing artist, Giovanni is a strong voice for the black community. One writer wrote of her: "She's got a smooth voice, 25 honorary degrees, and a 'Thug Life' tattoo on her forearm. And if you make it all the way through high school or college without reading her most anthologized poem 'Nikki Rosa,' something has gone terribly, horribly wrong." Many of her poems can be viewed at www. nikki-giovanni.com.

AT A time when there was not tv before 3:00 P.M.

And on Sunday none until 5:00

We sat on the front porches watching

The jfg sign go on and off greeting

The neighbors, discussion the political

Situation congratulating the preacher

On his sermon

There was always the radio which brought us

Songs from wlac in nashville and what we would now call

Easy listening or smooth jazz but when I listened

Late at night with my portable (that I was so proud of)

Tucked under my pillow

I heard nat king cole and matt dennis, june christy and ella fitzgerald

And sometimes sarah vaughan sing black coffee

Which I now drink

It was just called music

There was a bookstore uptown on gay street

Which I visited and inhaled that wonderful odor

Of new books

Even today I read hardcover as a preference paperback only
As a last resort

And up the hill on vine street
(The main black corridor) sat our carnegie library
Mrs. Long always glad to see you
The stereoscope always ready to show you faraway
Places to dream about

Mrs. Long asking what are you looking for today
When I wanted Leaves of Grass or alfred north whitehead
She would go to the big library uptown and I now know
Hat in hand to ask to borrow so that I might borrow
Probably they said something humiliating since southern
Whites like to humiliate southern blacks

But she nonetheless brought the books
Back and I held them to my chest
Close to my heart
And happily skipped back to grandmother's house
Where I would sit on the front porch
In a gray glider and dream of a world
Far away

I love the world where I was
I was safe and warm and grandmother gave me neck kissed
When I was on my way to bed

But there was a world
Somewhere
Out there
And Mrs. Long opened that wardrobe
But no lions or witches scared me
I went through
Knowing there would be
Spring

Seth Godin
The Future of the Library

According to forbes.com, Godin is "a demigod on the Web, a best-selling au-thor, highly sought-after lecturer, successful entrepreneur, respected pundit and high-profile blogger. He is uniquely respected for his understanding of the Internet." The following provocative piece was posted on his blog in 2011 and has been widely discussed, pro and con. His website is www.sethgodin.com.

WHAT IS a public library for?

First, how we got here:

Before Gutenberg, a book cost about as much as a small house. As a result, only kings and bishops could afford to own a book of their own.

This naturally led to the creation of shared books, of libraries where scholars (everyone else was too busy not starving) could come to read books that they didn't have to own. The library as warehouse for books worth sharing.

Only after that did we invent the librarian.

The librarian isn't a clerk who happens to work at a library. A librarian is a data hound, a guide, a sherpa and a teacher. The librarian is the interface be-tween reams of data and the untrained but motivated user.

After Gutenberg, books got a lot cheaper. More individuals built their own collections. At the same time, though, the number of titles exploded, and the demand for libraries did as well. We definitely needed a warehouse to store all this bounty, and more than ever we needed a librarian to help us find what we needed. The library is a house for the librarian.

Industrialists (particularly Andrew Carnegie) funded the modern American library. The idea was that in a pre-electronic media age, the working man needed to be both entertained and slightly educated. Work all day and become a more civilized member of society by reading at night.

And your kids? Your kids need a place with shared encyclopedias and plenty of fun books, hopefully inculcating a lifelong love of reading, because reading makes all of us more thoughtful, better informed and more productive members of a civil society.

Which was all great, until now.

Want to watch a movie? Netflix is a better librarian, with a better library, than any library in the country. The Netflix librarian knows about every movie, knows what you've seen and what you're likely to want to see. If the goal is to connect viewers with movies, Netflix wins.

This goes further than a mere sideline that most librarians resented anyway. Wikipedia and the huge data-banks of information have basically eliminated the library as the best resource for anyone doing amateur research (grade school, middle school, even undergrad). Is there any doubt that online resources will get better and cheaper as the years go by? Kids don't shlep to the library to use an out-of-date encyclopedia to do a report on FDR. You might want them to, but they won't unless coerced.

They need a librarian more than ever (to figure out creative ways to find and use data). They need a library not at all.

When kids go to the mall instead of the library, it's not that the mall won, it's that the library lost.

And then we need to consider the rise of the Kindle. An ebook costs about $1.60 in 1962 dollars. A thousand ebooks can fit on one device, easily. Easy to store, easy to sort, easy to hand to your neighbor. Five years from now, readers will be as expensive as Gillette razors, and ebooks will cost less than the blades.

Librarians that are arguing and lobbying for clever ebook lending solutions are completely missing the point. They are defending library as warehouse as opposed to fighting for the future, which is librarian as producer, concierge, connector, teacher and impresario.

Post-Gutenberg, books are finally abundant, hardly scarce, hardly expensive, hardly worth warehousing. Post-Gutenberg, the scarce resource is knowledge and insight, not access to data.

The library is no longer a warehouse for dead books. Just in time for the information economy, the library ought to be the local nerve center for information.

(Please don't say I'm anti-book! I think through my actions and career choices, I've demonstrated my pro-book chops. I'm not saying I want paper to go away, I'm merely describing what's inevitably occurring.) We all love the vision of the underprivileged kid bootstrapping himself out of poverty with books, but now (most of the time), the insight and leverage is going to come from being fast and smart with online resources, not from hiding in the stacks.

The next library is a place, still. A place where people come together to do co-working and coordinate and invent projects worth working on together. Aided by a librarian who understands the Mesh, a librarian who can bring domain knowledge and people knowledge and access to information to bear.

The next library is a house for the librarian with the guts to invite kids in to teach them how to get better grades while doing less grunt work. And to teach them how to use a soldering iron or take apart something with no user serviceable parts inside. And even to challenge them to teach classes on their passions, merely because it's fun. This librarian takes responsibility/blame for any kid who manages to graduate from school without being a first-rate data shark.

The next library is filled with so many web terminals there's always at least one empty. And the people who run this library don't view the combination of access to data and connections to peers as a sidelight—it's the entire point.

Wouldn't you want to live and work and pay taxes in a town that had a library like that? The vibe of the best Brooklyn coffee shop combined with a passionate raconteur of information? There are one thousand things that could be done in a place like this, all built around one mission: take the world of data, combine it with the people in this community and create value.

We need librarians more than we ever did. What we don't need are mere clerks who guard dead paper. Librarians are too important to be a dwindling voice in our culture. For the right librarian, this is the chance of a lifetime.

Erin Graffy de Garcia
The Bookmobile

Copywriter, author, historian and biographer, Graffy has written over one hundred books, articles, monographs and features for nearly twenty regional publications on Santa Barbara history, as well as such diverse subjects as business marketing, psychology, medical research, and society. For more about her and her work, see eringraffy.com.

THE LIBRARY is not only a storehouse of books, but a source of programs and events which draw in patrons to discover new authors, and topics and areas of interest. When I was nine or so years old, I remember a notice on the bulletin board that the Friends of the Santa Barbara Public Library was holding a poetry contest for grade school children. I was eager to try.

Not only did I win, but it launched a lifelong love of writing verse . . . and now as an award-winning poet.

The poem I wrote for that contest was inspired by the Library's "auxiliary shelves on wheels"—the Bookmobile. I recall being so excited when it was parked at Loreto Plaza, and would beg my mother to let me go in and explore.

The Bookmobile

I was riding in
Mom's car one day
when something I saw
made me jump and say,
"The Bookmobile!"
I gave a squeal,
"Oh mom, please stop!"
and out I hop
into the truck
and oh, what luck!

I find some books
for my report,
as a matter-of-fact,
of every sort!

There's story books
and do-it books,
books for artists
and for cooks,
books of football
(the passes and kicks),
books of magic and
slight-of-hand tricks,
books of knitting
and of sewing,
manners, jokes,
and bubble-blowing,
books that make reading
easy and quick,
books for spelling
and arithmetic.

There's a lady to help you
(the librarian, of course)
to find you a book
on a pony or horse
The truck is so neat
and clean, you see,
and all of the books
you can check out for free!

If you should go
you'll know just how I feel
—the nicest place is
the Bookmobile!

Sue Grafton
A Few Words About Libraries

The best-selling novelist is the author of the "alphabet series" of detective novels featuring private investigator Kinsey Millhone, set in the fictional city of Santa Teresa, California, not unlike Santa Barbara, where Grafton has a home. She has another in Louisville, the city in which she was born and raised. See www.suegrafton.com for more about the author.

THIS MORNING I found myself thinking about libraries, wondering how far back in time I'd have to reach to find the earliest evidence of the archiving of documents and books. I decided to research the question by doing what any serious scholar would do. I went to Google and typed "libraries in the ancient world" on the subject line.

I cribbed the following from the Internet and I freely confess to this so please don't think I'm plagiarizing the information and claiming it as my own. The first libraries consisted of clay tablets, some dating back to 2600 BC, which were discovered in temple rooms in Sumer. According to Google, these records of commercial transactions marks the end of prehistory and the start of history. The earliest private archives were kept at Ugarit and included correspondence, inventories, and texts of myths.

I'm still paraphrasing here when I report that there is also evidence of libraries at Nippur about 1900 BC and at Nineveh 700 BC, which showed a classification system. I don't know about you, but I'm impressed.

My own personal introduction to public libraries dates all the way back to 1945 when my mother first began to accompany my sister and me on our visits to the Highland branch of the public library in Louisville, Kentucky. In those days, there was a strict accounting by the staff. We were allowed to take out three books apiece and no more. This may sound stingy in the current era where such constraints have been lifted, but to me at ages five, eight, ten and onward, the three-book limit was challenging. I'd have to sit for quite a while in the wide aisle between rows of shelves in the children's section, assembling a choice pile of hard cover fiction (I favored tomes with lots of pitchers . . .) and then parse the number down to the three allotted. It was agony, but it did teach me to be discerning and it made me appreciate the bounty of good reading once I was old enough to buy books instead of borrowing.

Additional thieving from the Internet reveals the fact that "libraries in Louisville got their start in 1816, but it was not a free public library. It was a small collection housed in the old Court House. It soon folded for lack of funds as did others to follow it. In 1870 some progressive individuals decided to create a public institution for information and enjoyment where anyone could borrow books without charge." It wasn't until 1895 that the Louisville Free Public Library system was created. Organizers appealed to Andrew Carnegie, resulting in grant money for eight branches: Portland, Eastern, Crescent Hill, Highland, Parkland, Jefferson, Western, Shelby Park plus the Main library.

Andrew Carnegie? You gotta be kidding me.

Years later, this same branch moved to a new location and the building was put up for sale. I can't tell you how tempting that was to me. The edifice boasted three chunky two-story sections of a brownish brick. There were cornices, dentils, a frieze above the entrance, tall windows, and all manner of architectural folderol. I was certain the interior would smell the same as it did when I was in grade school. Imagine owning your very own library! Even empty, you'd have those marble floors, varnished woodwork, stacks where thousands of books could be housed, nooks and crannies, bathrooms with really low toilets, tyke-sized drinking fountains, perhaps a mysterious basement where you might come across who-knows-what.

Granted, most interior decorators would have thrown up their hands in despair, but that wouldn't have bothered me. If there had been a garage or any parking spaces provided, I might have plunked my money down. I have no idea what the sale price was, but I feel certain a little horse trading on my part would have done the trick . . . assuming I had a horse. Through the magic of Google, you can see a black-and-white photograph of that structure, which still sits at the intersection of Cherokee Road and Highland Avenue. If you're ever in Louisville, I would urge you to visit the site and think to yourself: this could have been Sue Grafton's personal residence if she'd just had a little more courage and imagination.

Betsy J. Green
Mrs. Frances Burns Linn:
The Heart and Soul of the Library

A writer for more than 25 years, Green writes about local history and architecture. She worked as an editor at Reader's Digest *and* World Book Encyclopedia, *and is the author of* MESApedia, *and the* Way Back When *series of books about Santa Barbara 100 years ago. See www.betsyjgreen.com for more about her writing.*

ON A balmy August night in 1914, fifty civic leaders—all male—sat on benches around a campfire in a leafy glen in the Carpinteria foothills. At the meeting, it was announced that the Carnegie Foundation had just signed off on a $50,000 grant to fund the construction of Santa Barbara's new library building (our present Central Library building). Mrs. Frances Burns Linn, Santa Barbara's head librarian since 1906, was not at the meeting. She knew about the grant, and was already on the road for her month-long fact-finding tour of ten major city libraries stretching from Oregon to New York State, and points in between.

Over the next two years, the library trustees raised another $50,000—as required by the Carnegie Foundation—and worked to acquire the land at the corner of Anacapa and Anapamu streets. Local architect Francis Wilson and Carnegie's architect Henry Hornbostel designed a building, described as a free adaptation of Spanish-Renaissance style, to complement the community's existing architecture. For the interior, they turned to Linn who they said "supplemented her experience and observation of local library needs and conditions, with the able judgement and authoritative advice of prominent librarians she had met on her 1914 tour. The Carnegie Foundation donated the seed money, the architect designed the building, and Linn gave the library a heart and a soul.

As the library was being planned, the trustees told the Carnegie Foundation that "the spirit of California, her people and their homes, is invitation and hospitality. Our library must express this from every viewpoint. Our librarian [Linn] has given nine years of study to the problem, and our present plans are the result of her efforts assisted through conference with the best librarians of the country. Her conclusions of the requirements [are] the basis of all our plans."

A native Ohioan, Linn graduated from Ohio Wesleyan University, married a classmate, but at age 30, was left a widow without children. Several months later, she enrolled in the New York State Library School in Albany, where she obtained a degree in 1904. She began working at the Santa Barbara Free Public Library in September 1906. The opening chapter of her sojourn in Santa Barbara set the stage for her three-and-a-half decades of relentless dedication. Less than 48 hours after she stepped off the train, Linn was on the job. On September 3, Labor Day (already a holiday in 1906), the local paper announced, "The new librarian, Mrs. Frances Burns Linn, arrived in the city Saturday night, and is at her post in the library today."

When Linn arrived in 1906, the library was just one room. A year and a half later, the little library doubled in size. When the library expansion opened in March of 1908, the local paper praised Linn "for the admirable performance of her arduous duties since she took her office about 18 months ago, and for her present effort and tireless energy in furthering the interests of the library in every way."

In 1910, under Linn's guidance, the library became the first in California to expand its services countywide. A contemporary wrote, "As a trained librarian and an administrator of high order, Mrs. Linn has brought [the library] to a degree of perfection that is most admirable in every particular. One of the first fruits of her efficiency was the establishment of [59!] county branch libraries, under which remote sections of the county can have the advantage of the Free Public Library." To Linn, a library was not just a repository of reading materials. It was a county-wide community resource. "The library can be the means of building up the neighborhood life and community spirit. It can be the common interest in the small towns where differences of creed and politics and social position separate the people, dissipating the forces for good."

While all this was going on, the City of Santa Barbara was growing at a phenomenal pace. The community's population more than doubled between 1906 and 1917. Fortunately, it had the right person in the right place at the right time. Linn's 1914 study-tour of libraries had equipped her to work with the architects to plan a new library that would be an efficient and welcoming center for the increasing numbers of books and citizens.

After the money for the library building was in place, it was time to dig in. "Mrs. Frances B. Linn had the well-deserved honor of turning the first shovelful of earth" on September 25, 1916. As the construction progressed, and the building took shape, Linn took charge of ordering and checking bids for furnishing the library interior. "The city librarian has to compare the prices submitted on each piece of furniture by all the bidders. The matter of design has also to be passed on by Mrs. Linn."

As the library neared completion, it was decided to open the library when children returned to school in August of 1917. With her typical "can do" spirit, Linn said she considered that the monumental task of moving all the books to the new library, in fruit crates loaned by local companies, was "the great adventure of the year." The library opened on August 27, 1917, three years to the day of the Carpinteria campfire meeting when the Carnegie grant was announced. The timing couldn't have been better. That same month, young men of Santa Barbara began leaving to serve on the World War I battlefronts of Europe, and the local labor pool began to shrink. As the community rallied to support the troops, Linn responded by setting up tables in the library that she filled with books and magazines on timely topics such as the history of the war in Europe, conserving food, and making useful items and clothing for American soldiers. On Christmas Eve, as the "war to end all wars" raged in Europe, residents found solace at the library as they listened to carolers and Christmas stories, while wood fires crackled in the massive fireplaces. Similar Christmas activities took place each year as the decades passed.

Perhaps Linn's greatest challenge was the devastating earthquake of June 1925 which left the library damaged and in need of urgent repair. As the city's residents reeled in the wake of the disaster, Linn racked her brain for a way to make the books available in time for the opening of school. A capacious and vacant carriage house on the corner of Chapala and Sola streets was found, and repurposed as a temporary library. The building was painted, repaired, and readied for the delivery of an estimated 20,000 books hauled in fruit crates. "The librarian was on the job every minute at the old library and the new library at the same time, keeping both telephones busy, directing, deciding, encouraging, demanding, knowing every worker by name and getting the best out of him." Five weeks after the temblor, the temporary library was open for business. When the damaged building was back in working order the following year, the monumental process of moving 20,000 books was repeated.

In addition to her work at the library, Linn also served as vice president and then president of the California Library Association. In Santa Barbara, she was the first director of the Faulkner Memorial art gallery, and was involved with numerous local organizations such as the Neighborhood House, the Community Chorus, the Recreation Center, the Community Arts Association, the Community Chest, and the American Association of University Women.

Linn took great pride in the library she helped to shape. She wrote about an episode that was oft repeated, "Two women met in one of Santa Barbara's larger hotels, one for many years a resident of the city, the other a visitor. The newcomer remarked with enthusiasm on the delights of the climate and the natural beauties, to which rhapsody the Santa Barbara woman assented with characteristic loyalty and exclaimed: 'Yes, God has done pretty nearly everything for us here. But have you seen our public library? That's all to our credit.'"

Linn continued her activities until she suffered a stroke in late 1942. She retired the following year. In 1958, on Linn's 85th birthday, civic mover and shaker Pearl Chase wrote a lengthy article in the local paper praising her influence on the library and beyond. "Her wonderful spirit of friendliness was felt by all who entered the library, and the Library Board supported the programs of expanding community service which she largely originated. During the long period of her leadership, the library grew astonishingly. Aided by a devoted staff, Mrs. Linn stimulated in the minds and hearts of the people of Santa Barbara, a love of good books and what was fine in all the arts."

In a similar vein, a former colleague noted, "Santa Barbara had the culture, wealth, and patronage essential to library development, but it was Mrs. Linn's personal charm, her warm hospitality, and contagious enthusiasm that served to bring about the desired relationship between library and community as few could have done."

Linn died in 1962 at the age of 89, leaving Santa Barbara with a library that it can be proud of as her legacy.

Jeff Greenwald
Who's Who

Jeff Greenwald has traveled extensively through five continents, working as a journalist and photographer. His writings are published in print and online worldwide, and his stories appear in more than 25 travel anthologies. Between 1980 and 1983 he lived in Santa Barbara, serving as editor of the weekly News & Review. *His first book,* Mr. Raja's Neighborhood, *was brought out by Santa Barbara publisher John Daniel. His website is jeffgreenwald.com.*

I WAS known to take refuge at the library. Then, as now, the lure of information was magnetic to me—so much so that whenever I ran away from home, which was frequently, my escape route inevitably took me the three miles from our split-level on Coronet Drive to the sheltering stacks of the Plainview-Old Bethpage Public Library.

At the time, this was one of the newer and more modern libraries on Long Island: a sprawling single-level building that opened two months before my tenth birthday. In a neighborhood that used to be covered with pumpkin and potato fields, it was a wonder. There were microfiche machines, study cubicles, an utterly silent Reference section, and a separate Juvenile Wing. And even though I can't remember what I had for dinner last night, I could probably recreate the entire floor plan of my childhood library with ease.

The first books I ever checked out were probably the Henry Huggins series, by Beverly Cleary. But by the time I was 12 the sciences obsessed me. I graduated to Tom Swift Jr.—along with *Danny Dunn and the Homework Machine*, which is still the bedrock of my opinions about artificial intelligence.

Though the Juvenile Wing was my shelter, I spent almost as much time in the adult-dominated Reference section, poring through atlases of the earth and heavens, studying old issues of *National Geographic*, and trying to find the home addresses of The Beatles, the astronauts, and Gilligan's Island stars in *Who's Who*.

I loved the *Who's Who,* a thick red volume with short biographies of every notable actor, scientist, architect, doctor and artist in the world. There was even a supplemental *Who's Who,* delivered to the library every few months, listing new bios and contact information for the recently famous.

Trivia like this fascinated me. And before the early 1990s, even the most banal information was something you worked for. If I wanted to know the genus of a clouded leopard, I had to look it up in the encyclopedia. Which film won Best Director in 1961? I'd call the reference librarian, or a film school. When were the weekend LIRR trains from Hicksville to Penn Station? If my Mom didn't have a schedule, we called the library. It's hard to imagine the world before the Web—and in a generation or so, it will be impossible. But during my teenage years, the quest for data was a thrill—and learning who played Ginger, or orbited the earth aboard *Faith 7,* was rewarded with a delicious endorphin rush.

During the summer of 1968, the Twin Theater in nearby Hicksville featured two films: Bonnie and Clyde, and 2001: A Space Odyssey. By now, my flight path away from home had changed. One humid afternoon I biked to the Mid-Island mall, my intention to see an air-conditioned matinee of the sensational, super bloody R-rated gangster movie. But I was a geeky 14, and the ticket seller turned me away. Instead I begrudgingly settled for the G-rated 2001. The film had just opened, and I had no idea what to expect. It blew my mind. I sat through the 161-minute movie three times—and emerged into a moonlit June night that seemed completely new and charged with dazzling mysteries.

The next day I went back to the library and looked up the film's credits. The co-writer was a science fiction author named Arthur C. Clarke. I determined to devour every book that he had ever written. There were whole shelves of them just waiting to be checked out—from *The Sands of Mars* to *Childhood's End,* and the novelization of 2001 itself. It took me more than a year to work my way through Clarke's canon, but I did it.

Once I'd read them, there was only one thing to do: write a fan letter to Clarke himself. And in 1970, if you were a high school junior eager to contact a famous author, there was only one way to do it. I returned to the library on foot, slogging through a fine January snow, pulled *Who's Who* off the shelf, and pored through the thousands of entries. Clarke, Arthur Charles—born December 16, 1917. I was amazed to see that his listed address was neither in

Hollywood nor New York, but in a country called Sri Lanka. This sent me dashing to the atlases, where I discovered that the small, teardrop-shaped island lay off the southeast coast of India.

A few weeks later, I wrote to Arthur Clarke. The letter was five pages long, and filled with earnest but harebrained sketches of zero-gravity wristwatches, rocket designs, and inanely complex variations on the Pentomino game played aboard the *Discovery* spaceship in 2001.

"I'm your biggest fan," I confessed, "if being the idol of a 15-year-old means anything."

Apparently, it did. In May of that year, I received a simple, hand-written postcard. "Will be in New York, at Hotel Chelsea, this month," it proclaimed. "Give me a call! Best, Arthur."

It is impossible to overstate my anxiety as I stepped off the LIRR at Penn Station that spring day, less than a year after Neil Armstrong and Buzz Aldrin stepped onto the moon. By the time I walked the half-mile to the Chelsea, I was drenched with sweat. When I informed the receptionist that Arthur C. Clarke was expecting me, he was clearly dubious.

"Is that so?" The clerk pulled out a notepad. "In that case," he said, "can you explain to me how a spaceship uses gravity to pick up speed?"

In fact, I'd just read about an article about that very subject in the library's magazine room. If the question was a test, I passed. The clerk told me Clarke's room number, and directed me to the lift.

In May of 1970, Arthur Clarke was 53. The science fiction grandmaster greeted me warmly, and I stepped into what seemed like a Space Age ready room. The walls were covered with 2001 posters, NASA photos, and news clippings. On the hotel desk, a sleek IBM typewriter cradled the manuscript of his novel-in-progress, *Rendezvous with Rama*. Clarke offered me Darjeerling tea, which he prepared with a heating coil.

I didn't know, at that point, that my awkward attempts at conversation (which Clarke graciously endured) would lead to a lifelong friendship and fuel the inspiration for me to write books of my own. During the decades that followed, Arthur and I stayed in touch, both of us passionate about writing, science, and a human presence among the stars... Nor did I dream, on that crisp Chelsea morning, that on four separate occasions I would visit Clarke in Sri

Lanka: at the very address that had seemed so impossibly exotic in the library's *Who's Who*.

My last visit with Arthur took place in Colombo in 2005. Sri Lanka had just been struck by a devastating tsunami, and I was working with a relief organization called Mercy Corps. Clarke and I shared a pot of Earl Grey tea on the veranda of the Galle Face Hotel, watching wistfully as an oblate orange sun sank toward the Indian Ocean.

Clarke, then 88, was trying to recall our first meeting. His memory, he told me, was fading. There were whole chapters of his career he could no longer picture or recall. It seemed inconceivable to me that this man—whose extraordinary life held so many experiences and so much information—could witness his own demise. Like the doomed HAL 9000 in 2001, Clarke's mind was going—and he could feel it. I recalled a comment I'd heard about a wise man in Africa: "When this man dies, it will be as if a great library has burned down."

The sun sets quickly near the equator, and now its huge crimson disk hovered just above the sea. Clarke seemed to remember something, and became suddenly animated. He reached for my sunglasses, and slipped them over his glasses. "This is the perfect time," he announced gleefully, "to see sunspots with your naked eye." A boyish grin lit his face as he stared intently at the Earth's nearest star.

There are some things one never forgets.

My dear friend died three years later. And though nearly fifty years have passed since that day—and my own name now appears in the modern avatar of *Who's Who* (Wikipedia)—I'll never forget the morning I sat in a tiny cubicle in the Plainview-Old Bethpage Library, leafing breathlessly toward the page that would change my life.

Susan Miles Gulbransen
Three Women Give Santa Barbara a Library

Raised in Santa Barbara, Gulbransen is a writer, book reviewer, Noozhawk *columnist and teaches writing at the Santa Barbara Writers Conference. She has been a major influence in enhancing the city's literary community.*

MY FIRST memory of a public library was the main door on Anapamu Street. The colorfully carved arch above it is still there. I would stop, fascinated by those images, but Mom grabbed my hand and led me and my brother on in to pick out books for the next two weeks. How could I argue when endless books creating magical worlds waited inside.

Until last year I had no idea that three women in the nineteenth century made our library happen. Who were they?

The first woman, Sara Plummer, received her education at Female College of Worcester in Massachusetts in the early 1860s. When teaching art in New York City, she became ill with pneumonia. A friend told her about Santa Barbara's climate as a good recovery environment.

After the long train ride across country she arrived in 1869. Soon Plummer, an avid walker, became fascinated with Santa Barbara's wildflowers and botany. Before long she was a self-taught botanist. Her artistic talent combined with love of nature evolved into a career as a botanical illustrator and official artist for the California State Board of Forestry.

During her second year in town Plummer was thrown from a horse carriage in the hills of Montecito. Reading would have made her recovery easier, but Santa Barbara had few books. No library, not even a bookstore.

This was nothing new. Thirty years earlier Richard Henry Dana wrote about the short supply in *Two Years Before the Mast*.

"Such a dearth was there of these latter articles [books], that anything, even a little child's storybook, or the half of a shipping calendar, seemed a treasure."

Local readers were either priests or wealthier citizens. Available books tended to fall into two categories: written in Spanish or law books.

Plummer appealed to a friend back East to help her, stating Santa Barbara's critical need for a public library. In those days most libraries were "lending libraries" with small fees to rent books. At the same time philanthropist Andrew Carnegie was changing America's reading habits by supporting the creation of more than 2,000 free public libraries.

Between Plummer's friend sending 200 books plus 200 collected on her own, she opened her first library in March 1871 located in a jewelry shop on State Street between Cota and Ortega Streets. Her "Lending Library and Stationery Depot" included books of fiction, the classics and nonfiction.

Membership was $5, or a ten-cent payment to rent a book. She also sold a variety of art and music supplies, gifts and greeting cards highlighted by the growing popularity of Valentine's Day cards.

Plummer used part of her shop for community events like art exhibits and lectures. Two years later in 1873 a local citizens' meeting held there formed the Santa Barbara Library Association.

Where were men in this saga? The first was Colonel W.W. Hollister. He stepped up in 1874 to purchase Plummer's collection of 1,500 books for $500. He donated them to the local chapter of the Independent Order of Odd Fellows, whose building at State and Haley he had built. They designated the top, third floor as the public library.

About this time Plummer joined the Santa Barbara Natural History Society. There she met botanist John Gill Lemmon, known for his study of Sierra Nevada plant life. They fell in love and were married in 1880. The newlyweds soon left to live in Oakland but never stopped visiting Santa Barbara.

The new library carried on, although too expensive for the IOOF to maintain. Along came the second important woman, Mrs. M.M. Childs, wife of a IOOF member. She had volunteered as librarian from the beginning with a passion for her work. When the IOOF wanted to close the library, she picked up the problem.

Few women worked as librarians back then. At the Centennial Exposition in Philadelphia in 1876, over a hundred librarians met to begin the American

Library Association. Ninety were men and 13 women.

Mrs. Childs realized that the library she and Plummer had worked so hard to create and operate faced failure. What's a girl to do? She began a campaign to save it.

A local paper at the time, *El Barbareño*, quoted her about the geographical isolation of Santa Barbara.

"We Barbareños are out of the world and must do something to make life endurable; home is here, and property not very salable. As we must stay here, we must make an effort to make life on its intellectual side agreeable."

The next step was to have the library deeded to the City and supported by taxes. Much like today those taxes did not cover the costs for a growing public library so Childs turned to private donations.

Up stepped Mary Ashley and her husband, a physician, from New England. They arrived in Santa Barbara in 1869, the same year as Sara Plummer. When Mary Ashley's husband died in 1876, she had taken on two projects: keep the library going and create Cottage Hospital.

First she set up a "Save the Library" campaign by reaching out to members throughout the community including several generous Montecito donors. In 1882 Santa Barbara Mayor Peter J. Barber declared it the "first free Public Library" in the area.

The library had occupied three venues before finding a home in its current location on East Anapamu Street. One of the moves in 1892 was from the corner of Carrillo and State Sreets to half-a-block away at 14 E. Carrillo Street. Volunteers took three days to move more than 10,000 books to the new store front. Walker Tompkins in his history of Santa Barbara book, *The Yankee Barbareños*, wrote that the books were re-shelved "according to the new-fangled Dewey Decimal System."

Andrew Carnegie's $50,000 grant in 1915 made possible the current location to be built one hundred years ago.

On a final note, Sara Plummer did more than start our community library. Whenever you look into your garden during the spring and early summer or hike up in the hills, you can thank Plummer for urging the state legislature in 1903 to designate the California Poppy as our state flower.

That little flower adds a charming brightness to the natural beauty of our area as does the library with its wealth of reading material and community activities.

Acknowledgments to Michael Redmon (librarian for Santa Barbara Historical Museum and columnist of History 101 in the Independent*), Walker Tompkins and Michelle Gibney for providing resources on the life of Sara Plummer and the Santa Barbara Public Library*

Deborah Gunther
My First Book Club
(Or How I Learned to Eat Books)

The UC Berkeley graduate taught high-school English and writing for twenty-five years and co-authored a book of writing exercises for teachers. She continues to work with young adults, currently helping facilitate an afterschool teen group. She has lived in Santa Barbara since 1997.

THE YEAR: 1949. I am in the 3rd grade. Every school day at 2:45 my twin sister and I escape out the gate in the cyclone fence surrounding Longfellow Elementary and trace the familiar route home. Swinging our pale green and gray metal lunchboxes, we turn up the familiar Pasadena streets of our neighborhood. We amble along the sidewalk of Mar Vista Street and cross Rio Grande Avenue, I, scuffing the heels of my penny loafers. I am careful not to get caught walking past a driveway when a car cruises by. That would be bad luck. This is my special magic to keep me safe from kidnappers. The papers have been full of scary news; recently, a little girl my age has been kidnapped and murdered.

Up Mar Vista, right on Elizabeth Street down our front walk. Inside, my mother is asleep—her daily nap. Because she has arthritis, my mother doesn't hug me much; it hurts her. I get a goodnight kiss but I don't feel much between us when she leans over me in bed to touch my cheek with her lips. Here's when I do feel something between us—when we have a little secret about a special food treat. That's when she throws me the look of a co-conspirator at the moment our maid carries in the groceries and I find a package of Parker House rolls, my favorites. Sometimes there is a pink box bound in string and I see my mother has been to the bakery. Éclairs!

I drop my lunch box on the sink, head for the bread bin and pull out a fresh package of Ralph's chocolate chip cookies—the soft kind my mother

112

knows I love. At the refrigerator I remove a big bottle of Welch's grape juice. With these supplies, I move to the room I share with Harriet. My sister is already flopped on her bed reading. She nibbles on a Peppermint Pattie from her stash under the mattress. From my pillow, I grab the latest library book I've been devouring, tuck it under one arm. and move out to the front porch. In the shade and quiet of the porch, I sit on the steps, lean on a wooden post, and read. One hand dips into the cookies, feeding myself in a leisurely rhythm. In this way I work my way through the entire package. Periodically I tip up the Welch's to wash down the cookie crumbs. I read and eat and fill myself. I am completely happy.

Every two weeks Miss Croft, my third-grade teacher, leads our class across the street to the neighborhood branch library. Crossing the street, we follow her erect figure with her head of tight white curls as crisp as her discipline. Marching double file, girls in one line and boys in the other line, we hold hands. Holding hands with Tommy Clark, (his hands are sweaty from playing dodge ball at recess), is exciting enough, but escape from the classroom into the world of books is pure bliss. Miss Croft holds the library as a sacred place and her pupils enter reverentially. Inside, I breathe in the quiet: only a few whispers, footsteps on the creaking wood floors, the thud of books being stamped at the checkout desk. Then there is that library smell—what is it? Old books with yellowing pages, dust, varnish on the wood floors?

For the next hour I float through the stacks, slowly adding books to my pile until I have ten, the maximum allowed for a two-week lending period. Each book is a small treasure. There is *Homer Price, Twig,* all the Laura Ingalls Wilder books. Elizabeth Enright's *The Saturdays* and *The Four Story Mistake, Five Little Peppers and How They Grew* and all the innocent pre-teen romance books—the Cherry Ames, Student Nurse books, Janet Lambert's books about Penny Parrish and her military family who grew older through the series. I consume my first "historical novels," the Little Maid books as in *Little Maid of Old New York*, and Cornelia Otis Skinner's *Our Hearts were Young and Gay.*

If my class does not get to the library, then my sister and I ride our four-wheeled, wide-platform Skeeters, to the neighborhood library to restock. I check out my ten books. She checks out her ten books. I go for the girlie stuff, she for adventure and fantasy. We balance our piles of books on the platforms of our Skeeters and wobble our way home. When we've each finished our own ten books I pick through my sister's choices and she picks through mine. *The Wizard of Oz* scares me and Dr. Doolittle seems silly. She goes for adventure, fantasy, and science fiction. They are not for me. She hates my favorite preteen romances- the Penny Parrish books, the Cherry Ames books. She hates even more *The Five Little Peppers*. I love *The Secret Garden* and *The Little Princess*. She loves Jules Verne's *20,000 Leagues Under the Sea*. We do, however, passionately agree on Laura Ingalls Wilder's Little House books, Noel Streatfield's Shoes books, *Homer Price, Heidi, Mary Poppins, Twig*, Elizabeth Enright's books, and, of course, *Pippi Longstocking*. By the time the books are due we each have eaten our way through more than a dozen books and I hate to think of how many chocolate chip cookies.

Naturally, all these years later, my sister and I both belong to grown-up book clubs. Neither of us has forgotten, though, the solitary pleasures of reading and snacking indulged in so long ago. There has never yet been anything quite as satisfying as that first "book club"—the visits to the library, and those dreamy after-noons when we read and read and fed ourselves with books and cookies.

Bruce Hale
Every Fish Tells a Story

Bruce Hale has written and illustrated over 40 books for young readers, including the award-winning Chet Gecko Mysteries and the Clark the Shark picture books, one of which ended up in a McDonald's Happy Meal (not the way you think). Hale is a popular performer and speaker, having presented at schools, libraries, and conferences from New York to New Delhi. A former Hawaii resident, he moved to Santa Barbara in 2001. For more about him see www.brucehale.com.

WHAT'S THE first thing that springs to mind when you recall the library you frequented in your childhood? The kind librarian who always knew the perfect read for you? The acres of enticing books? For me, it was the goldfish.

As a little kid, I would not have been named Most Likely to Become an Author. I was an unenthusiastic reader at best, but when your mom wants to visit the library, off you go, like it or not. Still, our red tile-roofed Malaga Cove Library did have a redeeming feature. On its sprawling grounds, the library boasted a fountain that poured into several levels of ponds, and in those ponds swam an amazing array of orange, white, and golden koi.

Whenever my mom would take us to the library, I always dragged my heels on the way in, slowing down to inhale the rich, mossy smell of the ponds and watch those fat fish drift through the water. Books? I thought they were boring. But goldfish? I could watch them for hours.

That all changed on a sad day in third grade, one that my family still calls The Day the TV Died. One minute I was glued to the screen, watching the thrilling climax of some Western. The next minute, our massive console TV gave a peculiar pop. Clint Eastwood vanished. The light on the screen shrank to a pinpoint and disappeared.

Disaster.

Even worse, my parents had some tragic news: We couldn't afford a new TV. After my shock and horror reached a fever pitch, my mom and dad announced that they had a better alternative than television. They would read to me.

From books.

Although skeptical at first, I finally warmed up to the idea—especially when my dad began reading me some (highly edited) adult pulp fiction: *Tarzan of the Apes*. Before long, my father's nightly readings couldn't keep pace with my desire to know what happened next. I began reading Tarzan on my own, with a dictionary on hand to look up words like "primordial," "simian," and "truculent."

The hunger for books swept me like a fever. And when I'd torn through all the Tarzan tales we owned, I went to my mom and said, "*Now what do I do?*"

She smiled. "We go to the library."

That's when I learned that the Malaga Cove Library was more than just a place to watch some cool fish. I fell in love with its comfy children's nook and its fireplace, the shelves and shelves of books, and the rich smell of the leather reading chairs.

The kindly librarians directed me to the rest of Edgar Rice Burroughs's pulpy tales. But beyond that, they steered me toward children's books, introducing me to Roald Dahl, *A Wrinkle in Time*, *Island of the Blue Dolphins*, *The Wolves of Willoughby Chase*, *My Side of the Mountain*, and much, much more.

I came to appreciate the way those book-savvy librarians knew just how to respond when I dumped an armload of returned books on their desk and said, "Now what do I read?" Together with my parents, those librarians turned me into a reader, something for which I will always be grateful.

Thanks to them, I now feel as at home in a library as a goldfish in a pond. And even though my library has changed from Malaga Cove to Santa Barbara, my appreciation for the gift of reading—and libraries—remains unchanged.

Jean Harfenist
Outdoor Life

Jean Harfenist's short stories have been published widely. Her novel-in-stories, A Brief History of the Flood, *received wide critical acclaim when it appeared in 2002. A native of Minnesota, a graduate of New York University, she has lived in Santa Barbara since 1994.*

YOU'VE SEEN it. The kid who gets dropped down the wrong chimney. The Rudolph Nureyev doppelgänger who's the son of a cattle rancher or the daughter of two Ivy League professors who can't see past her latest crop of non-GMO green beans. Or the book junkie who tumbles down the chimney into a family that doesn't read books. Which is not to say they couldn't. Our house was littered with well thumbed magazines: *Gun Digest, Hardware Age, Field & Stream, Sports Afield, Outdoor Life* and *TV Guide.*

It was a small house on the edge of a small lake three miles south of a small town in Minnesota.

A town without a library.

There was an old drive-in movie theater out next to the highway, and in 1961—the summer I turned ten—a man from Minneapolis opened a bowling alley in the space next to the VFW. But it closed before Christmas, and when the drive-in theater didn't open the following spring, people were angry, as if having something, even for a little while, proves you're the kind of person who deserves to have it.

We had never had a library.

Which explains why I've had this since October 23, 1962, when I clipped it from the weekly edition of the local newspaper. In short, it says that at 3:15 every other Wednesday afternoon for the next seven months a truck filled with books will be parked in town for thirty minutes. Like Meals on Wheels.

The bookmobile would park in the center of town on a dirt siding next to the railroad tracks. No one ever parked there, but the town kept it plowed all winter, as if they were expecting a crowd of sightseers, maybe out-of-town shoppers. It was the perfect spot for the bookmobile if you lived in town. But if you were five years short of a driver's license and lived three miles the other side of town, you needed a ride.

Think Minnesota. Think winter. Forget about kids riding bicycles and pretend you never heard about public transportation. Instead, imagine the sun starting to sink behind someone's snowed-over cornfield at 4 PM and think about air so cold that if you breathed through your nose too fast your nostrils would stick shut.

I thought about skipping the bus home after school, walking into town, and asking my mother to pick me up at 3:45 when the bookmobile left, but her old white Rambler refused to start unless the temperature topped zero, and even then it was iffy. When it did start, she'd say, It's a miracle! My mother believed in miracles, but they didn't happen to her all that often. Not that I could see, and I didn't want to be standing alone in the dark next to the railroad tracks, stamping my feet to stay warm, thinking it would be a miracle if she ever showed up.

That left taking the bus home from school and getting a ride back into town. I didn't make it the first few times the bookmobile was in town, but one afternoon as the school bus came to a stop in front of our house, her car was sitting in the driveway with its engine running and every window scraped clean. As I walked down the bus steps, she came out of the house. Dressed, jacketed and carrying her purse, she paused on the walk-way to wave at the bus driver and the few kids who were left on the bus. Then she took a deep bow.

At 3:20 we pulled off our gravel road onto the icy two-lane blacktop that ran straight as a ruler into town. When the roads were icy or if it was raining or snowing or if she forgot her glasses or if something made her nervous—which happened a lot—she drove leaning forward, gripping the steering wheel with both hands, as if getting her nose a few inches closer to the road would clear things right up. *Waa-la!* as she would say. She was nervous that day and it was my fault. I used an empty Marlboro pack to scrape away the ice that formed on the inside of the windshield, because she was breathing right on the glass.

It was 3:30 when we parked on a small rise just in front of the bookmobile. There were only a few other cars there, as if everybody in the county had been and gone, taking all the good books with them. It wouldn't be dark out for almost another hour, but when I climbed out of the car, the sky was the dirty gray of dusk. I had to fight the wind to shut the car door. When I turned around, I was looking down into the bookmobile through its front window. All the lights were on inside, turning everything gold. It could have been a cocoon lined with books. The shelves that covered every wall were so full that the extras were lined up neatly in baskets that sat on the floor. It felt as if someone had designed the inside of that bus with a photograph of my heart pinned to a bulletin board in front of them.

I don't know how long I'd been standing outside in the cold wind, staring into the bookmobile, when I realized that the driver, who looked like every farmers' wife I'd ever seen, had walked up to the front of the bus and was leaning over, looking up at me. I must have looked startled, because she smiled, then gestured that I should come in, and pointed to the side of the bus. I hurried the rest of the way down the rise, cornered the front of the bus, and as I reached the door, it opened wide.

Hillary Hauser
Walking in a Library
(A Literary Salute)

Hillary Hauser earned her Bachelor of Arts degree in English Literature in 1966. Since then she has written numerous travel and underwater adventure stories for magazines and newspapers, has published books on the sea as well as poetry ("Diamonds"), and compiled ocean-themed anthologies, worked as a newspaper reporter, covered California ocean politics for a Washington D.C. journal, written classical music reviews and interviews. She is Executive Director of Heal the Ocean in Santa Barbara, a 3,000-member citizens' action group, and is also a long-time classical pianist. Her work can be found at www.hillaryhauser.com as well as www.healtheocean.org.

I was stopping by woods on a snowy evening,
While Raskolnikov was escaping an encounter with his landlady on the stairs.
Sister Carrie was leaving on a train for Chicago,
And Vladimir and Estragon were waiting for nothing.

Egdon Heath embrowned itself moment by moment,
The bee was making its prairie,
While I the Native was returning
To wonder as I wandered out under the sky.

Tolstoy's Confession, What will come of what I am doing today,
What will come of my whole life?"
Is my Confession.
What is my last of life for which the first was made?

There are monstrous changes taking place in the world,
Forces shaping a future whose face we do not know.
It is in the new monarchy that difficulties really exist,
In years of magical thinking.

Can War find Peace?
And the Mohicans not be last?
Is it true that mercy is not strained?
One must not always think that feeling is everything,

If life had a second edition, how I would correct the proofs?
Anna Karenina would escape the tracks,
The Madding haystacks would not burn,
And Emma would be free of Bovary.

The broadening Floss hurries on between its green banks to the sea,
While Miss Havisham's gown catches fire
And the three musketeers clash swords.
Can I, like Edmond, swim from Château d'If of life with a smile?

Really, if the lower orders don't set us a good example,
What on earth is the use of them?
I pray God to keep me from being proud,
But have I made a difference?

Man is a rope stretched between the animal and the Superman.
The golden rule is that there are no golden rules,
The roads diverge in these yellow woods,
And every flower enjoys the air it breathes.

A library is a hospital for the mind,
Where words to the wise are sufficient.
And distance lends enchantment to the view.
The world is a grain of sand, heaven a wildflower.

What, Socrates, is the food of the soul?
The world is charged with the grandeur of God,
We are made wise not by the recollection of our past,
We are all made of stars.

I shall not die, but live on as one,
The journey of a thousand miles is at hand
I will walk in beauty, still,
Like a good book that has no ending.

* * *

With Apologies and Credits, line by line, to the following literary greats, whose works can be found in any library on Earth:

VERSE 1: Robert Frost, "The Road Not Taken"; Dostoyevsky, *Crime and Punishment*; Theodore Dreiser, *Sister Carrie*; Samuel Beckett, *Waiting for Godot.*

VERSE 2: Thomas Hardy, *The Return of the Native*; Emily Dickinson, "To Make a Prairie"; Thomas Hardy (ibid); Christmas Folk Hymn.

VERSE 3: Tolstoy, *A Confession*; Tolstoy (ibid.); H. Hauser; Robert Browning, "Rabbi Ben Ezra."

VERSE 4: John Steinbeck, "Letter to his Sons"; Steinbeck (ibid); Machiavelli, *The Prince*; Joan Didion, *The Year of Magical Thinking.*

VERSE 5: Tolstoy, *War and Peace*; James Fenimore Cooper, *The Last of the Mohicans*; Shakespeare, *The Merchant of Venice*; Flaubert, Letter to Madame Louise Colet.

VERSE 6: John Clare, Poetry; Tolstoy, *Anna Karenina*; Thomas Hardy, *Far from the Madding Crowd*; Gustav Flaubert, *Madame Bovary.*

VERSE 7: George Eliot, *The Mill on the Floss*; Charles Dickens, *Great Expectations*; Alexandre Dumas, *The Three Musketeers*; Alexandre Dumas (pere), *The Count of Monte Cristo*; Oscar Wilde, *The Importance of Being Earnest*; Oscar Wilde, (ibid.); William Blake, "The Divine Image"; H. Hauser.

VERSE 8: Friedrich Nietzsche, *Thus Spake Zarathustra*; George Bernard Shaw, *Man and Superman*; Robert Frost, "The Road Not Taken"; William Wordsworth, *The Golden Treasury.*

VERSE 9: Alvin Toffler, anonymous quote; Benjamin Franklin, *Poor Richard's Almanac*; Thomas Campbell, *Pleasures of Hope*; William Blake, *Auguries of Innocence.*

VERSE 10: Plato (quote); Gerard Manley Hopkins, "God's Grandeur"; George Bernard Shaw, *Maxims for Revolutionists*; Rowan Coleman, *We Are All Made of Stars.*

VERSE 11: *Holy Bible*; Psalms 118:17; Lao Tzu, *Tao Te Ching*, Chapter 64; Lord Byron, "She Walks In Beauty"; Robert Frost, (floating quote).

Eva Hoffman
Library in Paradise

Born in Krakow, Poland, shortly after World War II, she emigrated at age thirteen to Canada. She received her PhD in literature from Harvard and worked as an editor and writer for The New York Times. *She has written many books, fiction and nonfiction, but her best known work is* Lost in Translation: A Life in a New Language *(1989), the first "postmodern" autobiography written in English by an emigre from a European Communist country. The following remembrance is from that memoir.*

EVERY TWO weeks or so, my mother takes me to the library to provide for my next fortnight's reading. Every time, I anticipate the events as if it were a trip into Sesame itself. The library is located on a narrow, old street, in an ancient building, which one enters through a heavy wooden door. The interior is Plato's cave, Egyptian temple, the space of mystery and magic, on whose threshold I stand a humble acolyte. It is mellowly lit, smoky with dust and respectful whispers, and behind the counters, which stop the customers from entering farther, it reveals deep, ceiling-tall rows of shelves. When our turn comes, one of the guardians of the mysteries—most of them bespectacled women in black, satiny versions of a nurse's uniform—approaches for a consultation. My mother mentions some author or title she's interested in. And as for me—what might I want to read next? An adventure story? A boarding school novel? Something historical? The very thought of these possibilities makes the next two weeks a terrain of potential pleasure. The guardian then quietly vanishes into the cavernous interior, to emerge with a stack of musty, yellow-paged volumes. I open them; I sniff their aged smell; I read a few words; some of them have illustrations at which I look greedily; then I have to choose from the riches of Araby.

I come out, usually into the dim evening streets, enchanted with what awaits me, and as soon as I come home, I pounce on one of the volumes. Then there's the prospect of reading for the entire evening. My parents are worried that I read too much—it's not restful; it'll strain my eyes—and sometimes I sneak under the table in the hope that they won't notice what I'm doing. Sometimes they don't.

The boarding school novels, usually French, feature wicked girls who skip school and sneak out at night to do God knows what; I'm fascinated by them, but it's always the quiet, *bien pensant* girls who seem to end up with a boyfriend, so I conclude that I should wish to be like them—though I feel regret for giving up, even in my imagination, the titillating possibilities of badness. There's a book by an Italian writer called *Heart* about people so pathetic—deaf, blind, destitute—and children so filled with pity and kindness that I weep uncontrollable tears over the stories. There's Jules Verne and *Alice in Wonderland* and *Doctor Dolittle*, and *Quo Vadis?*—all of this very different from reading we're assigned at school, about boys and girls spending summers on a collective farm, being helpful to their hardworking mothers, of competing to do even more work that their two-week plans call for—reading that I know not to take seriously from the teacher's voice. "And what did you learn about the value of work from this story?" she asks the class with cheerful peremptoriness—and we answer in jaded tones, as if we were just disposing of a silly duty.

But this is not true of my library books, whose contents I take at face value and with complete suspension of disbelief. Like all Polish children, I am given lots of books by Sienkiewicz—the laureate of Polish nationalism—even though they might be considered strong fare by some standards.

*   *   *

[His] *Quo Vadis?* should teach me a lot about Roman history and the beginnings of Christianity, but I read it mostly for the hints of a whole other knowledge—sex. Its scenes of Roman orgies don't yield all that much detail but they're enough to stimulate tantalizingly pleasurable images, which fill my head at bedtime—fantasies of bare-breasted women feeding grapes to reclining men and people bathing each other languidly, behind which I feel something else I can't get to, but which go round and round until I lull myself to sleep.

*   *   *

Like so many children who read a lot, I begin to declare rather early that I want to be a writer. But this is the only way I have of articulating a different desire, a desire that I can't yet understand. What I really want is to be transported into a space in which every thing is as distinct, complete, and intelligible as in the stories I read. And, like most children, I'm a literalist through and through. I want reality to imitate books—and books to capture the essence of reality. I love words insofar as they correspond to the world, insofar as they give it to me in a heightened form. The more world I have, the more distinct, precise my perceptions become—and such lucidity is a form of joy. Sometimes, when I find a new expression, I roll it on the tongue, as if shaping it in my mouth gave birth to a new shape in the world, Nothing fully exists until it is articulated. "She grimaced ironically," someone says, and an ironic grimace is now delineated in my mind with a sharpness one never had before. I've grasped a new piece of experience; it is mine.

The yellowed pages I take out of the library draw me into them as into a trance—but only on the condition that they create a convincing mimetic illusion. I feel subtly cheated by *Alice in Wonderland*, because it is all pretend, a game, and of what interest is that? My reading is all mixed up, and it's not so long after I read *Alice* that I'm given *War and Peace*. This is something I should read carefully, my parents convey to me, a classic, something very important— but the usually discouraging invocation of duty has no effect on me this time. I don't notice that *War and Peace* is a book, something I'm reading. Surely, this is just life.

Melodie Johnson Howe
Finding Hemingway

Howe is a former actress and author of mysteries. She began writing as a child, composing plays such as "Nevada"—a Western that ended with the villain being sent to his room—and began acting in the mid-60s. For a decade, she worked in movies, but always wanting to be a writer. She left the Hollywood grind in the early 80s to write mysteries. Her first novel was nominated for an Edgar Award. An acclaimed author of short fiction, her most recent book is Shooting Hollywood: The Diana Poole Stories *(2012), a collection of short stories starring a forty-year-old actress trying to make a comeback. Her website is melodiejohnsonhowe.com.*

SUMMER, MASSILLON, Ohio. I'm standing in my uncle's home library. Ten years old. Short blonde hair. Long gawky legs. My family and I are visiting from Los Angeles. The sun streams in through a big paned window. I've never been in a house that has a room just for books. I pull one from the shelf titled *For Whom the Bell Tolls.* A man named Hemingway wrote it. I open it and begin to read.

My mother who has the ability to appear from nowhere sweeps in and grabs the book from my hands. "You're too young to read this."

The quiet room is suddenly full of adults. Talking.

My father, a sly grin on his face, says, "Oh, let her read it. She's not going to understand it." He has the ability to stand up for me and let me down at the same time.

"She understands enough," my mother snaps. Face knotted.

My aunt is asking if anybody would like iced tea.

My uncle, the lawyer, so pale he looks like he needs to be colored-in with crayons, says, "I have an appointment downtown. I'll take her to the library and she'll pick out a book that's appropriate for her."

Appropriate. My heart sinks. Mother pulls me from the room. I look back at the book now lost among the others on the shelf.

Soon my uncle and I are in his beige sedan. The hot summer wind blowing in on us through open windows. Then we are walking up a sweep of stairs to the Massillon Public Library. It looks like an enormous old mansion rising above us.

Inside, dark mahogany wood beams grace the ceiling and frame the long sash windows. Giant iron chandeliers speak of another time. Radiators line the walls. Polished tables have much-used leather chairs pushed against them. A rack for newspapers. And rows and rows and rows of books.

My uncle introduces me to the librarian. She shakes my hand. Her grip is firm not dismissive. She and my uncle chat like old friends. Her black hair is cut short, all sharp edges like a man's. Defiant. Not the Audrey Hepburn fad I have tried for. My uncle leaves me saying he will pick me up later. I turn shy. Awkward.

The librarian studies me. I'm waiting for her to ask my age. What grade I'm in at school.

"Well, you're obviously too old for the children's section. Let's see what we can find for you. What are you interested in?"

"Fiction." I've never spoken the word out loud. There is no need to in my family.

"Good. Follow me." And I do, past bookcases so high I have to crane my neck to find the very top. So many books. So many aisles. My heart is racing. Fear. Anticipation. How will I ever choose? What if it's wrong? What if it's another Hemingway and I have to return it? My outraged mother next to me. Mortified.

She stops. I almost run into her. "This section. Not too young. Not too old. To paraphrase Goldilocks." She sweeps her large hand along a row that seems to go on forever. Then leaves me.

Alone.

No one to watch me. To tell me what to choose.

I become aware of people wandering the aisles. Pausing to consider. Men in seersucker suits. Younger ones in jeans and T-shirts, sleeves rolled up like James Dean to show their muscles. Or tuck a package of cigarettes into the folds. Women, wearing cinched-waist dresses that sway around their ankles. Newspapers rustling. Discreet coughing. Ceiling fans whirring, wobbling. And the smell. A mixture of glue, paper, wax. The mustiness that smells old and stimulating at the same time.

I run my finger along the spines of the books. Most are about boys doing daring deeds. Nancy Drew! But I've read her. I want something else . . . something . . . adult. And there it is! A bright red book titled, *My Dear Wife*. That sounds adult.

I open the book. No pictures. Only chapters. The print is bigger than Hemingway's book and not so jammed together. I begin to read. A young pretty woman and a handsome young man have just wedded. But before they can consummate their marriage the American Revolutionary War breaks out and he must go fight. *Consummate*. I whisper this new word. I have no trouble figuring out its meaning. My heart races again. For a different reason. A hand touches mine. I leap.

The librarian smiles. She takes the book from me. "A perfect choice," she says. "Your uncle will pick you up out front." I wonder if she has read all the books in the library or does she say this to all the readers to make them feel special.

I feel special.

I sit on the stone steps. The sun hot on me. I miss the cool quietness of the library. Waiting, I read. The young woman decides she must do her duty for the war, too. She becomes a spy. Hiding messages in the hem of her skirt she crosses enemy lines to give them to George Washington. And all the time searching for her husband.

Alone in bed that night, I will finish the book. And feel the abandonment of having to leave this brave strong woman and the Revolutionary War. Years later when I am a writer I understand that I learned how to create suspense and strong women characters from reading *My Dear Wife*.

But sitting on those steps, waiting for my uncle, I am only a girl with a book from the library.

A horn honks. I look up. My uncle waves.

Driving home, he appears more colorful, even mysterious to me, than he did just a few hours ago. He says, "Promise me, Melodie, when you're older and the young men are flocking around you, you won't forget Hemingway."

I smile at him.

Pico Iyer
My Lifeline, My Livelihood, My Living

Pico Iyer is the author of two novels and nine works of nonfiction, and is usually to be found somewhere in the 900 section of the stacks. He has spent many years in Santa Barbara, where his parents taught at UCSB. For more about him, see www.picoiyerjourneys.com.

SOME TIME ago, deep in a book I'm writing on Japan, I desperately needed—what else?—a copy of Isabella Bird's *Unbeaten Tracks in Japan*, the intrepid Englishwoman's account of traveling, alone, to remote parts of Hokkaido, hardly seen by any Westerner, in 1878. I don't have access to a research library, and I'm not sure that the travel-diaries of indomitable Victorian gentlewomen are often to be found in the PR stacks in any case. And though Santa Barbara is blessed with some of the finest bookstores on the planet, I couldn't be sure I'd find a little-known work brought out 137 years ago even in Chaucer's, The Book Den or Tecolote. So down I went to our great hospital-cum-community-center-cum-sanctuary-cum-chapel on Anapamu Street, tucked (perfectly) between courthouse and art museum, and pulled down the volume in question. Within seconds, I was stumbling around the tatami rooms and kimonoed rites of Niigata sixty-three years before.

I wasn't entirely surprised to find Ms. Bird tramping across the second floor of the Santa Barbara Central Library; for more than fifty years now, that indispensable structure has been my lifeline, my oasis, my reason to believe. Each of its volumes opens out upon an entire universe, of course; but for decades I've gone there also to keep up with the *New Republic, Publishers' Weekly, New York* and any number of fine magazines I'm too stingy to buy. Friends of mine from Japan have all but lived in the Central Library, the one place in town so quiet and safe that they might (almost) be back in Japan. I've tapped away on the Library's Internet terminals, attended exhibitions and lectures in its Faulkner Gallery, even caught up on my thoughts (my sleep) in its astonishingly deep armchairs. Whenever I'm off on a trip, I head to the second floor, armed with dimes for the photocopy machine, and defraud some poor guidebook writer of his royalties.

Five years ago, after my eighty-year-old mother went through back surgery, she began to howl in pain. I raced into her bedroom and asked her what I could get her from downtown. Just a copy of P. G. Wodehouse, she groaned. Now that she's mostly around the house, after a stroke, I head to the library every three weeks and come back struggling under piles of Ursula LeGuin, P. D. James, Stefan Zweig and Jane Gardam for her to devour in bed. It's been a sadness, of course, in recent years to find the selection of periodicals shrinking each time I return, and more and more open space and machines displacing shelves of books. Yet it's thrilling to think how, in our book-unfriendly times, the Santa Barbara Public Library is celebrating its centenary, having outlasted VCRs, Walkmen, computer discs and even Pontiac Firebirds

An innocent friend might ask me, "Why support an institution that is cutting into sales of your own books?" The answer is that books teach us a different way of counting, on an account sheet written in invisible ink. They instruct us in subtlety in a world that is more and more bumper-sticker and sound-bite. They coax us into attention in a time of constant distraction and fragmentation. And they remind us of inner resources that are all we have to turn to when, in fact, a stroke (a forest fire, a dark diagnosis) comes down, and bank-account and business-card are clearly no help at all.

In fact, they deepen those resources and make us better able to face every eventuality in our lives. And all of this for free, as if to show us that what's given gratis is what is truly invaluable.

The Santa Barbara Public Library—not least in its branches in Goleta and Montecito—has been my abiding sustenance and haunt ever since the day I arrived in town from Oxford, England, a bewildered, tiny boy of seven. I can only hope that a hundred years from now it will be the same for my granddaughter's grandchildren, teaching them that a community is as rich as the wisdom that it stores inside itself and that a room in which everyone is silently absorbed in something passionate, intimate and deep is generally, and rightly, known as a place of worship

"When you are growing up," the great guitarist of the Rolling Stones, Keith

Richards, observed, "there are two institutional places that affect you most powerfully: the church, which belongs to God, and the public library, which belongs to you. The public library is the great equalizer." When Mr. Richards brought out his own book, the one public appearance he made for it in the U.S. was at the New York Public Library (he chose to forget, for the moment, that one of his most serious, non-fatal injuries had come when searching for a book on Leonardo's anatomical studies in his library at home).

Libraries are churches for people committed to conversation and exploration. And they're among the beautiful public spaces that are a collection of privacies, along their shelves and around their tables. If Santa Barbara—God forbid!—were to lose its Mission, its newspaper building, its finest restaurants, many of us would be bereft; but if ever it lost its library, we'd no longer be ourselves.

Beverley Jackson
My Reverence for Libraries

Born in Los Angeles, an inveterate traveler, Jackson ultimately moved to Santa Barbara in 1963. Her writing life began with a society column she wrote for the Santa Barbara News-Press *for 22 years. She has also informed audiences around the world about the culture and traditions of China through her award-winning books, art collections and lectures. Her last book,* The Beautiful Lady Was a Palace Eunuch, *was her first venture into fiction. For more about her books visit www.beverleyjackson.com.*

LIBRARY! THERE has always been a feeling of reverence for this one word. "Your father is in the library," meant he was in his special place surrounded by all his law books and could not be disturbed. "I'm going to the library to get some information," was my mother going on a serious venture. Then came the thrill of being taken to downtown Los Angeles to have lunch with my father and he walked me over to see the beautiful main Bertram Goodhue public library built in 1926. I felt so small and insignificant in that great rotunda knowing I was totally surrounded by those special things, books.

I was to have that feeling other times in later life. The Vatican Library in Rome. The wonderful 42nd Street Library in New York City. The magnificent library in the University Club in New York. The Liu Library in Nanxun, China built by three generations of my friend Edith Liu's late husband's family. Over 600,000 ancient rolls of books, carved rock books, paper books, woodblock printed books are found in the old buildings surrounding the ten-acre pond of lotus blossoms. This library incidentally survived the civil war and the Cultural Revolution thanks to the wise statesman Chou En-Lai who sent in special troops to protect the treasured books that otherwise would have been destroyed.

And somehow the same emotion of respect, reverence, slips into my thinking every time I enter the main library in downtown Santa Barbara or our dear little Montecito Library. These are special places filled with treasures. Treasures I need in my life to feed my brain and supply what I need for the books I write. I love to walk in and see the rows of books. Books I can pick up and feel. Books whose leather covering I can smell, whose paper I cannot only feel the texture of, but smell as well. I love books. I don't read online. I wouldn't give up the joy of walking into our libraries and having all my senses activated. I love books. I love our Santa Barbara Library.

Shakespeare Flower Festival - April, 1950

Sheila Golburgh Johnson
Libraries

Sheila Golburgh Johnson is a poet, essayist, and freelance journalist. She was the editor of, and contributor to, Shared Sightings *(1995), a collection of contemporary poetry devoted to birds, and author of the novel,* After I Said No *(2000).*

WHEN I think of libraries, I think of the years I used to write articles for Salem Press, the publisher of a literary series that used to appear in almost every public and university library in the United States. My husband used to write articles for them on Russian writers, since he was a specialist in Russian Literature. As the years went on, he grew busier and busier, and knowing that I would be just as competent as he was at writing about literature suggested that I should apply to Salem for a writing position. My field was different, though; I specialized in American and British writers of poetry and fiction. After sending them a test article and being accepted as an article writer, I was sent a sheet with preferences for subject matter. Literature, of course, but wasn't I a "fashion plate" as well? So I signed up for fashion, and this was all happening during the "feminist" era. And I had attended many consciousness-raising groups, under the impression that I had something to teach other women. After all, I had two small children, a husband, and I worked, as well. I just about had it all! I signed up for social movements, as well as literature and fashion.

They were lucky to have me. I was honest, I worked hard, and I cross-checked every article after I wrote it to make sure it was accurate. Impressed with the new (to me) technology of computers at the time, I usually cross checked my articles on Wikipedia, sure that they had the latest and most accurate information. Articles flew from my computer to Salem Press' editors, and I enjoyed writing most of the articles. I became reacquainted with favorite writers of mine, such as Alicia Suskin Ostriker, Pattiann Rogers, Sir V.S. Naipaul, Cynthia Ozick, and Marjorie Kellogg. I loved it. It wasn't until I wrote about Emma Lazarus, one of my childhood idols, that I became aware of the awful truth...Wikipedia, which I had been using as a test proof of my articles, was not always accurate! In 1903, sixteen years after Lazarus's death, her sonnet, "The New Colossus," was inscribed on a plaque at the base of the Statue of Liberty. Wikipedia had the date wrong, as I discovered when I checked the article for accuracy against the computer giant. I changed my methods after that, using only encyclopedia articles to check my own work against, and it changed my life. I first used the central branch of the Santa Barbara Public Library, leaving myself plenty of time to browse after finishing my work, which led to the discovery of hidden treasures that I didn't even know existed. What a wealth of books! Not only old classics that I had somehow never gotten around to reading, but all the newest works by established and newly-minted poets that I studied, learned from, and who influenced my own work. I was on fire, and the reading I did during that period enriched my life beyond my imaginings. Inspired by this abundance of material, I grew braver and signed up to cover musicians who were popular at the time, or whom I remembered from younger days. Articles flew from my fingertips.

Inspired by the wealth of topics in the Santa Barbara Public Library, I decided to take out a card from the UCSB library. Then, they were freely available to the public, and although I had special status as a faculty wife, I didn't need it. The most exciting thing about the UCSB Library at that time was its open stacks, which meant I could browse to my heart's content. It was there that I fulfilled my assignment on Iris Murdoch, an old idol of mine with whom I had once had lunch when she came to deliver a lecture at UCSB. I wrote a short biography of her, and then an analysis of six of her novels. Oh, what a reunion I had with Murdoch!

I don't write for Salem Press any more, since the company was sold to another firm which demanded more of me than I was willing to give. I mostly write poetry now, and my husband is retired from his position at UCSB. I am still thrilled with Santa Barbara's astonishing resources, especially the Santa Barbara Central Library. I use it now to access the works of other poets, and to keep up with the newest fiction and non-fiction. And oh, how my life is constantly enriched.

James Kahn
Library Memories

A medical specialist and writer, Kahn is best known for his novelization of "Return of the Jedi." His original work includes three novels in the New World series: World Enough and Time, Time's Dark Laughter, *and* Timefall, *He has also written the novelizations of the films "Poltergeist" and "Indiana Jones and the Temple of Doom" as well as episodes for television series such as "Melrose Place" and "Star Trek: The Next Generation."*

WHEN I was 7 years old, my family moved to Des Plaines, Illinois, a young suburb of Chicago. I didn't have many friends, but the library became my friend. Located on Graceland Avenue about eight blocks away from our house, it was a low, red brick building, a common architectural idiom of the time and place. My mother took me there initially—my first introduction to public libraries—and I was stunned at the number of books it housed. And the idea I could take home any book I wanted—any three at once, actually—unbelievable. Before long I was walking there twice a week. (Imagine a seven-year-old boy walking alone a mile and back in today's world—it would be called child endangerment.) Be that as it may, the library felt like a magical place to me—the equivalent of a Victorian study, to a child. It was unnaturally quiet. Everything felt old—unlike my parents' brand new split-level house—and it had a wonderfully ancient smell. Library paste, I suppose, mingled with the particular mildew that accumulates on seldom-used book pages. And there was a weathered, nicked piece of furniture, pine varnished orange with age, containing scores of small drawers filled with soft, well-thumbed 3x5 cards, thousands of them, displaying some arcane hieroglyphics, something they called the Dewey Decimal System.

There was a special program available only to children, too. On my first visit I was issued a page containing the outline of a map of the United States. Every time I returned a book I'd taken out and read, the librarian gave me a colorful sticker in the shape of one of the states and I stuck it to the outline it matched. When all 48 states were filled in (yes, that's how old I am), my limit of three books at a time was raised to four, and I got a new blank map.

Treasure Island, by Robert Louis Stevenson, was the first big kids' book I got there. Still one of my all-time favorites. After that they stopped giving me maps, though.

I went back once, a few years ago, only to find the building had been razed and replaced with a boxy lo-rise for municipal offices. They referred me to the new library downtown, near the train station. It was beautiful, well designed, lots of glass, big open areas, an atrium, a Help Desk, computers, the low murmurs of busy people.

But I missed the mildew, the dark silence, the mystical sense of this being some monastic, medieval Dewey Decimal scriptorium devoted to arts both sacred and profane which, deep in my soul, it will always be.

Carol Keator
A Director Remembers

The former Director of the Santa Barbara Public Library is now retired, and serves on a County commission and on boards of numerous non-profit organizations. She is an activist for feminism and social justice. She enjoys birding, theater, traveling and exploring, inevitably finding new public libraries and bookstores in which to browse.

RECENTLY AT a local business, I bumped into a former Friend of the Library member who queried, "Do you miss the library?" "Oh, yes I do," I truthfully replied. "I miss the people."

I came to SBPL to work as a reference librarian in 1972 thinking that it would be fun to spend two or three years in Santa Barbara before moving on. Thirty-four years later I retired from the position of Library Director for the Santa Barbara Library System.

Libraries have been special to me since I was a child. My family moved often, and in each new community I got a new and treasured library card and was taken to the library to choose books each week. It seemed a natural fit that I would acquire a degree in Information Studies and a job helping others find the right book or an answer to their questions.

As a reference librarian I was thrilled to be able to locate information that a patron needed—for a school report, how to fix a car or appliance, trace a family tree, find a job or just satisfy someone's curiosity. At the reference desk, it was a bit like traveling, as I made friends not only from here but also from all over the world and heard some of their life stories.

I left the Central Library downtown for a few years for a position as Supervisor at the Goleta Branch Library. In the mid-1970s there was a pressing need for more hours, more staff, more collection materials. I worked with an energetic volunteer group campaigning for a dedicated library tax. This was some of that "fun" I sought! "Yes on Measure L" won over two-thirds of the vote thanks to these wonderful residents who walked and talked on behalf of their local library.

Back at the Central Library, I became a Library Manager in charge of several public and non-public work units. Staff at the very public circulation desk has especially critical roles. In addition to checking library materials (yes, books, and also magazines, videotapes, CDs and more) in and out, giving directions and answering questions, they are often the only library representatives that some library users see, and therefore they are important library public relations representatives. I often marveled at the multi-tasking taking place, while still making time for a friendly exchange with the borrowers. I knew and chatted with many of these library users on a regular basis.

Technical Services staff do all the ordering of collection materials, affix spine labels and book covers, mend items as needed, and keep the catalog records. One example of the work of Tech Services that still makes me smile: as each new Harry Potter book was published, staff ordered 300 copies and got them catalogued, processed and delivered to each branch, ready for checkout to the first 300 people on the waiting list when the library opened on the official release date. I loved to witness the excited and happy children (and adults!) who rushed in to check out a copy!

When Library Director Robert Hart retired in 1988 I was appointed to succeed him. As Library Director my responsibility was to promote library services and to work to build collections, maintain, expand and improve services, keep facilities in good repair, and to make the Santa Barbara Public Library System the best it could be. It should go without saying that this cannot be done alone and I had many opportunities to work with and get to know other people who connect with the world of libraries.

Users of the library and the staff who serve are perhaps the most obvious inhabitants of the library world, but there are many others. I was pleased to work in partnership with members of the County Board of Supervisors and City Council, employees of other city and county departments (public works, finance, personnel, law enforcement and more), and colleagues from other library jurisdictions, to name a few. Special mention must be made of the legions of individuals who volunteer time and energy to assist the library—they shelve materials, listen to children enrolled in the Summer Reading Program give their book reports, tutor learners in the Adult Literacy Program, mend materials, and creatively find dozens of ways to support their library.

Over the years, I was privileged to meet with and accept monetary donations from caring individuals who believe in the value of libraries. Often I would hear about how libraries had been places of safety or a place to let the imagination run free or a place to inspire them as a child.

The Friends of the Library at all the branches are exceedingly generous in supporting programs and activities. Quite often the children's programs, furniture replacement, purchase of equipment and certain areas of collection materials were only made possible by financial contributions from these Friends. I greatly valued my friendships with these library lovers during all my years with the Santa Barbara Public Library.

The comments above are memories of what goes on at the public library to serve the community. I certainly remember the many parts of my library work life—serving at a public service desk, creating and balancing a budget, selecting materials for collections, mentoring young library professionals, raising money, networking with other libraries and organizations and so much more. However, it is important to know that many people are involved in creating and sustaining a public library that is used and valued by the community. As the saying goes, "it takes a village . . ." and I have been privileged to be part of the Santa Barbara Public Library village. I have learned many things, I have had a great deal of fun, and I have made friends who have enriched my life. I am grateful.

Hilary Dole Klein
Not for Animals

Hilary Dole Klein came to Santa Barbara when her father, William Dole, was hired to teach art at the new University of California. Her writing credits include books and articles on artists, food, travel, romance, bugs, heroes, and family. She is working on a memoir: Nothing Bad Ever Happened to Me.

MY FIRST memory of the Santa Barbara Library is seeing a stranger fish my two-year-old sister out of one of the reflecting pools that ran alongside the building. At the age of four, I didn't know how much my mother loved to read—had to read—only that she had parked in front of the library that day and left four kids to wait in the car while she rushed in to feed her habit. ("Stay here. I'll be right back," was one of the rallying cries of my childhood, mostly outside of hardware and thrift stores.) Our car, Peter the Pontiac, was hot and boring, so we got out to play around on the cool grass under the trees. The reflecting pool looked good to Deirdre, and in she went.

According to my mother, it wasn't long after that the lovely long pools were filled in with dirt—a great loss, I think, to one of the most beautiful buildings in the city. Yet my love for the architecture of the library pales in comparison with the promise within its walls, its limitless ability to satisfy my hunger for a good book.

I taught myself how to read in "junior primary" where I had been placed instead of first grade at Peabody School, which means that I flunked kindergarten. Was it my inability to draw the perfect orange concentric circles required for the body of the Thanksgiving turkey? Perhaps it was my voluble outrage when Mrs. Koenig told us that everything on earth is animal, vegetable or mineral, and we are animals. No way. Not me. I adamantly refused to accept this. At any rate, I ended up in the sad primary classroom, fretful with boredom, where I discovered a shelf of Raggedy Ann and Andy books, specifically *Raggedy Ann and Andy in Candyland*. I burned with urgency to know what the story was about. It still mystifies me how the black marks on a page suddenly organized themselves into words and sentences that opened the door to magical—and in the case of the Raggedies—scrumptious worlds, filled with creampuffs and lollypops, soda water icicles, and ice cream mud puddles.

My mother tried to get me to keep my reading a secret from my older sister, in order to spare her feelings. As if! And while she tried to get me to dim my own light, she welcomed me into her world of books and began taking me with her to the library. I loved going through the enormous door and racing over to the children's section, welcomed by the bright, colorful mural painted by our friend Don Freeman. Raggedy Ann and Andy had given me a taste for the weird, and I craved more, which led me to fairy tales. I couldn't get enough of them. I went straight to the end of one of the stacks, to the dimly lit bottom shelf where they resided. The books were big and fat, musty and old, their ornate silver titles embossed on cloth bindings: *Grimms' Fairy Tales, Slav Fairy Tales, Russian Fairy Tales, Hans Christian Andersen Fairy Tales*.... I worked my way down the shelf, often spooked by the ghoulishness of the stories, wanting only to have my urgent need for a happy ending satisfied. One of the more peculiar tales involved a village of wretched people whose feet were as big as row boats. After finishing the book that contained that one, I decided I'd had enough of the strange and spooky, and I discovered with some relief the books about pioneer girls and orphans.

Although I now walk instead of run into the library, and I use a computer to peruse its shelves, it still remains the most important building in my life, aside from my home. The library is where I learned that if you have a craving, it can be assuaged, and that unlike lollypops and ladyfingers, indulgence has few negative consequences—aside from occasional lack of sleep and neglect of family. Furthermore, there will always be more where the last pleasure came from, and it will always be free. Discovering the library was like walking into my very own fairy tale. Instead of a goose that laid a golden egg, or a little man who spun straw into gold, I had an endless, magical source of the greatest treasure of all: stories that provided escape, took me around the world—and proved we are definitely not animals.

Lise Lange
Unconditional Love and the Time Machine

UCSB graduate and a former high school English teacher, when not plying her trade the Nebraska-born, Corgi-loving author can usually be found reading or writing. Her vividly-written autobiographical novel, Scout, *is, as one critic put it, "raw, pure, and true."*

OH DEAR gawd I am not going to begin this love letter with one of those colorfully cheery stories of childhood at the library. It is a wonderful thing that some of us can recall those sessions with detail and charm, but seriously? There I was, walking home back in the day like a tiny cartoon character carefully juggling an immense tower of books. My growing up library had no stern division of adult and children's sections so I wandered like a wayward flea, making my way from the many-volumed girl detective collection to the young adult section of what appeared to be completely forbidden writing involving feelings I had not yet begun to experience and situations involving dark theatres and back seats of hot cars. So determined was I to know everything and so intense my curiosity and, ok, I will admit this, so all-encompassing my immaturity and naivete I soon found myself reading through volumes detailing the back alleys of literary scandal and discussing unlimited intellectual pagescapes. Seriously over my head. Way beyond my imagined capabilities.

Forcing myself to recover a bit more buried memory, there was a time when I sat in the sheltering arms of my vast treehouse oak and attempted Miller's book because I believed it would speak to my astrological sign. It must have been ignorance or I was too green to know or perhaps too daringly oblivious so my treasured Capote volumes stacked up next to picture books and stories of dogs and horses. Actually, thinking back on this literary chaos, my haphazard collection proved to be a surprisingly effective approach. In between scaring the wits from myself reading about a Midwestern murder that took place in a house freakishly like my own, I could return to a beloved pet's long journey home and a horse surviving an ocean disaster. All of this noise is not bragging and is no claim to my brainy capabilities, oh no no no, geez! I seriously blame that library without restrictions, and my book list that knew no boundaries for the plain and simple fact that to this day my could be well-read brain resembles a card catalogue emptied on the floor. And then . . . (should I say tragically here?) as the years are proving, you might as well turn on a fan and watch those titles and authors and words scatter. Oh dear, to where have all of those thousands of books read flown and will they be recaptured by me ever again?

Undeniably, what my childhood library did was to acquaint me with my first lovely stirrings of unconditional love. With each page turned I felt befriended, accepted, and transported. Such a fiend for time travel was I, for months I kept Wells' book and planned and schemed as to the possibility of finding or building a time machine for myself. Oh how very much I desired to travel to the deserts and planets, castles and oceans, and eras and settings that were my everyday library life. I spent hours, wow this was pathetic, days at a time, sitting with a flashlight in a cramped closet next to our water heater and counting to impossibly high numbers convinced completely that when I opened my eyes and the door, I would step out and into whatever book I was reading. Days I spent doing this. It never happened.

Unconditional love is a heady drug, however, and oh goodness I had become sweetly and forever addicted. Too young to understand just exactly how much out of step I would eventually find myself, I collapsed on the library floor under the weight of a man discovering himself a cockroach and women swallowing poison and crawling around a room with wallpaper and in all of that scholarly collapsing I could forget me. The library was old, the rug older, and the women behind the counters ancient and buried in books themselves. None of this was a bother to me because by this time adolescence had come and claimed me for its own. The outside world was painfully impossible, but the library provided shelter and comfort and was loaded with volumes that demanded only slavish curiosity and the reading skills I had spent an entire childhood developing on my own.

From this point on, with barely an understanding of what I was experiencing, I stepped into the time machine of my own reality. From that secluded and stuffy Midwestern library of flatland, flyover, vast prairies, conservative community, wide open skies, and judgmental normality I began wandering. And oh baby, I have wandered. The places I have seen, the experiences I have witnessed, the life I have led would astound you, or bore you to tears I am quite sure. Libraries came and went in my history like the lovers most of us would care to forget . . . there was the blessedly short and intense one-night stand of a library shelved within the walls of a desert post office, littered with wanted posters and cast off advertising inserts blowing about the racks of books like hot dirty moths. There was the traveling bus of a library that I sauntered into during my time living on the streets of a traffic choked downtown. The bookshelves inside were compact and well organized, flashy and color coded for efficiency and I spent a week riding from one location to another with that slick urban library on wheels. There were the stained-glass-window eyes of dazzling brightness in one tiny town library and I stayed captured there for almost too long. There was the teeth grinding, filthy, and oh why did I stop here, grey and dirty steel coldness of a dangerous criminal city library gone bad. All the sad and sorry books in that library had ripped covers, bent corners, and reeked of neglect and danger.

But eventually, after much delightful and dangerous traveling, and never, mind you, never without a book-heavy backpack, I arrive, finally and forever it now seems, to this city on the edge of the world. A jewel of a town where the sun sets last and I am convinced that for that reason alone I will live longer than the rest of the country and die a satisfied and dignified and respected wise woman of little renown but many, many years.

Believe me when I tell you that even though I mistake the exploding hills of local shrubs for lilac, and marvel beneath oranges and lemons growing on trees for an embarrassing number of days, the first place I look for in this town is the public library. Admittedly, no matter how many times I am book-struck by the free and unconditional love of every library I enter, it always takes my breath away for a moment. Remembering back to the first time I saw our library, such a sigh of gratitude as I stand there, one hand on the railing, and gaze skyward. The towering trees arching over the stately walls are graceful and patchworked with trunks of cream and moon shadow green and kids push past me laughing and an old man sits down next to me to tie his shoe. The stairs are well worn like the steps of that great cathedral I am sure and in I go, a stranger, but not for long. This is the beginning of a new love affair . . . a lifelong adventure with an unknown who seems to willingly share unlimited potential and promise. My city library, a brand new experience with challenges and surprises, pages of discovery and volumes of secrets. I instinctively know that I will spend the rest of my days here, in love with this library, curled up next to the sky-high windows and huddled in a small, walled-off desk.

For better or for worse, I am in the place where I am always welcome, always accepted, and always at ease. Within the walls of our library I am free to confess and own my inadequacies and find books to shore me up. I am free to compare my feelings and ideas with authors long dead or celebrated on the bestseller lists. I am free to find books with minutely detailed histories and biographies that help me to find and map my place in our worldly timeline. I am free to time travel my heart out, back to my beginnings here, back to my childhood far away, fast forward to imagined planets and future games, and double-click behind to centuries long gone. My time machine is right here, no hot water heater closet needed, the library rules are few and simple, judgements and criticisms are well hidden and I consider myself lucky and fortunate to have returned to the home that I know and love the best.

These days I am a regular patron once more and forever, and it is true that our library is changing with the times, as we love to say. The children's section has been moved downstairs and even though it is a glorious thing, I regret the loss of their energy and laughter and chatter upstairs. Light streams in, as always, through the sky-high windows. The wind still blows leaf pattern shadows across the newly carpeted floors. Readers sit all along the walls now and in every conceivable configuration of table and desk. Look for me when you go there. I am the one walking slowly and quietly among the stacks and the patrons, spying a tiny bit on the rows of computer users, occasionally checking out the happy, noisy downstairs level, climbing the glorious stairs and wishing eternally to see the angels, and hopeful again to find meaning and purpose and direction book by book and page by page. Our beautiful city library, where equality and acceptance are real and the sign says: YOU ARE WELCOME HERE. Unconditional love. A lifetime of it. And the books are free.

Ursula K. LeGuin
My Libraries

Nothing if not prolific, Ursula Kroeber LeGuin, born in 1929, has published twenty-two novels (including the science-fiction classics, The Left Hand of Darkness *and the* Earthsea Cycle*), eleven volumes of short stories, five collections of essays, twelve books for children, six volumes of poetry and four of translation, and has received many awards such as the Hugo, Nebula, and National Book Award. A complete listing of her work is at www. ursulakleguin.com.*

A LIBRARY is a focal place to a community; and its sacredness is its accessibility, its publicness. It's everybody's place. I remember certain libraries, vividly and joyfully, as my libraries—elements of the best of my life.

The first one I knew well in Saint Helena, California, then a small, peaceful, mostly Italian town. The library was a little Carnegie, white stucco, cool and sleepy on the fine August afternoons when my mother would leave my brother and me there while she shopped at Giugni's and Tosetti's. Karl and I went through the children's room like word-seeking missiles. After we had read everything, including all thirteen volumes of the adventures of a fat boy detective, we had to be allowed to go into the Adult Side. That was hard for the librarians. They felt they were hurling us little kids into a room full of sex, death, and weird grown-ups like Heathcliff and the Joads; and in fact, they were. We were intensely grateful.

The only trouble with the Saint Helena library was that you could only take five books out at a time and we only went into town once a week. So we checked out really solid books, I mean five hundred pages of small print in two columns, like *The Count of Monte Cristo*. Short books were no good—two days' orgy and then starve the rest of the week—nothing but the farmhouse bookcase, and we could recite everything in it by the time we were ten. I imagine we were the only people in the Napa Valley who regularly hit each other on the head with quarterstaves while shouting, "Varlet! Have at thee!"—"Why, fat knave, thunk's thee to cross this bridge?" Karl usually got to be Robin Hood because he was older, but at least I never had to be Maid Marian.

Next in my life was the branch of the Berkeley Library near Garfield Junior High, where my dearest memory is of my friend Shirley leading me to the N shelf and saying "There's this writer called E. Nesbit and you HAVE to read the one called *Five Children and It,* and boy, was she right. By eighth grade I sort of oozed over into the adult room. The librarians pretended not to notice. But when I arrived at the adult checkout carrying a thick, obscure biography of Lord Dunsany like a holy relic, I remember the librarian's expression. It was very much like the expression of the U.S. customs inspector in Seattle, years later, when he opened my suitcase and found a Stilton cheese—not a decent whole cheese, but a ruined moldy rind, a smelly remnant, which our friend Barbara in Berkshire had affectionately but unwisely sent to my husband. The customs man said, "What is it?"

"Well, it's an English cheese," I said.

He was a tall, black man with a deep voice. He shut the suitcase and said, "Lady, if you want it, you can have it."

And the librarian let me have Lord Dunsany, too.

After that came the Berkeley Public Library itself, which is blessedly placed just a block from Berkeley Public High School. I loved the one as deeply as I hated the other. In one I was an exile in the Siberia of adolescent social mores. In the other I was home free. Without the library, I wouldn't have survived the school, not in my right mind, anyhow. But then, adolescents are all crazy.

I discovered that the foreign books were up on the third floor and nobody ever went there, so I moved in. I lived there, crouched in a spiderwebby window, with *Cyrano de Bergerac,* in French. I didn't know enough French yet to read Cyrano, but that didn't stop me. That's when I learned you can read a language you don't know if you love it enough. You can do anything if you love it enough. I cried a lot up there, over *Cyrano* and other people. I discovered Jean-Christophe, and cried over him; and Baudelaire, and cried over him—only a fifteen-year-old can truly appreciate *The Flowers of Evil,* I think. Sometimes I raided the lower, English-speaking regions of the library and brought back writers such as Ernest Dowson—"I have been faithful to thee, Cynara! in my fashion"—and cried some more. Ah, those were good years for crying, and la ibrary is a good place to cry in. Quietly.

Next in my life was Radcliffe's small, endearing college library, and then—when they decided I could be permitted to enter it, even though I was a freshman, and what was far worse, a freshwoman—Widener Library at Harvard.

I will tell you my private definition of freedom. Freedom is stack privileges at Widener Library.

I remember the first time I came outside from those endless, incredible stacks. I could barely walk because I was carrying about twenty-five books, but I was flying. I turned around and looked up the broad steps of the building, and I though, That's heaven. That's the heaven for me. All the words in the world, and all for me to read. Free at last, Lord, free at last!

I hope you'll understand that I am not quoting those great words lightly. I do mean it. knowledge sets us free, art sets us free. A great library is freedom.

So then, after a mad but brief Parisian affair with the Bibliothèque Nationale, I arrived in Portland. Our first years here we had two little babies, and I was at home with them. The great treat for me, the holiday I wanted, the event I looked forward to all week or month, was to get a sitter and come downtown with Charles and go to the Library. At night, of course; no way to do it in the daytime. A couple of hours, till the Library closed at nine. Plunging into the ocean of words, roaming in the broad fields of the mind, climbing the mountains of the imagination. Just like the kid in the Carnegie or the student in Widener, that was my freedom, that was my joy. And it still is.

That joy must not be sold. It must not be "privatised," made into another privilege for the privileged. A public library is a public trust.

And that freedom must not be compromised. It must be available to all who need it, and that's everyone, when they need it, and that's always.

Shirley Geok-lin Lim
A Funny Thing Happened...

A Professor Emerita, Department of English, UCSB, Lim is an Asian-American/Malaysian-Singaporean writer of poetry, fiction, creative non-fiction, and criticism. Her first collection of poems, Crossing The Peninsula, *published in 1980, won the Commonwealth Poetry Prize, a first both for an Asian and a woman.* Among the White Moon Faces *is her American Book Award-winning memoir.*

IN FACT, several funny things happened on my way to address the Library Association of Singapore (LAS) in 1996. I was visiting the National Institute of Education as Fulbright Distinguished Professor, when the Head Librarian of the Institute of Southeast Asian Studies (ISEAS) invited me to give the keynote at the LAS Annual Dinner. Reading and the many fabulous doors in books it opened for me had rescued me from a poor, hungry, lonely, hard childhood. Much of who I am, and how I got to where I am, I owe to libraries—from the Convent School classroom shelves to the small-town Malacca public library stuffed with British children's favorites and popular fiction, to the University of Malaya Dewey-catalogued hard-covered texts fresh out of Cambridge University and Oxford University Presses. So, speaking to an audience of librarians raised an irresistible challenge: an opportunity to meet some of the godmothers who'd collectively gifted me with poetry, tall tales of romance and travel, and every resource of learning and imagination that's found its way into my head from a page.

The challenge, however, was daunting. How was I to speak to professionals whose work I knew so little of, except insofar as I may have called on them for assistance in chasing down a book? Whose lives I had seldom intersected with? Who were seen, as we academics too often also are perceived, as cogs in the machine of the research university? Library Science was not among my fields of research; and a post-buffet-dinner address, I feared, was not the most receptive time for philosophy, literary criticism, pedagogy, or worse, pedantry. My keynote was scheduled between a Japanese Drum Dance and a talk, "Dress for Success," before dessert and a "Lucky Draw."

Lost for ideas, I turned to the Internet and sent out a cry for help two weeks before the dinner, subject heading, "Librarians in Literature." "I am doing a brief piece on librarians, and wonder if anyone can advise me on representations of librarians in literature. Or are they such remote creatures that the literary imagination has not yet bothered with them?"

The next day, I received an email offering some arcane references, writing "there is a genre of literature in which immigrants and new arrivals to the city encounter the library and librarians. For most, the librarian opens doors to a new world of the imagination, but in some the door is shut by the librarian." I observed with a pang that the writer used the subject 'librarian' as the agent of welcome and rejection, and not what I had been thinking since I encountered libraries myself at the age of six, the actual building and the residents therein, its books. Fifteen minutes later, I received a referral to a Brian Castro novel where a librarian is "having a tortured affair with an author," a plot I took as a highly sublimated story, librarians to my mind generally suffering from tortured relationships with books. And about half an hour later, a professor emailed to note the movies, "Party Girl," "in which the heroine becomes a librarian," and "Ghostbusters," and leaped from the absurd to the sublime in reminding me that the genius Borges was a librarian "who often wrote about libraries." Clearly my query via the Internet had caused an instantaneous ripple in the limpid pond of librarians, scholars and book-related others who have found their setting in libraries.

The speed, intellectual level, carefully crafted, highly original, intensely concentrated nature of the collective sharing to a simple query from a small Asian state institution may be explained by the respondents' intrigue with the subject, "Librarians in literature." Shakespeare spoke of madmen, kings and queens, poets and lovers; novelists have portrayed soldiers and frustrated housewives, even men in grey and industrialists; but librarians have seldom been the central subject of scrutiny in literature, despite, as the emails emphasized, appearing in various literary genres as heroes, heroines, agents, major and secondary characters; appearing themselves as authorial genius—see Borges and Philip Larkin; and serving for children and ordinary readers and scholars, as admirable public servants—elevated, as I had viewed them when I was ten, through their daily immersion among the sacred texts of the human imagination. But because their interactions with me were almost always subdued (every library I entered holding sacrosanct the injunction to SILENCE), librarians remained, for me and many others, distant figures, not communicative authorities the way teachers are, and chiefly accessible in brief, narrow and ritualized ways. So many librarians sent titles, plot descriptions, character profiles, suggestions, lively ideas; did this exchange suggest a latent desire to see librarians emerge as fully developed literary figures via multiple texts; to see their behind-the-scenes profession step forward to claim its rightful shamanistic stature in the lives of children and minds; to drop the conventional image of the librarian shadowy among the book stacks and to insist how the librarian has been centrally cast in poems, stories, films, dramas, musicals, and more?

Alas, I did not dig much into the mine of dazzling librarian-related texts offered me in the eighteen days of email exchange. Had I been working on a dissertation, a book or even a scholarly article investigating the permutations of librarian-hood, my generous correspondents would have long received acknowledged thanks; and that publication might have contributed to an enlargement of how its readers "see" librarians–complexly emotional and richly intellectually endowed humans, whose choice of the profession suggests their psychological auras and which work has equally shaped them and the world in which books will always have their home. Instead, I wrote a short talk on my personal relationship with books coming out of early childhood obsessive reading (so obsessive that my eldest brother told his friends I read while in the outhouse, oblivious to its odiferous environment). The keynote quoted some of the humorous information on librarians my correspondents had sent, for I was determined to make the librarians laugh, a high bar to clear, as humor until then was completely absent in my writer's skill set.

And so I did. That keynote was published in the *Journal* of the LAS but is not included in my curriculum vitae, because two funnier things happened on my way to give a funny keynote. First, among the warm, thoughtful, wide-ranging, critically astute, even brilliant information I received (in what we might now call a crowd-sourcing endeavor), one email sent two days after my query went out sternly reprimanded me for my choice of wording: "I'm a librarian and do not consider myself a 'creature'. In fact, I resent your belittlement of our profession and the essential services that we provide to society, especially academics in the social sciences." This Library Director in a small college in Missouri had read my informal query, casually written—with a literary nod to the polite language of Romantics, as in Mr. Bingley's "She is most beautiful creature I ever beheld" (Jane Austen, *Pride and Prejudice*) and to the sacred association in the Anglican hymn, "All Things Bright and Beautiful"—as a put-down where I had intended to suggest an idealizing distance. Her message was my first experience of being flamed; and even as I cringed at the burn, I was amused to see she could not help adding her knowledge to the crowd source: "Librarians are most often represented in fiction as a detective or sleuth." Still, her rebuke stung.

After the keynote, as I stood in line for dessert, the Dean of the Division where I was Visiting Professor said to me huffily, "Wah, so easy to write your keynote. Simply ask for help and write what people tell you." I could not return a quick comeback; could not then launch into the nature of inquiry, which seeks sources and different expertise; sifts through a wide range; catalogues, selects, organizes, arranges according to a thesis schema; and writes to illuminate, illustrate, discover, persuade and perhaps even entertain if not enthrall.

These three funny things persuaded me in their instruction:

1. to never send out a cold query to unknown correspondents.
2. to never write with my tongue in cheek in academic writing, particularly when addressing an unknown audience.
3. to not include humorous keynotes in my curriculum vitae.

Still I have never regretted that special experience, if only for eighteen days, of being Internet-connected to a hive of librarians and librarian-loving scholars and immersed in their provocative, highly charged, and yes, honey-humored passages: as in the sharing of Elizabeth McCracken's *The Giant's House*, in which "The plot revolves around a 25-year-old single woman (i.e., spinster) librarian who falls in love with an 11-year-old 6'2" boy" and another referring to "Neal Klugman in Roth's *Goodbye, Columbus*, who worked the reference desk at the Newark Public Library—and who had a sex life". Two decades later,

I am still grateful for having learned that Batgirl was a librarian. Wikipedia records that Batgirl arrived in DC Comics in 1967 with a doctorate in library science, and she directed the Gotham City Public Library before serving in the U.S. Congress. Librarians in the literary imagination had come a long way by 1967.

Why then are they still also greatly invisible half a century later, in 2017?

Information desk, 1925

Leon F. Litwack
How the Santa Barbara Public Library Radicalized Me

The author of Been in the Storm So Long, *which won the Pulitzer Prize in History and the Parkman Prize, Litwack is the recipient of a Guggenheim Fellowship, two Distinguished Teaching Awards, and a National Endowment for the Humanities Film Grant, and is the A & M Morrison Professor Emeritus of American History at the University of California, Berkeley, which he attended after graduating from Santa Barbara High School in 1947.*

DURING MY childhood and teenage years, the Santa Barbara Public Library exerted an extraordinary influence on my life. In the sixth grade I applied for the position of library page. Several years later the job was mine. I enjoyed assisting many of the authors who lived nearby, such as Alfred Noyes and Franz Werfel. By high school I was sitting at the library's information and reference desks and zealously reading the books surrounding me. My neighborhood (Milpas and Alphonse) exposed me at the same time to a diversity of cultures, languages, and histories. I found my upbringing in Santa Barbara to be an intoxicating learning experience.

What drew me to history, even as a child, were the stories I read and heard. My parents told me about coming to New York from Tsarist Russia, and then finding their way to Santa Barbara, where I heard the stories related by Italian, Greek, and mostly Mexican neighbors, almost all of them immigrants. Neither my mother nor my father had any formal education but even in my childhood they introduced me to a cultural world that helped to shape my reading and listening, my thoughts and writings. They spoke often of the people they most admired, and the public library gave me easy access to such voices as Tom Paine, Frederick Douglass, and John Peter Altgeld, to Henry David Thoreau, Emma Goldman and Walt Whitman, to Leo Tolstoy, Nat Turner, Ida B. Wells, John

Reed, Mother Jones, Tom Mooney, W.E.B. Du Bois, and the abolitionist and labor movements. Rebels and misfits, many of them, they enlisted in struggles for racial and social justice, challenged authority, repressive legislation, and hostile courts, and defined for me at an impressionable age the limits of dissent in America.

These were important lessons vividly imparted by literary and political outlaws, revealing what Alfred Kazin has called the "raw hurting power" that a book can exert over an individual. The public library became my sanctuary, and I mined its riches, reading passionately, feeling the words, discovering the world outside of Santa Barbara: the USA of John Dos Passos, Theodore Dreiser, Mark Twain, William Faulkner, Richard Wright, Nathaniel West, Sinclair Lewis, Langston Hughes, John Steinbeck, Woody Guthrie, and Paul Robeson.

But my extracurricular education, aided and abetted by the books I read, came increasingly into conflict with the patriotic drumbeat, the uncritical celebration of the American Dream, a growing awareness of the uses and abuses of the past, the impoverishment of public life, the macho posturing, and the elusive and intractable barriers to racial justice. These did not prepare me for the textbook's America: Pilgrims. Puritans. Founding Fathers. Anglo-Saxons and northern Europeans. That was someone else's history. Where were my people, my parents and neighbors? Their stories were not to be found. If Mexican Americans appeared, as in the textbook, they were appendages to the Europeanized mainstream. In Santa Barbara, the postcard icon—the Old Mission—rendered invisible the Mexican field hand. And if African Americans were noted in my history course, they were docile and contented slaves or easily manipulated field hands.

The public library provided sources that helped to undermine the conventional wisdom. It was a librarian who urged me to read historians Charles Beard and Richard Hofstadter, and a Santa Barbara High School teacher who gave me class time to refute the textbook's version of slavery and Reconstruction. That led me to the public library and the exciting discovery of Du Bois's *Black Reconstruction*, with its provocative subtitle: "An Essay Toward a History of the Part which Black People Played in the Attempt to Reconstruct Democracy in America." (Several years later I met Du Bois in Berkeley to discuss his work and its impact.)

In my senior year, I edited *The Forge*, my high school newspaper, only to find myself embroiled in a running conflict with the Vice Principal, who several times threatened to shut us down over editorials he deemed subversive or obscene. They were. We demanded, for example, the removal of the Reader's Digest from English classes, on the ground that it imposed right-wing values in the deceptive guise of building vocabulary. We opposed the ROTC and the prospect of compulsory military training. We thought the funds used every year to stage Fiesta could be better spent on low-cost housing, and in a special issue for Brotherhood Week, we focused on the persistence and virulence of racism in American society and the urgent need for a national civil rights movement. For the 1940s and 1950s this was an unusual high school newspaper but it did reflect a growing uneasiness in American youth and in many of the returning World War II veterans.

Throughout history the fear has persisted that that teachers, librarians, writers, poets, artists, and musicians are more likely than most to disturb the peace, that they are peculiarly susceptible to subversion. We are. The fears are well grounded. Intellectual activity and inquiry have a way of undermining old dogmas, values, and systems of thought. I still think about that day in high school when I hoped (with all of my youthful idealism and enthusiasm) to change the way my classmates and teachers thought about slavery and Reconstruction. More than half a century later I would like to think that my work has made a difference, not only my books but my courses, the more than 30,000 students I have sent to the library. Teaching and writing remain for me that unique opportunity to force students to see and to feel the past in ways that may be genuinely disturbing. I want to bring into their historical consciousness the experiences and voices of people ordinarily left outside the framework of history, many of them losers in their own time, outlaws and rebels who—individually and collectively—tried to give meaning to abstract notions of liberty, equality, and freedom, those who chose to dissent from the national consensus and who opted for the highest kind of patriotism and loyalty to their country—a willingness to unmask its leaders and to subject its institutions to critical examination. The more we absorb our literary heritage, the deeper we probe our past, the more likely we are to ask the most searching questions about who we were and who we are today. The Santa Barbara Public Library taught me that lesson—and much more. I will always be grateful.

Perie Longo
Journal Entry Found on the Internet About a Library

Poet Laureate Emerita (2007-2009) of Santa Barbara, Longo has published five books of poetry. Her poems have been published nationally in many journals, anthologies and texts. She has been Poet-in-Residence in many local schools through the California Poets-in-the-Schools program (1984-2014) and has been on the staff for the annual Santa Barbara Writers Conference for over twenty-five years. As a psychotherapist, she integrates poetry writing for healing and is a past president of the National Association for Poetry Therapy. For more information about her work, see www.perielongo.com.

> *Be a little careful about your library.*
> *Do you foresee what you will do with it?...*
> *the real question is what it will do with you...*
> *turn you inside out or outside in.*
> — *Ralph Waldo Emerson, 1873*

I'M NESTLED in the window seat, my favorite spot
at our neighborhood library between the A&P and bakery,
flutter of snow outside, lost in the latest Nancy Drew mystery.
A stack of toppled other books I'll lug home two blocks away.

Worlds later, early for a meeting, I enter the Faulkner Gallery
hung with paintings of local bluffs and coves,
the Thousand Steps. I cross to the main library,
stunned.

Where am I?
    What have I been doing?
Barely any books, all that space like a prairie
    and so much light gushing through windows.

Readers lounge at the edges, others in rows
plugged into laptops, computers, upstairs and down,
attached as if from outer space to earphones,
any information desired delivered with a click,
     no waiting for the word.

Gone the cumbersome indexes, card catalogues,
all collapsed into the efficiency of a chip. Gaze
drifts to the ceiling cathedral high, a refuge still
hushed as any church, unwanted fractures left outside.

Breathing in the must of age, a librarian ascends
from the archives with my requested out-of-print book,
bears it like a sacred trophy, her importance unquestioned.
    Be careful, she whispers, *it's rare.*

Gayle Lynds
Reading Can Get You into Trouble, Or...
Why I Love Librarians, And...
How the Santa Barbara Library Captured My Heart

A New York Times *bestselling novelist and award-winning author of ten international espionage novels, Lynds spent many years in Santa Barbara raising her children. She honed her craft by writing male pulp adventure novels before her first thriller,* Masquerade, *hit the bestseller list. She currently lives in Portland, Maine. Her website is www.gaylelynds.com.*

I'M TALL. That's for those of you whom I've not yet had the pleasure to meet. Yep, five-foot-ten. I love parades, theater seating, and looking for my husband because I can see over almost everyone's heads.

I grew fast, eventually having to take my mother along to vouch that I wasn't too old for folks to give me Halloween candy. As fast as I grew, so did my love of reading. Books were my friends, my teachers, my allies, my secret under-the-covers companions to ward off the evil hand that lived in the dark under my bed.

Our family lived in Council Bluffs, Iowa. My mother loved books as much as me. She introduced me to the local Andrew Carnegie library before I could read. We didn't have money for books, but library cards were free. My mother and the librarian knew and liked each other. Her name was Mildred Smock.

Mildred was stylish. Although she was thin, there was something sturdy about her, especially when she picked up a stack of hardbacks. She had a good face, long fingers, and a brown bob that curled more than it bobbed. She wore serviceable pumps and dark dresses with narrow little belts. Her expression was serious. To a child like me, she was intimidating. It never occurred to me that what she looked like was merely her dust jacket, that there was far more inside.

Summers were grand. The day after the last day of school, I'd ride the city bus downtown to the library. With awe, I'd enter the Mark Twain Room of children's literature. The first time I returned the books I borrowed by myself, Mildred checked them closely for abuse. Mildred followed the rules, and she expected everyone else to do so, too.

She and I seldom talked, except when she'd stop me and put a book in my hands. And then she was gone, while I'd be entranced by a new author or genre to follow.

I worked my way through the stacks, devouring novels, adventure tales, fantasies, and mysteries. By the age of nine, thanks to Mildred, I went through a period of biographies and histories—Marco Polo, the Empress Josephine, Mozart, Madame Curie, the kings and queens of England.

Then I discovered the sports section and the works of a fine writer who eventually became my friend—William Campbell Gault, of Santa Barbara. From him I learned about baseball, football, hockey, soccer, and the life lesson that all great athletes must learn: never give up.

When I was eleven, I got very lucky—a neighbor joined the Doubleday Book Club and gave me her books as she finished them. The world of popular literature opened up to me with Pearl Buck, Graham Greene, Daphne Du Maurier, and James Michener. I was riveted by the breadth of their stories. So many interesting characters trying to solve problems, create new lives, and operate in cultures that were foreign and fascinating.

I remember my mother discussing my latest reading habits with my aunt, who was concerned about the sex in adult books.

"Don't worry," my mother assured her. "She won't understand what's going on."

As every child knows, there's power in eavesdropping. After that conversation, I was suddenly interested in the sex scenes. Thank you, Mom.

As I neared the age of twelve, I was almost five-feet-seven and looked like a teenager despite no makeup. I kinda liked that, except I could no longer convince bus drivers and ticket-sellers at movie matinees that I was young enough to pay the kid price.

As soon as school was out that summer, I rode the bus through the June sunshine to the library and climbed the familiar granite steps. I had that wonderful stirring in my stomach. What great tales would I find?

In the children's section, I walked up and down the aisles. I'd read so many of the books. Devoured them, really. But now all of them seemed somehow too familiar.

161

I turned on my heel and left. I wanted books like I'd been reading. Adult books. But there was a problem—Mildred of The Rules. Mildred knew I was too young to be allowed into the adult stacks.

I spotted her at the card catalog, her back to me as she bent over, working. I skirted the room and sneaked into the tall shelves packed with hardcovers. Oh, to be able to read every one!

Thus began my short life of crime.

Avoiding Mildred, I checked out my prizes with other librarians, even though my library card was marked for the children's section. My tall height and teen appearance had its advantages.

For a month I sailed through.

Then one day I set my latest choices before the young librarian at the counter.

"Your card?" She picked up the books.

As I handed it to her, Mildred's voice sounded: "Wait. Is that Gayle again?" She was coming around the corner toward us.

I felt a chill. "Yes, Miss Smock."

Her stride was purposeful. Serious as always, she picked up the novels. She examined them. "What's your telephone number?"

I had no choice. I gave it to her.

She dialed and identified herself to my mother. Then she did the unexpected, the shocking, the act of the book saint: She winked at me.

Then she said, "Would you object if I gave Gayle an adult library card?"

And that was that. She'd been monitoring me all along and realized I wasn't going back to the Mark Twain Room. Thank you, Miss Smock.

While I grew up to be a writer, Mildred Smock continued on at the Council Bluffs library, enriching people's lives book by book. She began as a clerk in 1941, rose to be director in 1957, and after more than a half century, retired in 1992. Continuing to contribute to the community in numerous ways, she died in 2014, much lauded and much loved. Her imprint continues to echo.

As for me, I moved to Santa Barbara in the late sixties and within a week started frequenting our beautiful library on Anapamu Street. The lavish inventory of books with all of their possibilities embraced me. The librarians met me with a smile, asking how they could help. By the mid-seventies, my children were attending story readings and checking out books. We were eager participants in art and cultural events downstairs. As the editor of *Santa Barbara Magazine*, I often called over to the reference desk to make sure the facts in a story were correct.

When the library's 75th birthday arrived, in 1992, I was honored to be invited to be one of the speakers. By then I was writing novels, and I was spending days there researching. Even though the library could seem vast, I felt cozy sitting at one of the wood tables surrounded by books in various stages of being studied. For my spy novel, *The Coil*, I remember discovering *The Encyclopedia of Violence* and needing nearly $100 in coins to copy pages. It was an ordeal made easier and far more pleasant by the company of one of the reference librarians, who'd made time to help me.

Now that I live far away, in Maine, I can still picture the library's tall columns, soaring staircase, and sense of civility and promise. Oh, to open a book I'm unacquainted with. To read words knitted together with skill and thought. To be in the company of those who love the Santa Barbara library as much as I do.

Lance Mason
At the Heart of the Art of Learning

Author of four novels and a nonfiction collection, Mason's award-winning writing has appeared in many publications, including Best American Travel Writing. *Based in Santa Barbara, he has spent over twenty years traveling, living, and working abroad, including a half-dozen around-the-world adventures. Interested readers can find out more at his website, www.lance-mason.com.*

OXNARD'S LIBRARY was on The Plaza, our town square, and faced the Bank of A. Levy and Juan Holquin's Shoe Repair, among a clutch of established shops. Built in 1906 with funds from Andrew Carnegie and local citizens, the library was Norman Rockwell Americana, its neo-classical style and marble-work giving this Far West farming community the sense that it had arrived at some cultural milestone in a country that would become the twentieth century's namesake.

At twelve years old, c. 1960, I sat at the library tables memorizing "The Gettysburg Address" for class recitation at Santa Clara Grammar School, and felt Abe Lincoln standing over me. If my mother was on swing shift and my father delayed at work, for ten cents, at the food stand across C Street, I would buy toasted cheese sandwiches, browned in butter on the grill, sometimes with sliced dill pickles. That library was a cathedral of quiet, of card catalogues and discipline, of classmates struggling with their own civics assignments under the owlish gaze of Mrs. Gowdey or Mrs. Kerr. The odors of aged paper and book-bindings were, to our young noses, the incense of learning—less an intoxication than an abstract magic that made us bigger and better people just by being in its thrall.

During my high school years, the books and administration were moved from "the Carnegie" to a new brick building a few blocks away, but the original building is still my image of a library. Yet I attended the new one, and even studied there in breaks between learning how to flirt with girls. Decades later, in fact, when my friend Vic tried to cure my IT ignorance by comparing a harddrive to a library's stacks, and RAM to a work table of open books, the stacks-and-tables scene I conjured was from that library.

As an undergrad, and in UCLA's very serious bio-med collection during grad school, a trek to the library upped the ante in that week's study schedule, raising one's sincerity quotient regarding the target topic (not that gender-based flirtation was off the menu!). Later, whether in the States, Brazil, or New Zealand, library research assignments (pre-Internet) told my students that the material under investigation was not for empirical hypotheses alone, but required broader, evidence-based learning, derived from the scientific method and recorded in journals, monographs, and textbooks by disciplined professionals in that field.

Most stored knowledge is now available without the need for buildings and books, and so it's logical to question the role of traditional libraries when cyber-sources can reach so many more readers. Moreover, it may be pointless to argue a case for Google vs. bricks-and-mortar centers, of paper-and-ink galleries vs. "data-stacks" ad infinitum because, regardless of how information is stored and accessed going forward, those societies and cultures rich, blessed, and privileged enough to have access to learning, to advancement, will continue to derive value from the records of both the remote and the immediate past. Our more relevant challenge lies in disseminating to the wider world that wealth of experience, imagination, artistry, logic, conflict, insight, compassion, forgiveness, and forward movement that books, and the protection of books, have allowed and provided over these many centuries.

Postscript: The week before I was asked to write this, I was reflecting on the role of the Carnegie Libraries in America and on the synergy between libraries and art—as with the Faulkner Gallery and the Santa Barbara Library. In a search to update myself on my childhood library, I found it is now Oxnard's "Carnegie Art Museum," giving us another concrete chapter in the contributions libraries make to art—and to life.

Marcia Meier
I Found the World in a Library

Marcia Meier is a writer, editor and writing coach. Her work has appeared in numerous publications and she is the author of three books. She initially moved to Santa Barbara as a high school senior with her parents, left to go to college, and returned in 1985. It's been her home ever since. Visit her website at www. marciameier.com.

HACKLEY PUBLIC Public Library's wide steps, huge oak doors, and stone façade were an imposing entrée to the world of books when I was seven. The library was just a few blocks from my home in downtown Muskegon, Michigan, and I spent many a Saturday morning there with my older sister and younger brother.

I remember wandering through the tall stacks of books, searching for an armload to take home for the week. I hear the footsteps on marble floors, smell the delicious cardboard-y scent of the books and glue, feel the airy silence of the cavernous rooms splashed with colored light from huge stained-glass windows at either end of the main hall.

Heavy wooden tables bisected the room, dividing fiction from nonfiction, historical from mystery, romance from the children's section, where posters and chapter books piqued my seven-year-old interests. But there was no children's reading area, as you often see in libraries today. I would choose six or eight books, then climb up on one of the big oak chairs with my potential take-homes, spreading them out in front of me on the broad table.

The librarian who sat at the front desk in the entry (always a woman) was kind and helpful (if a bit of an authoritarian; she often shushed me—I could never quite keep quiet or still).

As I grew, so did my literary appetite, and soon she was suggesting classics like Madeleine L'Engle's *A Wrinkle in Time*, Harper Lee's *To Kill a Mockingbird*, Anne Frank's *The Diary of a Young Girl*, Louisa May Alcott's *Little Women*, and many other titles.

Hackley Public Library is still there, in all its stone-faced glory. Completed in 1890, it was commissioned by lumber baron Charles H. Hackley at a cost of more than $200,000. Architecturally, it is considered a classic example of American Romanesque style, with a tall eight-sided turret on one side and massive blocks of bluish-grey syenite granite trimmed with rich Marquette terra cotta sandstone for walls. Inside the great oak doors are fine marble, plaster carvings, metal work, and multicolored Italian marble mosaics on the floors. The arched stained-glass windows transform the great hall into a space of light and color. These impressions remain etched in my earliest memories, and the library truly became a place of mystery and solace for me.

I found equal refuge in my high school library, where I discovered Steinbeck, Hemingway, Salinger, Fitzgerald, Vonnegut, and Faulkner, not to mention Shakespeare, Dickens, and Homer. And, too, my all-time favorite trilogy: J.R.R. Tolkien's *The Lord of the Rings*, which I read at least three times before I graduated.

When my daughter was young, the Santa Barbara Public Library became a favorite Saturday morning destination. There she developed her deep love of reading, and discovered so many then-contemporary young adult writers, like Judy Blume and J.K. Rowling. We read all of Rowling's Harry Potter novels together, first with me reading to her at bedtime (she was eight when the first came out), and then as she got older, we'd read them together, alternating pages. By the time the fourth Potter book came out, Kendall was reading them on her own, and she had become a Potter fanatic. When she traveled to Europe the summer she turned thirteen, she bought the fifth book while she was in London, and still has both the American and English versions with differing covers. When the sixth came out, she stood outside Chaucer's to get her copy at midnight, and read the entire thing in two days.

As I think about the influence of libraries on both of our lives, I'm reminded of the incredible power of the word, and its ability to change our lives and perspectives. I would not be exaggerating to say that thousands of stories have enriched and enlivened my life through the pages of a book. I'm grateful for the literary journeys Hackley Public Library inspired me to take, and will always hold that stone façade in my book lover's heart.

Joseph Mills
The Ideal Library

Joseph Mills has degrees in literature from the University of Chicago (BA), the University of New Mexico (MA), and the University of California Davis (PhD). As he was working on his third one, his mother asked, "Don't you know that stuff yet?" A faculty member at the University of North Carolina School of the Arts, Joseph Mills holds the Susan Burress Wall Distinguished Professorship in the Humanities. His work includes poetry, fiction, drama, and criticism. He has published six volumes of poetry. See www.josephrobertmills.com for more about the author. Here is a short essay and a library poem.

I TAKE my six year old son to the library to get his first card. As we pull a bunch of books, movies, and CDs from the shelves, he becomes increasingly concerned and finally says, "Daddy, we can't afford all of these." I explain, "They'll let us take them. For free." His expression turns to amazement as if he can't believe this is true. When I explain, "But we have to take care of them, and we have to bring them back," he nods and says, "That's fair."

I know how my son feels. Forty years after getting my own first card (at the Shawnee Public Library in Fort Wayne, Indiana), I still feel a sense of amazement at having access to so many materials. It is almost, as Vizzini says in *The Princess Bride*, "inconceivable." Wait, you're going to let me take home anything in here? For free? What's the catch?

Lending libraries are beautiful in their basic ideals. In enabling people to educate themselves, they are the most empowering and humanistic of institutions.

In a very real way, libraries have shaped who I am, so perhaps it's not surprising that when I gave my wife a tour of places where I grew up, it turned out to be, in part, a tour of libraries. Some of these were rundown. Some no longer existed. None of them were architectural wonders. Yet I loved each one because when I walked in I felt a sense of possibility.

I still feel it.

When I move to a new place, something I've done dozens of times, one of the first things I do is get a library card. It makes me feel both more rooted and as if I've secured a type of life line.

While I'm grateful for any library where I live, what is my ideal one?

My ideal library is open whenever I want to go. Mornings. Evenings. Any day of the week.

My ideal library is easy to get to. I can walk or ride a bike.

Whatever book I think of, my ideal library has it. More importantly, it has books that I may not think of, but still should read.

I can browse all the stacks and storage areas of my ideal library and make discoveries. (And the stacks are well-lit and spacious.)

My ideal library has comfortable places to read, windows that let in natural light, and good non-fluorescent lighting as well.

My ideal library is staffed by people who respect my privacy, leave me alone to explore, and yet also suggest books that end up being important to me.

My ideal library hasn't been given to the community by a wealthy donor, but is of the community and is the community.

When I walk into my ideal library, it feels like optimism and hope. It simultaneously offers a sense of adventure and safety. And it instills in both six-year-olds and forty-six-year-olds a sense of amazement.

If Librarians Were Honest
"... a book indeed sometimes debauched me from my work...."
– Benjamin Franklin

If librarians were honest,
they wouldn't smile, or act
welcoming. They would say,
you need to be careful. Here
be monsters. They would say,
These rooms house heathens
and heretics, murderers and
maniacs, the deluded, desperate,
and dissolute. They would say,

These books contain knowledge
of death, desire, and decay,
betrayal, blood, and more blood;
each is a Pandora's box, so why
would you want to open one.
They would post danger
signs warning that contact
might result in mood swings,
severe changes in vision,
and mind-altering effects.
If librarians were honest
they would admit the stacks
can be more seductive and
shocking than porn. After all,
once you've seen a few
breasts, vaginas, and penises,
more is simply more,
a comforting banality,
but the shelves of a library
contain sensational novelties,
a scandalous, permissive mingling
of Malcolm X, Marx, Melville,
Merwin, Millay, Milton, Morrison,
and anyone can check them out,
taking them home or to some corner
where they can be debauched
and impregnated with ideas.
If librarians were honest,
they would say, No one
spends time here without being
changed. Maybe you should
go home. While you still can.

Shirley Morrison
Some Thoughts on Libraries and Librarians

After earning a BA in Education from UCLA, Morrison taught for a few years before returning to UCLA to earn a Masters of Library Science. As a librarian, she worked in Los Angeles before moving to Santa Barbara, where she held library positions at Hope School, the Santa Barbara Museum of Natural History, Ventura County Library Services Agency and Santa Barbara Public Library, where she served as Children's Librarian for 20 years.

I GREW up in the library. I sometimes have been known to call myself a librarian's librarian. By that I mean my mother was a librarian and so was I, so literally, a librarian's librarian. My mother was widowed very young. With two kids to support, she went back to school and got a degree in Librarianship. She went to work in Los Angeles Public Library's Benjamin Franklin Branch in East Los Angeles.

Benjamin Franklin in those days was a classic old Carnegie Library. There were stately marble steps leading up into the library. Straight ahead, at the top of the stairs, was the library check-out desk. To the left and right were huge plate-glass windows. Behind the left window was the very quiet adult reading room. Behind the right window was the children's room which was anything but quiet because my mom worked there. She was the perfect Children's Librarian—charismatic, funny, vivacious, enthusiastic and loud. When she held her storytimes, even folks sitting in the back rows could hear her very well. She told stories in schools, in the parks, at PTA meetings, even in the shopping malls, always hauling her library books with her in canvas bags. Because my brother and I were the library kids, we sometimes had access to the staff room, where there might be cookies and, although we didn't have a Christmas tree at home, we got to decorate the Library Christmas Tree.

Years later, I met a woman who was by then a grandmother herself. As we talked about the old neighborhood, I must have mentioned my mother. She touched her heart and said, "You are Mrs. Peltzman's daughter! She was my librarian! I loved her. She loved me, I was her favorite." The same thing happened when I went to library school. There were about seven of us in a class of 70, who knew my mother as their librarian, and were inspired to do the same thing that she did so well.

Both my brother and I began working in libraries as teenagers. My first job at 14 was shelving books at my local library, John C. Fremont, off Melrose Avenue. I earned an unbelievable 75 cents an hour. I worked in the children's room for a children's librarian who was very near retirement. Sometimes when she was asked for help or the location of a book in the stacks, she would point to me and say, "go ask that girl, she will find it for you." And I did. I shelved books all through high school and only left the library when I entered UCLA. My older brother worked at the Downtown Central Library during high school as well. We both could probably recite some favorite numbers in the Dewey Decimal System: 629.13 (airplanes) for my brother who grew up to be an engineer and 636.8 for me because I still love cats. I think the Dewey Decimal System is still the only numerical sequence I actually understand.

Except for four years teaching elementary school, most of my professional positions have been in public libraries, school libraries, and a museum library as well as a few stints in bookstores.

My own two daughters grew up going regularly to Santa Barbara Public Library, participating in the Summer Reading Programs, getting their first library cards and learning to read. I remember, as a library patron, sitting in the Children's Room with them and watching as they chose books. I also could gaze outside at the beautiful Santa Barbara Courthouse or inside at the wonderful Don Freeman mural. When I started work at Santa Barbara Public Library as the Children's Librarian I felt I had come home. And the Don Freeman mural was mine to share with library patrons, young and old. Like my mother, I too could be funny and loud and during Halloween lead a noisy group of costumed preschoolers all over the library trick-or-treating. My years at Santa Barbara Public Library were definitely happy years. The library itself with those high ceilings, long windows, double staircase and small, yet cozy, children's room was the place to be. It was not a charming old Carnegie Library but a place to settle in and get comfortable. My two daughters became the "library kids," and sometimes there were even cookies in the staff room.

Piri Korngold Nesselrod
The New Library

In her Biography of a Library *(1977), Nesselrod (1907-2002) relates how the original Santa Barbara Public Library, constructed in 1892 at 14 E. Carrillo Street, outgrew its space. The wife of the historian Ralph Korngold, she was also an author in her own right and served as President of the Friends of the Santa Barbara Library in the mid-1970s.*

THE USE of the library expanded so rapidly that by 1914 it was necessary to plan a much larger building on a larger site. The Chamber of Commerce purchased the old Library for its home, and with the money from that sale the land for the new building at Anapamu and Anacapa Streets was bought.

Again public-spirited residents, in the persons of Charles L. Taylor and Dr. Henry S. Pritchett, both Trustees of the Carnegie Corporation, came to the aid of the building fund, by procuring from the corporation a grant of fifty thousand dollars, which was matched by the city.

The building committee desired a structure of definite architectural beauty. Much credit for the accomplishment of this dream goes to Library Trustee Charles A. Edwards, first appointed in January 1900, who, with one short interruption, served until his death in 1930. He was not only dedicated to establishing a great institution, but was intensely interested in beautifying the town and adjoining hillsides by saving live oak trees and ceanothus and planting eucalyptus trees.

The first sketches for the present library building were the gift of an eastern architect, Henry A. Hornbostel. However these plans had to be simplified to fit local conditions and materials. The revision of the plans was done by Francis W. Wilson, aided by conferences with [Library Director] Mrs. Linn, who journeyed east to visit libraries and to study the latest trends in library design and facilities.

Ground for the new building was broken on July 5, 1916, and in November, 1917, the Library was opened to the public. In Spanish Renaissance style, the low building with its impressive breadth and dignity was admirably suited to its purpose. The main reading room opened to a sheltered patio with tropical plants, tables and chairs. There was also a beautiful fountain, which unfortunately had to be sacrificed in a later remodeling.

Spanning the arch of what was then the main portal is a wood carving of great beauty, an anonymous gift, designed by architect Carleton M. Winslow and executed by Marshall Laird. At the center of the tympanum is the coat-of-arms of the city. On either side are figures of Plato and Aristotle. Surrounding the center are the shields of four famous libraries: from the left, the University of Bologna, the Bibliothèque Nationale in Paris, the University of Salamanca and the Bodleian Library, Oxford University.

Enid Osborn
The Summer I Was Nine

Santa Barbara's poet laureate (2017-2019) produces and supports poetry venues and small press publications in Santa Barbara and Ventura counties under her moniker, Green Poet Project. Her poetry has appeared in regional and national journals and in her book When the Big Wind Comes. *She co-edited with Cynthia Anderson the celebrated anthology* A Bird Black As the Sun/ California Poets on Crows & Ravens.

THAT SPRING, I fell from a tall horse and wore a cast for six weeks from my left hand nearly to my armpit, with a ninety-degree bend at the elbow. I still went to ballet class, but my arm movements were one-sided and unlovely. I didn't play army games with the boys on my block, or get into water balloon fights. I walked instead of running. Couldn't ride my skateboard or my horse or my bike. Instead, I read.

Mrs. Sims, the librarian at Valley View Elementary, kindly set aside books about dogs and wolves with courageous hearts and uncanny powers of reason. Books about wild horses, unbreakable horses, and the horse who saved all the other horses from a burning barn. I read the Silver Chief series, *Call of the Wild*, and everything they had by Ernest Thompson Seton.

I was running out of dogs and horses. One Saturday, my mother promised to take me shopping. To my surprise, she turned the Chrysler into a parking lot on Fourth Street, right next to the Carnegie Library. I had never been there, had only dreamed of the limitless stacks of books inside.

We climbed the steps and passed through the double doors. I was struck by the shining waxed floors and the musty mix of old wood, ink, and clothbindings. There were rows and rows of catalog drawers. My mother and I exchanged smiles of delight and stepped forward.

After that, she took me nearly every Saturday. I quickly graduated from the children's section to the youth section. I was reading novels now, stories about people. I checked out all that I could carry with one arm. I grew to love the sound of the date stamp chunking on the first page, the sound of a book cover flapping shut, and books being stacked—my books, at least for two weeks. And I loved the smell of library books, more soulful than the smell of bought books.

I endured the sixth week of the cast in quiet mania. It was spring, and I longed to go swimming and to play with my friends. But when the cast was sawed off, the arm that was returned to me was weak and unsightly. It no longer matched my other arm in size or color. The doctor, seeing my face, assured me that this was temporary. But for several more weeks, I was kept indoors, where—you guessed it—I read.

Finally, at the very end of the spring term, I was allowed to ride my bike to school. But I was a different child. I no longer played the roughest games or took a dare to prove myself to our pack of neighborhood boys. I wasn't afraid to, I just didn't see the point. I had discovered worlds without limit, other people's thoughts, and adventures more grand than winning at kick-the-can. My best friends and my models were characters in books. When June came and the bell rang on the last day, I went home and climbed the giant mulberry tree in my front yard with *Misty of Chincoteague* tucked in my shirt, and read until the bell rang for supper.

I lived in that leafy house for most of the summer. Each morning, I would put on my baseball cap, say good-bye to my mother, climb the tree, settle into a high fork, hang my cap on one snag and my transistor radio on another, and then, I would open my book and begin the discovery.

From time to time, I would look up to admire the light that shone through the leaves.

From time to time, I would eavesdrop on the boys as they argued over their games. How childish they were!

From time to time, my mother would come to the window and look for me among the leaves. At noon, she would call me down for lunch. And so the days of summer passed. My arm grew strong and tan. I went swimming. I climbed back on my horse and rode. But mostly, I was in the tree with a book. The boys stopped calling from below, though they brought the occasional argument for me to settle from my lofty perch.

My teacher had given us a summer reading list, which I finished by the end of June. After that, I was free to explore any book in the youth section. By August, I was allowed to ride my bike into town with a short grocery list and three to four books in the wire basket on my handlebars. The library was my first stop. Now I was reading books on astronomy, insects, how to collect miniatures, poetry... and novels!

To this day, if you look very hard, you can see a groove worn into the asphalt by my Schwinn Debbie, running between my house and Fourth Street, where the Carnegie Library still stands. Forty years ago, they built a sprawling, one-story library just a block from the old one, but I still drive by and smile at that smaller, older building— the one that held wonders and seemed so big inside, the summer I was nine.

D. J. Palladino
How I Got Away with It:
Public Library As Scam

A former editor at the Santa Barbara Independent *and* Santa Barbara Magazine, *Palladino is also a long-time film reviewer and freelance writer. His first novel,* Nothing That Is Ours, *was published in 2017. Not only does he write books, but he sells them as well, as the co-owner of the Mesa Bookstore.*

PUBLIC LIBRARIES always seemed suspicious, always seemed too good to be true. Beginning with my first visit to a Los Angeles-area branch, circa 1958, I doubted even my own sainted mother's lavish claims for my brand new card's limitless powers: good for any book I wanted. Free.

Any book, I asked? Even this hardbound green volume that tells Earth's origin story in some strange theoretical framework called Big Bang, the one that seems blasphemously contrary to the version promulgated by Sister Mary Aidan's Genesis recitation? (I spoke like that back then.) Even that book?

Indeed, that one too, she solemnly replied.

From that day forward, public libraries have seemed to me like something I was getting away with, a magnificent scam. And a decade later, in the city of Santa Barbara, my gaming of the system dramatically increased.

I was the new kid at Bishop Garcia Diego High School in 1968, and, like most new students, shy, alone in my private history, and eager to make new friends. The guys I met on the school bus, Mesa rats Don, Charlie and Michael, seemed surprisingly hip for villagers—I moved here from a comparatively huge Catholic high school in the San Fernando Valley. My first bus interaction with them involved practical jokes, subterfuge, pickpocketing and contraband Pall Malls. So I was confused, no flabbergasted, when my new friends later invited, no expected, me to join them Wednesday, and every Wednesday henceforth, when one of their parents would drive the whole motley desert-booted crew to the public library for study time. Listen: these kids were surfers who dabbled in every imaginable late-1960s vice before graduation. They liked Cream, Hendrix and Buffalo Springfield, so they couldn't be lame. But a weekly library date? If they said they loved square dancing, I would hardly have been more astonished.

Turns out, it was a pretty good con. Our parents, idealistic lovers of education for its own sake, chose to encourage this midweek excursion from home because we boys were always careful to come back with new books. That part of the ritual wasn't faked. We spent the first fifteen minutes scrupulously returning books and scouring the stacks for new volumes, or, very occasionally, something we needed for school. Then we dumped our swag on the long tables, this being the old downtown library, which was mainly two big rooms and a basement, and headed out through the ornate children's section with its emblematic but puzzling empty diver's suit, onto Anacapa Street and crossed to the Sunken Gardens, where we talked about life and smoked while gazing across at the wing of the courthouse that then held prisoners. We shivered in the night air considering our own lucky taste of freedom. Then it was down State Street to buy snacks at the Thrifty's—the only store open after 6 PM back then, and finally trundled back to the library where we sank down into the chairs and sifted our glommed books until the designated sappy parent picked us up again.

Our favorite section was the new books, and our greatest discovery was Claude Brown's *Manchild in the Promised Land*. Reviewed by an over-eager UCSB professor who deemed it one of the greatest novels ever written, (it was not) but it was (for suburban white boys at least) a festival of gaudy sinning. An expose of inner city life, we learned many things from the fine writer Brown, details of household DIY contraceptives, for instance, as well as a glowing review of cocaine; though, of course, it also showed us the corrupting stench of racism, and the alienating hand of poverty, and became the gateway book to Eldridge Cleaver's *Soul on Ice*.

On another visit, we turned our admiring eyes to E.M. Forster's "The Celestial Omnibus," which John Lennon had recently cited as inspiration for "The Magical Mystery Tour." The connection seemed strained yet Forster's myth-enriched story glows in my mind to this day.

Charley liked spy thrillers, Don was keen on cars and surfer lore, everybody loved *Kon-Tiki*. Michael found volumes of strange art and Herman Hesse. I was let loose in a bookcase brimming with poetry, and learned the difference between Keats and Yeats, which somehow led me to Richard Brautigan, right about the time he became a thing. We all read Brautigan's short books and one day grabbed a freshman in the Bishop quad and wrote "Trout Fishing in America" in chalk on his back, just as his protagonists did. We marveled at the anti-war anger in *Catch-22*, but we also participated in its jokes with book-provoked phone pranks. One day at home the phone rang and a croaking voice (Michael's mother, put up to the game) said "T.S. Eliot," and then hung up. If you don't get the joke, for God's sake read the book.

I discovered Gerard Manley Hopkins in those stacks, a Victorian-era Catholic bishop who wrote in a jumble of rich alliteration and assonance that seemed to belong more to our psychedelicized world than his post-Romantic England:

Squandering ooze to squeezed' dough, crust, dust; stanches, starches
Squadroned masks and manmarks' treadmill toil there
Footfretted in it. Million-Fueled,' nature's bonfire burns on.

I passed the book to my friends in the dark there underneath the Courthouse tower. "Far out," was the group's measured response to Hopkins's "That Nature Is a Hercalitean Fire and of the Comfort of the Resurrection." They liked him even better when I read "Jack, joke, poor potsherd, patch, matchwood, immortal diamond," alongside the Beatles' "I Am the Walrus" lyric: "crabalocker fishwife,/ Pornographic priestess/ Boy you've been a naughty girl/ You let your face grow long." I wrote an English paper citing the comparison and got an A for the effort.

Good. Right? For me many more ruses were to be used in following years, made possible by this early abuse of the public library. Like the time a decade later when I got a job at a newspaper and my first assignment was a feature story covering a succulents festival at Earl Warren. "Succulents," I repeated. "You wanted to be a staff writer," said the editor. A trip to the same downtown library (though rebuilt by that time with many floors) replaced my nonexistent interest quotient with evolutionary factoids, making me sound erudite when I interviewed real succulent aficionados. My editor was impressed as well.

Maybe you might argue that though the worldwide web was on the corner of Anapamu and Anacapa Streets back then, Wikipedia is easier to reach today. To tell the truth, I remember the nights of stolen freedom as fondly as I do the books. Hippies settled into the grassy area outside the library back in those days, playing flutes, burning incense and reading, and nowadays, the downtown stacks seem like a haven for lost souls as much as a resource for hungry researchers and the reading-obsessed. But that's not so bad. Memories and ideas are forming all around you in a public library. People are reading Yeats, Nora Roberts and even Richard Brautigan in there. You should keep it to a whisper but you can talk about books there. And besides they have internet access for people who can't own computers as well as movies, magazines and CDs, too. Diverse strands entwine inside the library, hushed together summer or winter in refuge. And it feels like an inalienable right though it's not in any Constitution I know. A grand illusion civil society created, a rare example of freedom that is free, and something too good to be true: the library is just there, unbelievably, for the taking

Lynelle Paulick
Over Time Within the Timeless

A freelance editor and proofreader since 1993, Paulick's primary activity is nonfiction writing. She also teaches writing at Santa Barbara City College's Center for Lifelong Learning. For more about her and her work, see www. lynellepaulick.com.

AHHH, SANTA Barbara, California . . . ahhh, Santa Barbara Central Public Library in downtown Santa Barbara, California.

I close my eyes and see the always-pristine building and grounds in my mind's eye. I see several incarnations of my own self sitting in, or perhaps walking through, the inside of this massively high and broadly situated structure. Right now, I feel excitement at having found the book I wanted. I feel heavy-eyed at the amount of work sitting in front of me as I hide somewhere upstairs in the late day, studying for, let's see—could be junior college, university, freelance writing or editing work, or . . . maybe not studying at all. Who knows, who remembers....

I always appreciate the bathroom located so conveniently right down those same stairs just for a short change of scenery. Why do I add this to the narrative . . . well, if nothing else, it's an essential addition to the main edifice, a vestibule whose presence I can vividly remember appreciating many, many times; and not just for its offering of a momentary change in scenery. Yes! The famous, beloved, and timeless bathroom break. I can hear applause as I write.

On an off-day sometime later, perhaps years later, driven to this sanctuary by established habit, I feel enlightened and inspired by a randomly chosen reading of Jim Morrison's biography. And Janis Joplin. And Camus. And Gertrude Stein. And *Homeowners: Electrical Wiring Made Easy.*

I am reminded of how poor and always-financially strapped I was when arriving at the main desk to be told by a familiar face, one of the longtime, loyal employees, that I owe $5.00 of late fees on a book I didn't return in time. One book from a stack of about 10 that I carried out in a single backpack one fine day.

I am bug-eyed and amazed when I walk in one other fine day and see that the great main desk on the first floor has now been replaced, whenever that was, with some kind of plant and a couple of computer stations. At first, all I see are a lot of now-unemployed individuals replaced by a clean-washed and metallic, darkly lit atmosphere, and it makes me very, very sad; I wonder if there are any humans left here at all of whom to ask questions and enjoy their professional demeanor and quiet sense of pride and satisfaction in working for this public library, especially the majestic downtown Central location. Then I am met by a single individual at a desk strategically placed in the very center of the first floor. And to my delight, she comes with the very same professional demeanor and quiet sense of pride and satisfaction. She is forthcoming and helpful, just as everyone at the Santa Barbara Central Library has always, always been. I am satisfied, so I walk on down the hall.

I leave the main library and walk across the foyer to the Faulkner Gallery. In my mind, I am greeted, through a collage of impressionist memories, by many of the smallest, largest, most colorful, and/or most uniquely interesting paintings and sculptures I can recall from years of stopping in momentarily to change the mental scenery inside the weedy garden of my mind. The colors and shapes scroll through the desktop monitor behind my eyeballs like a screensaver, random and undated.

On another day, on an invisible number pad, my fingers mindlessly dial the indelible seven digits leading to the reference desk. Ah, how I love the reference desk . . . I recall spending aggregate hours or more sitting on the speaker phone waiting for some one of the always-slammed-busy librarians to kindly take my call. And even if it has been twenty-plus minutes, she or he who finally answers the call or speaks to me in line is just as kind, patient, and willing as though I am asking the first question of the day.

I am now standing at the first-floor reference desk or, no, wait, it's now the upstairs reference desk, hopeful that one of these great gods of library science will show me The Way and The Light. Many names come to mind, names like Ken-something, an employee who, among all the rest, dazzles me with his vast knowledge and fingertip access to the most obscure information. They wonder politely why I come to the desk, or call, with such odd queries. Yet they never do and never did remember my name, my face, my voice, and why should they?

The end of the day—a special time indeed. As I fidget, still sitting upright in my familiar, favorite cubicle, I pack up my coveted stash: Books, pens, papers, scribbles, ancillary notes, take their rightful and usual places in my rusty back-pack. I glance at the ceiling, silently say good-bye to all of the familiar friends whose names I'll never know, and leave the world of *Survival in Auschwitz* or *Man's Search for Meaning*. No Cliff Notes here, I mutter with pride as I exit.

I sashay down the stairs, slowly, sometimes sleepily, and leaving my brain up-stairs in the otherwise empty cubicle, I wander past the turnstiles, the Faulkner Gallery, the bathrooms, and the ever-heavy doors of the library, exit out to the world of varying barometric pressure, and heave a great sigh. I am so proud of myself today, and every day, when I sit for hours in this great house of learning; I appreciate the respect I know to have for the code of quiet, for the priceless re-source that is this place. I appreciate it in others who sit just as quietly, for hours and days and weeks and years. I say good-bye, once again.

Over time, I will continue to rely on this timeless resource. Over time, and through all the changes, I have come to see the value of timeless resources and thus the nature of timelessness itself. May the Santa Barbara Central Public Library live forever. And if it does not—no matter—the immovable, multi-dimensional mosaic that it represented and the silent breath of eternal mind that lives on the inside of this edifice will live on even without the edifice for those of us who ever stood in its vastness.

Sara Plummer
Santa Barbara's First Library Efforts

Suffering from pneumonia, in 1865 Sara Plummer (1836-1923) left New York for Santa Barbara to regain her health. There she would establish a lending library that would become the cultural center of the city. Decades later she wrote about it, portions of which are below. While walking about Santa Barbara, she acquired an interest in botany. In 1876 she met John Gill Lemmon, a renowned botanist, when he was giving a lecture in Santa Barbara. They corresponded, married a few years later, and left Santa Barbara together to travel and categorize botanical specimens.

AFTER REVISITING Santa Barbara after an almost unbroken absence of thirty years, I am urged by former friends and newfound ones to give a personal and reminiscent sketch of . . . what I did to establish Santa Barbara's first public library.

During the middle of the year 1870, the continued daily walks and unflagging interest in the new plant life on the beach and the foothill region and the mountain slopes were constantly attracting, filling and feeding the mind, thus greatly assisting in regaining strength and vigor. . . When the flora became less in evidence, when the ground grew dry, a growing hunger for books and literary companionship took possession of my thoughts. My mind often turned to New York's literary centers and their rich storehouses of books; such as the fine Astor library, over which Washington Irving presided for several years. I began to ask myself why we in the far-off region should not have some literary center—with a library attached, if ever so small, to share with the incoming tourist and at-leisure invalids. This thought quickened into a determination. I wrote to my cousin in New York . . . stating the need of establishing a literary center and public library and my determination to make a start for that purpose. Back came the word: "A happy thought to take up the work of establishing a public library. It will be both a light and illuminating work. The next steamer will bring you a box of two hundred or more of good miscellaneous books." . . . I talked up library .

. . to the citizens and available county residents. In two weeks this preliminary work was done. A goodly number of the two hundred citizens pledged to the amount of about two hundred dollars. Without exception both men and women enthusiastically favored the plan. Many could not afford the fixed sum of five dollars for the year, but with families to support they felt the needs of a library and agreed to pay ten cents when they drew a book on the time limit of two weeks. This plan would establish a circulating and public library.

As soon as the permanent rooms were ready, all the books were placed on their "very own" shelves. And "opening night" was announced and a general invitation extended to all patrons and visitors, through the *Times* and the *Press*; and from eight to ten o'clock the cozy rooms were filled to an overflow. It proved the occasion for general greetings and congratulations that this real need for the growing town had been accomplished. During several successive years, when any public social function was to be projected, the library rooms were where the first gatherings centered.

* * *

My leading care during this decade was for the library and its value to the community. The time came for it to be merged into a larger library when, previous to 1880, our state legislature passed an enabling act for the establishing of free public libraries throughout the cities of California. Then it was deemed best to fall into line and with the private library of the Odd Fellows turn it over for the larger and broader plan. It had done its good work during a crucial period of Santa Barbara's new growth, and what better surrender towards the present result of a fine public library, keeping pace with the city's growth, and now, as then, meeting the intellectual demands of a city like the present, with its many plans of public benefit in all directions.

[editor's note: The Library, by then a tax-supported entity, was housed in a second-floor room of the Odd Fellows Building at State and Haley Streets. In 1888 it was moved to the "upper Clock Building' at State and Carrillo Streets. When more space was needed a library building at 14 E. Carrillo was built. There it remained until the present building on Anacapa Street was constructed in 1917.]

Lawrence Clark Powell
What's Wrong With Librarians?

Powell (1906-2001) was a legendary librarian, literary bibliographer and au-
thor of more than one hundred books. He founded the UCLA School of Library
Service and built the fledging UCLA library into an institution of renown. He
had a special relationship with Santa Barbara, where his friend Noel Young
of Capra Press encouraged Powell to publish a 1941 manuscript, which he re-
vised and Capra published as The Blue Train *in 1977. He is buried at the Santa*
Barbara Cemetery, where he enjoys a perpetual ocean view.

THE ANSWER depends upon who you ask. A library user might say that li-
brarians are austere and unapproachable, that they lack the human touch, are
timid, and, worst of all, dull. Ask a librarian and he will say that librarians do
too much clerical work, and that if only someone else would do the dirty work,
the librarians could be the professional people they really are.

I shall never forget my wife's response when one day in the Depression I
came home from my job in a bookshop and announced my intention of becom-
ing a librarian.

"You a librarian?" she exclaimed.

"Why not?" I asked, defensively.

"You're too lively. Besides, you read books."

Then I had to explain that the idea had come from a librarian, not from
me; and from Los Angeles's leading librarian, Althea Warren, head of the Pub-
lic Library, who had interrupted my sales talk when I called at the library to
sell books with a sales talk of her own, and had persuaded me that liveliness
and a bookish bent were the things library work needed. Miss Warren was her-
self lively, bookish, and so persuasive that I quit my job, borrowed money, and
went back to school to add a library credential to my other degrees, which were
proving useless in those bad times.

Neither administration nor research was my goal. All I wanted was a job with books and people that would pay $200 a month. I never got one. I started in a public library at $125, went on to a university library where in six years I rose from $135 to $185. Then I became head librarian of the university at $500. I have always had a feeling of intermediate failure.

Althea Warren was right; my liveliness and my bookishness proved assets. My wife modified her opinion of librarians as she came to know them better, but she has never overcome her first impression that librarians, like many others who are completely immersed in their own work, are more interested in rules and penalties and having things tidy than they are in giving people their own way, are in fact unable to see patrons as they see themselves. She derived this early and ineradicable impression from a prim librarian who could not see the library for the rules and routines.

I was luckier in my first impression of librarians. It was formed by a little gray-haired lady in the town library of South Pasadena, where I grew up. She seemed always to be behind the desk, making the date stamp smoke. I never saw anything but the upper half of her, particularly her twinkling eyes; but she saw all of me, and realized that I was a swift reader.

By the age of twelve I was through Tom Swift and the Rover Boys, the Texan and Civil Wars series of Joseph Altsheler, devouring Zane Grey, and moving on to D. H. Lawrence. All of this was apparent to deaf Nellie Keith, and for me she waived the rules that to this day make many librarians nay-sayers rather than yea-sayers. A library should have as few rules as possible, someone (not a librarian) once said, and break them all whenever necessary. Mrs. Keith let me take out any books, regardless of the color of the stars on their backs, and in quantities limited only by the number I could carry home. When I appeared with a laundry basket wired to the back of my bike, she let me fill it with books and pedal off to my idea of an orgy.

Thus my philosophy of librarianship was formed by my good fortune in knowing these two good librarians whose favorite word was yes. Even though a librarian is going to have to say no in the end, for example, to a patron who wants to take the library's only unabridged dictionary home with him, it should be said this way: "Certainly you may, if we only had a duplicate. Why not get someone to give us another, then you can take this one home."

Patrons don't like to be asked why they want a particular book. The cynical librarian believes that people usually don't know what they want or how to explain what they want. Patrons hate librarians who are condescending. Although I would not urge surrealism in reference work, I do like to see a blithe spirit on the public desk. Something of the lightheartedness with which Henry Miller taught English in a French high school. Remember? About the love life of elephants. You will find it in *Tropic of Cancer*, but you may not find that book in your library. It is often banned.

To be inspiring without being nosy is a fine art. How absurd to proclaim librarianship a science! It is an artful craft, a crafty art, to be practiced with a trinity of talent: hands, head, and heart.

Joe Queenan
Some Thoughts on Public Libraries

The famously dyspeptic humorist and self-proclaimed "sneering churl" is the author of a dozen books, including Closing Time: A Memoir *and* One for the Books. *By his reckoning, in his 66 years of life he has read at least 6,500 books. Should he continue to read at his current clip (100 to 200 books annually), he calculates that, given natural life expectancy, he has only some 2,000 books to go. The clock is ticking, he warns, for him and for us all.*

WHEN TAKING my first steps toward literacy, I lived in a neighborhood that had no public library. Luckily, the city of Philadelphia sent around a bookmobile that visited my street every week. It was, for all intents and purposes, a magic bus. Each Friday night I would borrow as many books as permitted, devour them, and come back the following week for more. They were mostly things like *The Call of the Wild, The Black Rose, Journey to the Center of the Earth,* and *Swiss Family Robinson*, or books about chippy underdogs like Vercingetorix and the Count of Monte Cristo and Cochise. Simultaneously, I would read any palatable materials my sisters brought home, excluding obviously unsuitable items like *The Child's Mansfield Park* or *The Adventures of Trixie Belden*. Like many children growing up in crummy neighborhoods, I had neatly believed that if I read enough books and learned the root causes of the War of the Austrian Succession and the location of the final resting place of the Persian tyrant Ahasuerus—sometimes known as Artaxerxes—I would one day come into possession of a demure but well-appointed three-bedroom Colonial, with two cars, two children, a white picket fence, and a spectacular river view. This is exactly what came to pass.

When I was eight years old, a brutal recession hit the nation, and my father lost his job. Shortly thereafter we were evicted from our house—a cute little redbrick affair—so we had to move to a housing project. The project was no picnic—the tenants, by and large, were not avid readers—but about a mile away there was a well-stocked public library. Unfortunately, the stately old stone building was at a considerable distance from our new home, and books were heavy, so I did not visit it anywhere near as often as I had visited the bookmobile.

Maybe another deterrent was at work here. The bookmobile had a driver and some sort of factotum in charge of checking out books and collecting fines. I recall nothing about this person's identity, physique, or gender, except that he or she must have been fairly inoffensive. The East Falls Library, by contrast, was staffed by grumpy, autocratic, middle-aged women who seemed to dislike children. The crotchety librarian is a vicious stereotype, but like most vicious stereotypes, it is rooted in truth. You could sense the staff's animosity as soon as you walked in. *What, you again?* Maybe, sensing that we were from the housing project, they feared gunplay, though my sisters and I were fairly young for that sort of thing. Years later, when my children grew up directly across the street from the public library in Tarrytown, New York, they would form a strong bond with the patient, affectionate assistant children's librarian, Mrs. Firmin. A diminutive, theatrical Englishwoman who seemed to have matriculated from the Beatrix Potter Academy of Small-Town Librarian Charm, she would read them stories and sing songs and teach the crafts and play educational board games and host Saturday afternoon get-togethers showcasing sporadically competent magicians and harmonica-brandishing folklorists and industrious clowns whose comedic reach too often exceeded their greasepaint grasp. The children reveled in these outings because until the age of seven, children think that all adults know what they are doing, even the ones manhandling the harmonica.

I had no such formative experiences in East Falls· no magicians, no musicians, no clowns. The closest we ever got to edification or diversion or laughter was when my sisters and I sat through an interminable routine by a local TV personality named Chief Halftone. His act suffered from a dearth of variety, and he was a bit on the catatonic side. I long thought he was Polish, but learned years after the fact that he was a full-blooded Seneca. His performance did little to elevate the reputation of Quaker City Native American television personalities.

There was another contrast between the bookmobile and the public library. The bookmobile had a finite number of books on hand, so you never felt intimidated or paralyzed by the possibilities presented to you. The public library,

191

by contrast, had thousands of books bivouacked in rows that seemed to stretch forever. The presence of all these books that I would never have time to read discouraged and saddened me. But I also felt sorry for the authors. "No place affords a more striking conviction of the vanity of human hopes than a public library," wrote Samuel Johnson; "for who can see the wall crowded on every side by mighty volumes, the works of laborious meditations and accurate inquiry, now scarcely known but by catalogue."

It also didn't help that so many of the books were atrocious. The problem in public libraries is that the wheat and the chaff are commingled. Especially today. Unlike museums, which conscientiously segregate the Bronzinos from the Bouguereaus, sticking the hideous paintings out in the stairwell, barely lit by forty-watt bulbs, where they can inflict no further damage on a society that has done nothing to merit such mistreatment, and where rodents or insects or mold might finally get to them, libraries jam every thing together in one vast, alphabetically organized maw, with James Patterson sharing a shelf with Marcel Proust. Putting James Patterson next to Marcel Proust is like displaying Babe Ruth's uniform alongside Three Finger Brown's. It's as if the library expects some knucklehead, discovering that *Along Came a Spider* is currently out on loan, to declare, "Oh, well, I guess I'll just borrow *In the Shadow of Young Girls in Flower* instead."

But it's not just that libraries are filled with horrible books that I am never going to read. They are filled with books I have made a deliberate point of never reading. I am never going to read *Sister Carrie* or *An American Tragedy*. I tried Theodore Dreiser once, and I am not going back. James Gould Cozens is out, as are John Galsworthy and Jean Rhys and any book connected in any way with the exploits of Studs Lonigan. I have read *The American, Washington Square, The Apsern Papers, Daisy Miller*, and *The Portrait of a Lady*, but I am not even sure I will get to *The Golden Bowl* or *The Wings of the Dove*. Still, the presence of these menacing titles on library bookshelves makes me nervous. It's as if they are stalking me, taunting me. *Think you're so smart, do you? Think you're so urbane and sophisticated? Well, we keep track of these sorts of things, and we know for a fact that you've never read* Go Down, Moses, The Birth of Tragedy, or the Collected Stories of V. S. Pritchett, *much less Madame de Lafayette's* La Princesse de Cleves, *or* Freedomland. *You're not fooling anybody, pally. If you haven't read* Ulysses, *you're still a pathetic rube off the streets of Philadelphia. And you always will be.*

I am not afraid of these books. I do not fear their gibes and threats. What I do fear is that they may one day catch me in an unguarded moment and overpower me. Then, I will find myself bound, gagged, and bolted to the floor in the musty library reading room, and forced to suffer through the complete works of William Styron or, if my assailants are in a particularly sadistic mood that day, all four volumes of *Joseph and His Brothers*. How I will turn the pages, fettered like that, I have not yet determined. I am not being facetious when I say that some of those unread masterpieces may have it in for me. I honestly believe that they are preparing an ambush, with the seemingly harmless Gertrude Stein luring me into a box canyon where the murderous Alice B. Toklas can take my scalp. These books think that if they can catch me at just the right moment, I will break down and finally read *Middlemarch* from cover to cover in one sitting. Dream on, public libraries. Dream on.

Grace Rachow
*For Hope is Always Born at the Same Time as Love**

The author is the director of the Santa Barbara Writers Conference and a columnist in the Montecito Journal. *She was the editor of seven Community of Voices anthologies and has been a supporter of the Santa Barbara literary community since 1980.*

I MOVED to Santa Barbara as a young woman and fell in love with everything about this city, including my husband-to-be, who had as much of a passion for reading as I did.

It was not long after we married in the summer of 1980 that the two of us first walked into the downtown Santa Barbara library. A massive mural of Don Quixote by Channing Peake and Howard Warshaw greeted us as we entered the library.

It was my first time seeing this mural, but it was not the first time I'd met Don Quixote. That had happened twenty years before and half a continent away.

I grew up in rural Nebraska in the 1950s. The nearest town had a population of only 99, but it had a small library.

When I say "small" I mean one room, ten-feet by twelve-feet. The bookshelves were arranged around the four walls, and the librarian sat at a table in the center. Her name was Jenny, and she was a friend of my grandmother's.

The library was open on Saturday night when all the farmers and their families came to town to buy groceries and socialize.

My grandmother was a constant reader. Every Saturday she went to the library to return the book she'd read the past week and pick a new one.

The checkout system at the library was simple. Once a book was selected, Jenny wrote the title and person on her list. There was no time limit, but if you checked out a book, it had to be returned before another could be checked out.

The winter I was four-and-a-half, I was allowed to pick my first volume, a Big

* *Miguel de Cervantes Saavedra,* Don Quixote

194

Little Book. I chose it because I liked the shape and color and how the book felt in my hands.

I couldn't read yet, so I had no idea of the title, but I grasped the book tightly for the rest of the evening in town. I fell asleep on the ride home, and somehow my library book disappeared.

It was not found until a few months later. I'd dropped the book in the snow when my father carried me half asleep from the car to the house. When the snow melted that spring, I found the ruined book. My grandmother went with me to talk to Jenny and explain what had happened.

Although no adult scolded me for this, I understood all too well how serious it was to ruin a library book. I promised Jenny I wouldn't do it again.

That was the rocky start of my love affair with reading. I was given a second chance, and I continued visiting the library every Saturday evening with my grandmother.

Over the next few years I worked my way through all the books for younger readers, but I was hungry for more. This one-room library was a portal to the rest of the world, and I didn't want to miss any of it.

I had a few arguments with Jenny when I picked books beyond my age level. She'd point out a book she thought was more age appropriate.

I'd say, "I already read it. Check your list."

So that's how I came to take home *Don Quixote* long before I had the capacity to read it. I needed a dictionary for every third word. It was hard.

When my grandmother saw me reading with the dictionary, she said, "You might as well just read the dictionary."

I waded through the pages, and I'm sure I missed 95 percent of the gist of the novel. I was a stubborn kid, and I kept at it. I would not admit defeat to anyone.

I lived with the book for several weeks and read on and looked up many words . . . never mind my lack of understanding. When I returned the book, Jenny was kind enough not to ask for a book report.

The impossible challenge of reading *Don Quixote* before I was able gave me a touchstone for every other difficult thing in my life. All I have to say, is, "Well, at least it's not *Don Quixote*," and immediately I feel more able to keep on keeping on.

Whenever I enter the Santa Barbara Central Library and see the mural, bigger than life, I am reminded that the love of something does not necessarily make it easy. But it is the love that creates hope that the impossible can be achieved.

Mahesh Rao
An Elegy for the Library

The Kenya-born Rao has written that "probably unsurprisingly for a writer, I was a bookish child and spent a lot of my time wandering around the school library or the few bookshops that Nairobi had at the time." His short fiction has been shortlisted for various awards, and appeared in The New York Times *and numerous other publications. His debut novel,* The Smoke Is Rising, *won the Tata First Book Award for fiction.* One Point Two Billion, *his collection of short stories, was published in 2015. See www.maheshrao.info for more about the author.*

MYSORE, INDIA — It's an unseasonably hot winter day in this southern city, and the midmorning sun is turning the crumbling yellow stucco of the 100-year-old City Central Library a shade paler. A hawker is yelling on the busy road, trying to drum up business for his collection of old coins and medals. As I take the stairs to the main level, I can see a bit of a line at the water fountain.

The occupants of the small reading room are all middle-aged men poring over newspapers in at least three languages. The ceiling fans whir. Pages rustle. Not one man is looking at his phone. Overhead a framed poster features a paraphrase of a line from the novelist Neil Gaiman: "Google can bring you 100,000 answers but a librarian can bring you the right one." Fighting words.

In the larger reading room the crowd is mixed. An elderly woman looks up from her notebook; a lanky boy is mouthing the words he reads. Every seat is occupied, and I wander between the stacks: Astronomy, Home Economics, Satire in Kannada Literature.

Every so often, there are rumblings, among students gathered on the front steps or in the local press, that the library will close: the predatory gaze of developers is never far. And I'm more conscious than ever of the many things we would lose.

Wherever I've lived, I've used the library. When I was growing up in Nairobi, Kenya, I would sometimes go to a tiny community library run by a church organization. It was a stronghold of stalwarts; there were hardly ever any new faces. The dust was thick. Branches of a jacaranda tree pressed against the single large window. The place had a vaguely medicinal smell, as though along with tonic for the mind, it administered tinctures and liniments. One evening a few minutes before closing, the librarian and I were packing up at the same time. He glanced over at one of my books and did a cinematic double take.

"That's not from this library?" he asked.

"No, it's mine," I said, telling the truth but sounding cagey. I was in early adolescence, and everything I said seemed like an admission of guilt.

"I'm reading it too," he said, whipping out his own copy.

It was the same edition of Iris Murdoch's *A Word Child*. Its cover even seemed to have the same fold as mine in the right-hand corner.

I looked at my copy for a few seconds and put it in my bag. I felt a sudden rush to the head: After years of longing to leave childhood behind, it felt as though I had finally become an adult.

In later years, I would sometimes go to a library in North London, a drab hulk of a building where I became friendly with one of the chattier librarians. Ms. R. was a middle-age woman with close-cropped hair and scarlet fingernails that flipped absently through the cards of her Rolodex.

"Oh, that Hemingway," she would say. "And Scott Fitzgerald. Such drinkers. They'd drink you out of house and home. It's amazing they were ever clearheaded enough to plan a novel."

She would describe Daphne du Maurier's Cornish home in detail, as though they spent summers there together.

Ms. R. favored dangly earrings, often of sea creatures—gold crabs, diving dolphins—and I came to associate their dainty glamour with the stories she told.

She once handed me a copy of *Wide Sargasso Sea*, while describing Jean Rhys's bohemian life in Paris.

"Her book is much better than *Jane Eyre*," she said.

Ms. R.'s anecdotes bridged the gap between those semi-mythical beings with great imaginative powers and we ordinary individuals who borrowed their books from libraries. Authors may have had spells of adventure and excess, but they weren't that different from the people around me, after all: They also fought with their spouses, worried about money, cheated and lied, and then mowed the lawn. If they had got it into their heads that they would write, maybe some of us could, too.

Today I do write, and as I drift around the central library in Mysore, that still seems like a bit of a miracle. At Botany and Horticulture, a woman is dusting old volumes with the vigor normally reserved for beating carpets. The prim, desiccated formality associated with libraries is absent here. On the other side of the bookcase, a woman dozes on a stool, a mop clutched in one hand.

Once, as I wandered past her office enquiringly, the librarian, H.N. Poornima, beckoned me in. We chatted about the books that were most in demand, and I told her that I was surprised by the large number of shelves of Kannada poetry.

"Oh yes," she said, "poetry is very popular with housewives."

"Do you think the library is in danger of closing down?" I asked.

"No chance."

The library has 28 branches around the city, in addition to a few reading rooms at community organizations. Ms. Poornima tells me each branch regularly orders books at readers' request from the state's central library system.

Computers are much too costly for many families. Even books remain out of reach. The library's website lists "uninterrupted lighting" as one of its services—a real draw in a city that suffers from frequent power cutoffs. This is a place of refuge. It offers a respite from the heat, from office life, from noisy households, from all the irritations that crowd in.

It also offers the intangible entanglements of a common space. One of my favorite descriptions of the public library comes from the journalist and academic Sophie Mayer, who has called it "the ideal model of society, the best possible shared space," because there "each person is pursuing their own aim (education, entertainment, affect, rest) with respect to others, through the best possible medium of the transmission of ideas, feelings and knowledge—the book."

Libraries may have their idiosyncrasies, but the fundamentals of their ecosystem are universal. They are places of long breaks, of boredom and reverie, of solace and deliberation. They offer opportunities for unobtrusive observation, stolen glances and frissons, anticipation and nudging possibilities. And when the sensible realization strikes that a thrilling plan is better left unaccomplished, they might also become sites of abandonment.

I once discovered a gorgeously caustic letter of resignation on a library desk, unsigned and presumably unsent. I can't remember now what words it used, but I remember leaving it where I'd found it so that as many patrons as possible could enjoy its fruitiness.

As I read of libraries closing around the world, I worry that these ideal models of society will soon recede into sepia. Mysore's City Central Library, where every seat is occupied, may one day exist solely as images in a database.

And it'd be my fault, too. A little bit.

You see, I have a confession to make. About a month ago, I came upon a book on one of my shelves that I hadn't spotted for years. It was a copy of François Mauriac's *Thérèse* in English. When I opened it, the slip on the inside cover told me that I had borrowed it from the library of my school in Nairobi on March 2, 1991. It was due back 14 days from that date. I felt a little sick. I couldn't even remember if I had read it.

I mailed the book back with a letter of apology and a donation to the school alumni fund. But surely further penance was required—some expression of how much I valued every library I had ever spent time in, every librarian who had told me a salty anecdote, every book I had signed out. Well, here it is.

John Ridland
For the Santa Barbara Public Library: a Tribute

Critically-acclaimed poet, critic, translator, Ridland taught for over forty years at the University at California Santa Barbara and is currently professor emeritus at the university. For more than twenty-five years he was faculty advisor for UCSB's award-winning literary magazine, Spectrum. *In 2017 Ridland was honored by the Ventura County Arts Council as a Mid-Coast Literary Treasure.*

AS IT happened, when asked to contribute to this celebration of the Santa Barbara Public Library's centennial year, I had just resumed my direct use of its collections for the first time in several years. Projects not requiring library materials had been occupying me, and teaching for over forty years at UCSB had all but forced me to keep getting books in my field from its rapidly expanding facilities, and wandering out of them. However, UCSB used to display a couple of cases with new books from all fields, but as the quantity of books published exploded, that became impractical.

So I've slowly come to realize that my Santa Barbara Public Library card could be much more practical now than the UCSB one, besides which, the Library is right downtown, where I spend much more time now, and has parking lots across the street. In 1976 I wrote a poem for a reading at Santa Barbara City College. It described how I felt coming to read my poems in the college of my adoptive city—why it meant a lot, and how it differed in a good way from reading at my out-of-town university:

> A city is real,
> It is crammed with history,
> anthropology,
> drama and speech, psychology.

They are not forts in this college,
galaxies remote
from one another
as from the city.

And the public library is where these "real people, the ones who really live here," go for what they need to read, or don't know they need but stumble upon. So, a couple of weeks before the invitation reached me, I'd stumbled upon four new books, conveniently on the top shelf of New Non-Fiction, which were just what I wanted: a handbook on literary agents (no poets need apply––I did know that already); a slender little paperback translated from the Czech (!) on Indian and Chinese philosophy; a large, lavishly illustrated volume by Ernest Shackleton on his heroic British Empire expedition to cross the continent of Antarctica (they failed, but lived for him to tell the tale, and this edition has scores of splendid photographs and paintings as well as his text). The fourth has occupied me at every meal for three weeks, a book called *The Book*, by Keith Houston, which accounts for every element of itself through concise histories of all the components of a book: paper, writing, inks, printing methods, binding, etc.—a heartening pep talk for "the most powerful object of our time"—which the Library is dedicated to looking after and keeping from going extinct.

My childhood experience of a public library was in Pasadena, where I signed up for a Summer Reading Program, which very likely was duplicated in Santa Barbara. I had a gold star stuck on my chart for every book read. I don't recall any testing on contents to assure our claims of reading were true. The librarians must have trusted us, or figured that if we cheated we were only cheating ourselves. And I, at least, was still too innocent to think of such a thing. A friend my age, the sculptor Nina DeCreeft Ward, who grew up in Santa Barbara, doesn't remember any such program here, and clearly she didn't need one. She and her brother Billy would check out four books (the limit) every two days and hide in the bushes, where they couldn't be called for chores, to read them. She remembers doing the Doolittles also, but outdid me by reading the whole run of Tarzan books and one of *Boy Scouts in the Wilderness*, among many others. They couldn't wait to turn twelve and be allowed into the Grown-Ups section of the Library.

It's a bit of a shock to realize that if 2017 is the centennial of the Santa Barbara Public Library, it had only been going for twenty-three years at the time Nina and Billy were plundering it, and I was dipping into the Pasadena Library, which was ten years younger, although to me as a boy, it had an atmosphere of great longevity about it. I would have felt the same in Santa Barbara. Both were and are beautiful buildings, but I am here to talk about Santa Barbara's. Perhaps its loveliest detail is all but hidden from view—the ornate, unused doorway nearest the corner of Anapamu and Anacapa Streets. On either side stand the sculpted figures of Aristotle holding a book, and Plato, who disliked the fixity of texts, because they "always say only one and the same thing" (so I read in that Keith Houston book), talking and gesturing Socratically. (Their names, by the way, are spelled in Greek.) They are framed by "a polychromed wood carving, bearing the city's coat of arms... and the shields of four famous [European] libraries." I am quoting the 1941 Federal Works Project Administration *Guide to Santa Barbara*, in the American Guide Series, which otherwise was occupied with much bigger cities along with all the States. It's no digression to note the WPA's spoken and unspoken assumption that Santa Barbara deserves the term De Tocqueville provided politicians for our nation among all the others, "Exceptionalism."

The *Guide's* Preface begins in a flurry of fluffy historical clichés:

> Questing galleons and swift pirate craft once plied the waters of the Santa Barbara Channel; priests, explorers, soldiers, and adventurers tarried on both the mainland and the four islands—lived and died there.
>
> *Tierra adorada* (Sp., beloved land) of that day it was [notice the rhetorical inversion of word order] and not less so today.

Although here the *Guide* calls the town "it," truer to the sentiments of 1940 would be the feminine pronoun "she"—and the *Guide* reverts to this form in declaring that "In her venerable adobes was made not only the history of California, but also the history of Spain, Mexico, America." Here Exceptionalism merges with Boosterism, always a booming industry in Santa Barbara, from the huge floating cities of cruise ships popping up offshore from time to time, or as early as 1886 in a tourist-enticing little book, *Santa Barbara and Around There:*

Santa Barbara does not need to have untruths published regarding its climate, surroundings, and natural attractions. They are so nearly perfect, so varied and beautiful that it is superfluous to exaggerate them.

Further proof of the city's fame is more relevant to the present subject: an extended sequence in the long-lived comic strip "Mary Worth" was very clearly set in the Santa Barbara Central Library, the strip's background illustrator living here. And when my wife and I were opening a bank account in Melbourne in 1993, a strange gleam came to the teller's eyes when we named our hometown: its soap opera was more popular in Australia than over here. And finally, Santa Barbara has been located at or near the spiritual center of the Earth by more than one guru. I am sure there must be books about all of this in the library.

Countless times I have gone into the Faulkner Gallery, a 1930 add-on designed by Myron Hunt, for precisely these purposes: concerts, poetry readings, films, and displays of local artists' work, whose excellence thrives well away from the Manhattan tastemakers. Across from the Faulkner and flanking what is now the library's main entrance, after Plato and Aristotle's doorway had been closed off, we are confronted with its two floor-to-ceiling murals of Don Quixote. The one by Channing Peake is more clearly representational, the other, by Howard Warshaw, more sophisticated in style. The two have represented the library for a long time (though they had to be transferred from another wall to their present site during a major remodeling), and for me they haven't dated any more than the story of the Don intoxicated to madness by—the reading of books! What an ironic subject for the wall of a library that seems, and yet what a faithful image of all who read books seriously: sallying forth with our borrowed volumes under one arm like a lance, searching for windmills to tilt against, and finding ourselves knocked off our feet instead by the richness of the reality that lies beyond our imaginings.

But having exhausted ourselves with one pile of lances, we ride back to the spacious, well-lighted stable of our library, this time to find the right, the essential book to take into our hands and read—aloud if possible—to change our world.

Elizabeth Ann Robinson
The Skill of Women Built the Library

A fourth generation Californian, the author has been a nurse since 1986. Good at science, yet searching for the feminine, she found her sisters in nursing school, fast became enamored with the nurse, and has been dedicated to her ever since. She has a MA in Nursing and a PhD in Mythological Studies with Emphasis in Depth Psychology. Her book, The Soul of a Nurse, *draws from her personal experience as a nurse and patient in traditional healthcare.*

INSCRIBED IN stone on the magnificent facade of the Santa Barbara Courthouse are the words, "God gave us the country, the skill of man hath built the town." Santa Barbara is a city of breathtaking beauty and legendary climate, so I would agree with the first part. The second is where I take issue because it was the women of Santa Barbara who built the town. Cottage Hospital and the Santa Barbara Public Library are prime examples.

California officially became part of the United States in 1850, accessible only by stagecoach or steamers sailing around Cape Horn. It was a treacherous journey until the last track of the transcontinental railway connected the west. In 1869 two women, seeking health benefits, arrived in Santa Barbara and altered the social landscape of our city forever. Both were independent thinkers with their own beliefs. Both were intrepid and wouldn't let anything stop them once they had a good idea.

The first, Sara Plummer, was a graduate of the Female College of Massachusetts and teacher in New York City who became ill with pneumonia and sought the healthy climate of Santa Barbara. Hundreds of books were sent to her during her convalescence and she opened a lending library on State Street between Cota and Ortega in 1871. Art exhibits and lectures were held there and in 1873 a local citizens' group formed the Santa Barbara Library Association. As the city of Santa Barbara continued to grow, the library moved several times. Also in the early 1880s women's temperance groups were opening reading and coffee rooms, specifically for men as an alternative to the many saloons up and down State Street. A public library in Santa Barbara was a natural progression, where people could gather for conversations about literature, art, and social justice reminiscent of salons familiar to the educated in Europe and on the East Coast. It was women who conceived of a public free library where people could meet to further their education and exchange ideas.

The second arrival, Mary Powell Ashley, would prove especially fortuitous for Santa Barbara. She was fifty and seeking a healthy climate for her husband, a physician, in poor health. She spent the rest of her long life advancing social causes in Santa Barbara. Soon after arrival she became known as a mover and shaker and was sought by groups who wanted to get things done. Sara Plummer married and moved to Oakland in 1880 and Ashley took on the cause to establish a free public library in Santa Barbara. She set up the "Save the Library" campaign.

A few more words need to be dedicated here to Mary Ashley. Her efforts are gargantuan and breathtaking. Not only was she President of Santa Barbara Equal Rights League for women's suffrage and financier of the Spiritualists of Summerland, she organized hundreds of women's fundraising efforts, like the five-day Trades Carnival in 1890 at the Lobero Opera House, to raise the money for Cottage Hospital that opened in 1891. Ashley was President of Cottage Hospital for its first ten years. For twenty-six consecutive years the hospital's Board of Directors were exclusively women until the first men were allowed in 1915. With suffrage on the ballot in 1896 she penned a compelling pamphlet describing women as "hardworking, intellectual with moral worth and usefulness—women should not be crippled."

The library was in transition for years but Ashley remained the steady hand. Simultaneously, women organizers across the country led the movement to establish free public libraries with the help of the Andrew Carnegie Foundation. The Carnegie endowment required each town to contribute ten percent of the annual funding, supply its own building site, and provide free service to the public. Santa Barbara women took Carnegie up on the funding, making possible the opening of the new Free Public Library at Anacapa and Anapamu Streets in 1917. This is one of the many examples demonstrating that it is not just brick and mortar that makes the town, it is the social fabric created by the skill and perseverance of women that makes Santa Barbara such a wonderful place to live.

Sojourner Kincaid Rolle
The Cloistered Door

Santa Barbara's sixth Poet Laureate (2015-17), Rolle is the author of Common Ancestry, Black Street, The Mellow Yellow Global Umbrella *and other titles. She has maintained a relationship with the Santa Barbara Pubic Library for over 30 years, serving as Poet-in-Residence at the Eastside branch in the early nineties and, more recently, presented programs throughout the system under the auspices of Children's Services and the Adult Literacy Program. This poem celebrates the original door and painted arch that was the main entrance to the Central Library.*

In ample view of all who pass
A shuttered cove by hedges bound
Ensconced in inarticulate brass
A treasure trove of erudition found.

Above the door, the emblem of an ancient maze
Adorns the mast that serves this public nook
Tandem columns hold our enthralled gaze
Two giants of mind extend the realm of book.

An ornate entrance to the deep-spun pearl
Where printed tomes held precious reign.
A tribute to great libraries of the world,
our past ephemeral moments to maintain.

Where once we read but could not talk.
An ode stands mute before a sheltered walk.

Abby Schott
Our Trusted Friend

Daughter of a writer-father and a bookseller-mother, Schott grew up surrounded by books and became a dedicated library "consumer." She moved to Santa Barbara in 1993, has volunteered at her children's school library and founded a book club that has been going strong for over 20 years. When not at the library, she works in publishing.

THE SANTA Barbara Public Library was there for our young family, like a trusted friend who has your back; a coffeehouse of readers and explorers. Our kids had a variety of fleeting interests: Fire trucks. Whales. Spies. Dogs. Surfing. All seven installments of the Rick Riordan series. In the words of that old Staples commercial, "Yeah, we've got that."

The bonus beauty was we could enjoy these gems, renew them multiple times or borrow them from libraries far away, and then (wait for it) *give them back.* My recycling, striving-to-be frugal-environmental/minimalist nature especially liked that. Let's be clear. I don't consider books to be clutter. They are all beautiful, tactile, warm and fuzzy reminders of imagination, creativity, possibilities and memories. That being said, it's nice not to own every single one, don't you agree? We have plenty. My now-teenaged daughter has arranged and accessorized several of our bookshelves in our home by color and style.

Is it possible to talk about libraries without reminiscing and using buzzwords like "progress" and "change"?

There are still books, glorious books. There are fuzzy play areas and "old school" experiences: Puppet shows. Musical performances. Story time. Magic shows. Craft projects, Legos, Makerspace. Summer Reading Programs. My own hometown library sported a groovy shag-carpeted amphitheater for story hour. It was the best.

Back in the day, after the books got stamped, the kind librarian would then stamp my daughter's tiny hand at her request. This analog version of checking out books with the very satisfying "clunk clunk" (think Marion the Librarian in *The Music Man*) has been replaced with self-serve kiosks with Space Age infrared lasers flashing. There are also computers, the option to download books onto your device without stepping foot in the library, and "how to use your iPad" tutors. Progress. Change.

I see old wooden card catalogs (where we learned about things like alphabetizing and the Dewey Decimal System) are now being repurposed into chic coffee tables for our living rooms.

Progress. Change.

At the very basic level, libraries are the keeper of books for all to enjoy. It's fun to imagine aliens or anthropologists in 5,000 years studying libraries. Will they be flummoxed by the gathering place of books and people?

I like to think they will immediately recognize it.

Kathleen Sharp
My Long, Bibliolatrous Journey

Kathleen Sharp is a prize-winning journalist, film producer and author of four books, including Mr. & Mrs. Hollywood, *which* Kirkus Reviews *called "enthralling." A contributor to* The New York Times, *she's won a dozen awards including a grant from the Investigative Fund at the Nation Institute to research her next book in Rome. Her website is www.kathleensharp.com.*

I WASN'T quite six years old when I received my first book, an unhappy occasion. I was learning to read and proud of it. My father, I now realize, was proud, too, and presented me with Rudyard Kipling's *The Jungle Book*. Written in 1894, the book had an unattractive brown-and-black cover. I flipped through its pages, searching for pretty pictures, and was crestfallen. Not only were the pages dense with words, the words were hard to understand. "(T)hou art very like my Nathoo," I read.

No pictures, no color, or easy words: this was not my idea of fun. Even so, I thanked my dad and put the gift in the closet.

For years, *The Jungle Book* was the only children's book in our house. My parents had six energetic kids, and there were more pressing things than books to buy, like shoes and socks. A library was a foreign concept even though my father had a large collection of paperbacks. These books weren't shelved but splayed around my parents' bedroom, their lurid covers like decorative touches on window sills and bureau-tops. Most nights, my dad would send one of us kids into his room to fetch his reading material and one evening, my sister was given the honor. After being told the title of a particular book, she returned, holding an old John Updike book. "Here it is!" she said triumphantly. "Bunny, Hop." The book of course was *Rabbit, Run*.

To my schoolgirl mind, books were a telling apercu into an adult world I wasn't sure I wanted to join. Why work so hard to read dark, unillustrated tales? What was the big deal about this grown-up pastime? A few years later, however, I entered a real library and discovered how exotic books could be. Our Catholic elementary school room held lots of works written by saints but few matched the passion of St. Teresa of Avila. "He appeared to me to be thrusting it at times into my heart, and to . . . leave me all on fire." Okay now! The life of a cloistered nun seemed more exciting than that of a gadget salesman or a boy raised by wolves.

I began checking out historical romances featuring heroines such as Margaret of Anjou and the War of the Roses (such a lovely name for a bloody struggle). There was a fictional spy in England's Reformation who rode her horse through forests to deliver a coded message, a slip of paper tucked into her bosom, racing to deliver the note to a male spy and admirer. Would she make it without being captured? And then what? I devoured these books at midnight armed with a flashlight and some apples as my sister snuffled in the next bed, dreaming no doubt of Bunny, Hop. One night, my mother caught me reading under the tent of my blanket. She was furious at me for ruining my eyes, but I didn't care if I had to wear glasses. At least I could now see where I was going: to a writer's life.

Years later, I joined the *Santa Barbara News-Press* as a cub reporter, and one of the first places I visited was the Santa Barbara Public Library. Compared to the majestic Santa Barbara County Courthouse across the street, or the enchanting pathways of La Arcada, the library building did not impress. The plaza felt cramped. The touches of Spanish Colonial Revival were muted. The path from library's front door to the Santa Barbara Museum of Art was dim. But the towering gum trees that guarded the front entrance welcomed me with their arms wide open, their trunks thick and steady, their fragrance a lemony scent that hit like a two-by-four.

I stepped through the library's glass door and met a reference librarian on the first floor. He introduced me to Santa Barbara by lending me books about the industrial barons and rebellious women who helped shape this region. The Moody Sisters built whimsical cottages; Beatrice Wood created brazen sculptures; Ganna Walska planted a lotus garden; Margaret Millar wrote twisted mysteries. As I read their stories, they became muses who accompanied me on my daily beat.

Descending into the bowels of the library, I met another librarian who taught me how to use the archives. I spent hours in that basement staring at sheets of microfiche or scrolling through spools of microfilm on a dependable if noisy machine. I got lost in the faded, old-timey stories about local characters, from the bewhiskered writer hired by the railroad to lure tourists here, to the consort-turned-millionaire's wife who lived in a manse overlooking the sea. Every now and then, I unearthed a nugget from the library's basement that informed a story I was writing—or birthed a new one. When I got stuck, I'd walk to the Historical Society and bother the director of research, Michael Redmon.

I wasn't the only genius to haunt the stacks. I'd see the late Joan Crowder, theater critic, checking out a Tennessee Williams biography, or the talented Teri Sforza, balancing stacks of music books, or features editor Cissy Ross, flipping through a photography book. After a rendezvous at the check-out desk, we'd occasionally head down the street for a cocktail at Jimmy's or Mel's. Mining the riches at Anacapa and Anapamu produced a lot of great stories, and we reporters grew in discrimination and skill. We won awards, got promoted, married and moved away to bigger cities, where housing was affordable and libraries varied. Friends left for Kansas City, Tulsa, and San Diego, but I remained, writing about this region for glossy magazines and East Coast newspapers, always checking in with my local librarian.

When I expanded into narrative nonfiction books, I had to leave town to immerse myself in the places where these stories took place. I lived in the meat-packing district in New York for a spell and roamed that city's numerous archives. Compared to Santa Barbara, I found the public library in midtown Manhattan to be dark, dingy and downright spooky. (This was before its renovation.) Combing the archives in the basement was a test of nerves and, after a day of musty confinement, I'd run out of the Beaux-Arts building and down the stairs, clearing my head on the steps by the marble lions, Patience and Fortitude.

My second book took me to Chicago to research the birth of American radio. In the early twentieth century, mobsters such as Big Jim Colosimo and Al "Scarface" Capone ran Chicago's clubs and speakeasies, and the talent agents who booked bands for these guys grew rich enough to move to Hollywood. To understand this, I'd walk every morning through the Loop to the Harold Washington Library Center, the crown jewel of the Chicago Public Library System. Inside, I'd take the switch-back escalators to the eighth floor, where I'd burrow into the archives. My book took shape under the library's stunning glass roof, which was tinted green with Depression-style glass—or was that the shade of the Winter Garden above me, or perhaps the faux foliage on the rooftop where sculpted owls perched? No matter: I reveled reading in what I thought was the most beautiful library in the world.

I took bibliolatrous journeys to places far and wide but always came home to Santa Barbara. I settled down, had kids and kept a house full of Slinkies and Legos. The kids and I would visit the downtown library on occasion, making sure to greet the stately old gum trees. After smelling the lemony thicket, the children would run inside to the aquarium that marked the first-floor children's section at the time. Pop-up books; stories of magic; illustrated tales of dragons: visiting the library was always a happy outing. But after researching in other cities, I considered the local facility to be a quaint vanilla version of what a learning cathedral could be.

Then one afternoon, I stumbled upon something I had never seen before: the original wooden double door of the library. Beautifully carved, the doorway stands to the side of the main modern entrance and back from the street, easy to miss. The door was crowned by a magnificent tympanum set within an arched niche. The tympanum itself is a riot of color and, in the center, is Santa Barbara City's coat-of-arms: a brilliant yellow sun, two galleon ships and the blue ocean. On either side of the seal are two men, Plato and Aristotle. Fanned around the center are the shields of four other big-city libraries: Bologna, Paris, Oxford and Salamanca. Someone else had traveled far and wide, too, only to return and create this marvel. The side walls enclosing the tympanum are smooth and adorned with two plaster pilasters that could hold giant candles.

It blew me away.

Lately, I've come to see that there is nothing ordinary about the Santa Barbara library. How wonderful that steel baron Andrew Carnegie helped build this library and other sanctuaries around the country. How tragic that libraries in Goleta, Lompoc and other American cities are under siege today with budget cuts, electronic diversions, and the shrinking of public spaces. So when a fellow author in 2013 invited me to join the Honorary Author's Committee of the Santa Barbara Public Library Foundation, I didn't hesitate. I admit that I mourned when the library closed the basement where I had spent hours squinting at yellow microfiche. But when it reopened as a children's library, I rejoiced.

Now, every child in the area has an entire cozy floor in our public library, a mental playground where they can find an easy-to-read edition of *The Jungle Book*, an actual book called *Hop, Bunny*, or a bracing tale about heroines and spies. Easy access, pretty pictures, fun to read: The Children's Library holds everything my six-year-old self could ever want in a book.

Children's Easter event, 1964

Lida Sideris
Simply Irresistible

Like the heroine of her novel, Murder and Other Unnatural Disasters, *Sideris hails from Southern California and worked as an entertainment attorney for a film studio. She has written numerous magazine and newspaper articles, a poem or two and a teleplay. She shares her home with her family and an assortment of dogs and chickens. She was the recipient of the 2014 Helen McCloy/Mystery Writers of America scholarship for mystery writing. By day she serves as the executive director of the Santa Barbara County Bar Association. Her official website is www.lidasideris.com.*

I'VE HAD several love affairs in my literary life. I've carried a torch for little used words and old books, for fine writing tools that inspire beautiful penmanship, and for the misunderstood semi-colon. But my long-standing love affair has been with the public library. Now that I've met and gotten to know many of those who create the steam that runs the library engines, all I can say is wow! Librarians serve in a noble, imagination-steering, knowledge-heavy profession. I'm so grateful to have discovered the public library early in life.

The library became my escape hatch long before I picked up a pen. My family had immigrated to the United States just before I was born, so when I started kindergarten, English tiptoed around in my vocabulary. While my classmates ran out to play in the playground, I stayed indoors, suffering from shyness that inhibited any attempt to speak the few words I knew. And it seemed everyone else already had friends. I felt very much alone.

The classroom had a small library, a shelf or two housing mostly picture books, which became the star attraction for my attention. My first favorite was filled with bold, terrifying drawings of large, fierce monsters. But what captured my imagination was the small person in the pictures. If he could command an army of monsters in *Where the Wild Things Are*, maybe I could command my classmates into playing with me. I learned all about drawing your way out of a predicament (more like imagining yourself out of one) in *Harold and the Purple Crayon*.

By the time I exhausted the school library, my English had sprung to life. And I'd found a teacher who fanned my newly discovered passion. She turned me in the direction of paradise: the nearest public library. It was the only place I'd ever ask my mother to take me. All other children's attractions paled in comparison to the adventures the library offered.

Many a kindly librarian pointed me toward books that entranced and happily consumed me. When I couldn't decide which books to check out, the librarians stood by, ready to recommend. In the sixth grade, a wonderful librarian suggested *Gone with the Wind*. I carried that book everywhere with me from start to finish. So absorbed was I in reading, my grammar school teacher once slammed a ruler on my desk to recapture my attention. Did he seriously think sixth-grade math could hold a candle to Scarlett and Rhett?

Since I checked out my very first book, I've been a devotee of public libraries. And not just as a patron. The library provides the perfect opportunity to assist the connoisseurs of all things literary by volunteering. I've had the pleasure of doing just that at the wonderful Solvang branch of the Santa Barbara Public Library for several years. By helping the library, I helped myself. Just being in the company of marvelous books and readers of all shapes and sizes is an instant mood lifter, jump-starting a low-energy state of mind into something more promising. It happens every time.

I blame my addiction to libraries for my myopic vision. For my preference to view things up close and personal, to understand and make sense of people and their actions. For sparking and expanding my imagination. For my becoming an author. And for making my world a wondrous one. Shelves lined with books brimming with conversations waiting to be had, lessons to be learned, and friends eager to be discovered—all these things make the library irresistible.

Ralph B. Sipper
Confessions of A Serial Fetishist

Ralph Sipper and Carol Sipper established Joseph The Provider Books, an internationally known rare-book firm, in 1970. Since 1996 he has been conducting business under his own name. He is a member of the Antiquarian Booksellers Association of America and has served on its board of governors.

I LIKE to ogle books. I like to sniff them unobtrusively. I like to—dare I say it—fondle them when no one is looking. This assessment, flip as it is, nonetheless has its basis in truth.

My love affair with books began three-quarters of a century ago when my mother took me to the local public library branch in the Bronx of my misspent youth to get a library card. I was at that time an antsy seven year old who prized playing ball—any kind of ball—over sitting still for more than a minute at a time. We were informed by the librarian (who could have been enacted by Anne Revere or Fay Bainter) that I could borrow up to four books at a time and that they were to be returned after not longer than two weeks.

I opted for the full complement of four children's stories, in all probability having chosen the likes of a Hardy Boys adventure, a Civil War juvenile with an intriguing title like *The Rock of Chickamauga* or *The Guns of Shiloh*, and perhaps *The Kid from Tomkinsville*, an inspirational baseball tale that hoped to instill in boys with yet unformed characters the enduring values of fair play. Clutching my printed haul, I hurried back home and chugalugged all four volumes—the last of which was consumed surreptitiously after lights-out from under the bedcovers with the aid of a flashlight.

Call it hooked, call it smitten, call it bewitched. To be able to decode those abstract symbols we call words into emotions was nothing less than thrilling, and catalyzed imaginative powers with me I had not known were there. The train to a lifetime of reading for knowledge or pleasure was at the station and I was on board.

The very next day I returned the books, eager to take on others, only to have the librarian ask if I had not liked them. When I assured her that I much enjoyed reading all of them, she was skeptical and informally quizzed me on their contents—a test I easily passed. Little did I know then that down the line I would be commenting formally on dozens of books as a moonlighting reviewer in those early bookselling days when I sought to supplement the modest profits slowly accruing to a financially shaky enterprise that was struggling to equipoise. Nor did I know that in the fullness of time I would be selling university libraries first editions for their special collections or appraising those that were given to them.

Libraries have existed since ancient times. Two foundational repositories of knowledge that readily come to mind are the Alexandria Library, established in the third century B.C. by the polymathic Macedonian, Ptolemy, and other leading scientists of that time. Several hundred years later the power-hungry Medici family established its own formidable collection. It was truly book hunters who jumpstarted the Renaissance because canny Florentine dynasties like the Medici and the Borgias understood that the consolidation of knowledge was a key step to political control. Today a staggering amount of information is available on Wikipedia. Whether this sometimes chancy online form of education is an improvement or a step back I will leave for others to debate. What I will say is that there are more books in my reference library than books for sale simply because I prefer having a particular volume on hand precisely when I wish to consult it. This, I suppose, pegs me as a cultural reactionary or an antediluvian aberration. Either way, so be it.

Through the years my heartfelt attachment to reading has evolved into what can only be described as spiritual reverence. Even so, I still like touching books—which, the last time I checked, was not considered a capital crime.

Kimberley Snow
Libraries Mean Us Well

After completing a PhD from the University of Kentucky, Snow took a job teaching at the University of California, Santa Barbara, where she helped to found the Women's Studies Program. Two of her books, Writing Yourself Home *and* Keys to the Open Gate, *grew out of her involvement with Women's Studies. Over time she moved on to teach other classes at UCSB: Writing, Science Fiction, Women's Science Fiction, and, in 2003, "The Art of Peace." In early 1991, she and her late husband, the poet Barry Spacks, moved to a Tibetan Buddhist community in Northern California where she spent the next six years studying Dzogchen. She currently lives, meditates, and writes in Santa Barbara and can be better known by visiting her website at www.kimberleysnow.net.*

MY MOTHER was a talker. If she wasn't talking to someone in the household, she was on the phone. As a child in South Carolina, one of the things I loved about going to the library was that she wasn't allowed to talk there. She still did, of course, but not as much, and only in whispers.

As the youngest, smallest, and most fearful of our neighborhood gaggle of children, I spent a great deal of my time hiding from them. Eventually I learned that the library provided the safest of havens from all their rough and tumble. Not only was the place quiet and safe, but also full of books. Each one provided different places and new characters to populate my imagination: tigers and cockatoos talking to each other; fairies so small they could hide in your ear and sing you to sleep; typewriters that wrote their own adventure stories on the sly. On nearly every page endless possibilities popped and bloomed in vivid colors.

The inventive children's librarian created a summer reading program in which each child was given a short bamboo pole with their name on it. For each book we read, she would tie a string from which dangled a colorful paper fish. By the end of the summer, I had earned more "fishes" than anyone else in the program, even my older sister, much to her irritation. But I hadn't even been trying to get ahead of her. I just liked books, loved to read.

When I graduated from the children's section and was allowed into the main collections, the first book I checked out was *Out of This World:* Across the Himalayas to Forbidden Tibet by Lowell Thomas, Jr. I was drawn to its cover of snow-capped Himalayan peaks and also to the words "forbidden" and "Tibet," which held a sort of magic for me. The book itself expanded and stretched my view of the world in unimagined directions, introducing me to an exotic culture that turned into a life-long passion for all things Tibetan.

In graduate school, I'd sometimes leave my carrel just to walk up and down the stacks, feeling a sort of reverence for the huge number of books collected there. That floor after floor contained a neatly catalogued wealth of knowledge, information, and wisdom, all open to the public, seemed almost too good to be true.

I never made it to Lhasa itself, but thirty years after checking out a book on Tibet from a little library in a small Southern town, I moved to the Trinity Alps in Northern California to work and study in a Tibetan retreat center. I lived there for six years, writing books of my own, editing Tibetan texts, and delving into subjects so vast and deep that I've yet to touch bottom.

All along the way, no matter where I found myself, libraries and librarians have come to my aid again and again to provide a sense of order, stability and kindness, affirming over and over that libraries, and the people who help to maintain them, mean us well.

Gary Soto
The Mystery and Wonder
of a Marked-up Library Book

Born and raised in Fresno, California, Soto began his career writing novels for young readers, before beginning to write poetry in the early 1970s. Since then, he has earned a place in American Letters, particularly with his collection New and Selected Poems, *a finalist for the National Book Award. He is also the author of a collection of essays,* Why I Don't Write Children's Literature, *from which the following piece is excerpted. For more about the author see: www. garysoto.com.*

I USE the public library weekly and, when I return home, stash my haul on a bookshelf. On the shelf at this moment are several histories, a gardening book, and Ian McEwan's *The Child in Time*, a novel about the abduction of a three-year-old girl and the unraveling of her parents' marriage—guilt, anger, grief, loneliness. I'm a quarter of the way through this tidy novel but may return it to the library, unfinished. Words are underlined in pencil by one of the previous readers, who, I suspect, was trying to improve her vocabulary—deciduous, reptilian, affability, provenance, slow loris, averse, etc.

The underlined words have halted my progress and not because of annoyance. As a poet, invariably searching for the right words myself, I began to consider the author of these pencil strikes. I couldn't help wondering about this previous reader—the culprit, let's say. She was female, near my age (early 60s), and reflective about the years lost on a no-good husband. Like the dainty pencil marks, she was understated in every way—touch, voice, makeup, and clothes. I began to imagine her as a reader of admirably crafted contemporary fiction (I still consider McEwan's novel, published in 1987, "contemporary"). Perhaps a nurse attracted to the novel's theme. Or a psychologist—but no, that was wrong too. A psychologist would have known most of the underlined words, as would have a nurse. Maybe an inexperienced bookworm on her way to the morning shift by bus?

Who was she? I assigned her the details of a life story. A widow, she read the novel late at night, with cotton balls in her ears against the noisy neighbor above, while a moth batted around the lamp and a cat the color of smoke slept at her feet. No—she was an office worker on her lunch hour in a park with graffiti-marked trees. A duck with a white ring around its neck was eyeballing her from three feet away. Did she have a crust of bread to quiet its quacking? But no, I was hasty: She was really a florist in rubber boots, her breath condensing in the cold, with a surplus of roses in tall buckets to sell by late afternoon.

Conjecture, all of it, but one fact remained: A reader had underlined words. In doing so, she had embraced the view that learning doesn't end. She might have been a mail carrier padding about in corrective shoes (this is how I saw her by page 180), but she was not about to give up on her head, now capped with grayish hair.

There are thousands of words we don't know, long or short, soft or clunky, seen in print or heard in conversation. We can just let them go, like passersby, and be none the worse because of it. But we can also give new words a try on their own. Who is this person who looks like a dogmatic priest? What sort of fluctuating shopper is she? Where did they get that dubious car? These adjectives may not quite fit the nouns, but the attempts are interesting. Why don't we forge the refrigerator? Close but not quite.

In a recent novel, I paused at this sentence: "'She's fly,' said Mathew to his best friend, Ronald." Fly? I mouthed the word, quietly befuddled. Was this a typo? Did the author mean to say "She's flying"? That wasn't probable, because the scenes in the novel were grounded—nothing about planes, terminals, check-in, and such. Failing to grasp the meaning, I asked a young man eating lunch on a bench, who said that fly meant "lovely" or "pretty" or "hot." Then the young man put down his sandwich and informed me that the word was like a Black-Berry—no longer in use.

Oh.

I might finish McEwan's novel—it's very good, after all. But as my eyes peruse his prose, I can't help thinking of the previous reader—nurse, psychologist, florist, or mail carrier—as concocting a subplot, a sleuth with a pencil poised.

With affability, she turned the reptilian page and, through reading glasses as thick as mine, made aversive check marks on her dubious self-improvement, while her cat and her stuffed slow loris watched with provenance from the end of a very comfy and deciduous bed.

Lawrence Spann
Thirteen Words

Spann was the founder of LAMP (Literature, Arts, and Medicine Program), which received national attention as the first hospital-based writing program ever to appear on "Literary Row" at the prestigious Dodge Poetry Festival. He facilitates writing groups at Santa Barbara City College and in private practice, and is a physician assistant in the anticoagulation department at Santa Barbara's Sansum Clinic. For more about his work see www.spannrobinson.com.

"This is a library, open to all who pursue knowledge, truth, and learning."
– Santa Barbara Library, a public library system

I WALK down the street three blocks from the tiny cottage where I live. I like to get to the door at 10 AM when the library opens. Sometimes I don't shower so I can mix with the smells and aromas of patrons who stand in line, especially in winter, when the library is the only refuge from cold and rain. We stand and mill like cattle, one foot to the other, until the locks open. Some have been loitering since dawn. Both entrances, east and west, are clogged with ragged people.

In the lobby there is a digital sign with thirteen words, "This is a library, open to all who pursue knowledge, truth, and learning." The main room is spacious with high ceilings and floor-to-ceiling windows. Books are stacked politely in neat and orderly rows, along with DVDs and CDs that encompass a renaissance of human thought. This is our library. It belongs to the people. It offers free Wi-Fi and a bank of computers where you can search the web and connect on email. People sign up and wait for this privilege that is time limited.

The library is across the street from our handsome Spanish Colonial Revival courthouse, adjacent to the Santa Barbara Museum of Art (which was originally the post office) and Myron Hunt's distinguished La Arcada, all forming a pre- and post-World War I corridor of elevated thought and beauty. To me, the Santa

Barbara Central Library represents liberty, freedom and equality. Library patrons are treated by staff not for their place in society or how they are dressed; it doesn't matter. All present are treated equally. The library is a beacon of democracy, whether you're on the street or behind a large hedged estate in Montecito.

There are hundreds of thousands of print books you can borrow for free and rotating scores of books on the sale rack. Paperbacks are fifty cents and hardbacks two dollars. It's a place where everyone belongs. Such an egalitarian idea doesn't exist much in our city. The library with its arches expresses free trade among people. Intellect reigns supreme.

I love the library and it has made me a better man, more tolerant, more patient, less judgmental, and that has nothing to do with the wisdom of books. It has to do with the commingling of people. It's an outpost for intellectual curiosity and dignity. Some might say I am romanticizing this public institution. It is dirty, full of homeless who carry disease and filth, they say. Sometimes patrons break out in Tourette's-like outburst and need to be reprimanded. True, it is not a hallowed or holy place like the temple where the twelve-year-old Jesus drove out the Pharisees and sellers. It is often an unkempt place kept clean by broom, polish, stain remover, vacuum machine, under constant disorder and reconstruction.

I've been to the other branches; all are smaller, some more tidy, but like the Santa Barbara Central Library all are free and open to the public. There is no entrance fee. This is the kind of world I want to live in, one that is not exclusive and cut off from the common person, a place open to those down on their luck and those who never had any luck at all. I want to wear the sweat of humanity on my brow, go to the library every day, spend time among books, maybe buy a book on the sale rack, take care of this public treasure. Guard it with my life.

Thank you, Mary Ashley, mother of Cottage Hospital, for making our public library system real. This fine building exists one hundred years later as a tribute to your persistence and tenacity. The people who live in houses, and those who don't, thank you for your foresight and wisdom. Libraries are places to feed the soul. A book never rejects its reader. The library is an extension of that ecumenical need for people to read each other's hearts and communicate through the magic of dialogue found in books.

David Starkey
In Praise of the Public Library

David Starkey served as Santa Barbara's 2009-2011 Poet Laureate and is Director of the Creative Writing Program at Santa Barbara City College. He has published seven full-length collections of poetry. His Creative Writing: Four Genres in Brief *is one of the best-selling creative writing textbooks in the country.*

Where would we go if not here,
this place of astonishment
and weightlessness, where
our floodlit eyes—readjusting
to the interior—focus
on the slow, Zen-like attention
of the browsers? Here,
the muddled lives of individuals
intersect with the clutter
of history, though diligent hands
have untangled and classified it all:
art partnered with recreation,
philosophy sharing space
with psychology, economics
nudging up against the law.
Fiction stands alone, of course—
there is so much of it: pooling
in obscure corners, wispy
as the reasoning that runs
through so many of our favorite

books, slumbering among the sleepers
who have wobbled in from the unkind
streets. If you, too, shut your eyes,
you will hear the rustle of newspapers,
the rasping wheels of the reshelving
carts, the questions answered
and the murmur of those
unresolved. Above it all,
the musical chattering of children
rising like a soprano's descant—
their voices not yet trained to silence.

Dean Stewart
Public Library: An Appreciation

An autodidact of the first order, this native Santa Barbaran is probably one of the city's most well-read writers. He is a former journalist who contributed literary essays to The Los Angeles Times Book Review *and other regional publications, as well as the co-author of* Literary Santa Barbara: Between Great Mountains and a Great Sea, *and co-editor of* Tales of Santa Barbara *and* Published & Perished: Memoria, Eulogies & Remembrances of American Writers.

I HAVE some friends who, like myself, are lifelong residents of Santa Barbara. Inevitably we play a kind of game, testing recollections of time and place. It is the game of "what used to be there?" or "when did something come about?" or "when did something disappear?"

Do you remember the milk bottling plant on the corner of Castillo and Carrillo streets? Where was the Greyhound Bus Depot? Do you remember the Repertory Theatre? It was a wonderful place for live theater that occupied the corner on Arlington Ave. and State St. and is now shops and restaurants. If the Earthling Bookstore was at State St. and Anapamu St. for many years, what preceded it? Do you remember the old Woolworth's store that was there? Or do you recall that there was a very beautiful stone Presbyterian church directly across from the public library where there is now a city parking structure?

I grew up in Santa Barbara and started going to the public library in the early 1960s when I was ten or twelve years old. Much of my childhood and adolescence was spent on the Westside, but that was not too far to walk downtown. I remember getting my first library card and how pleased I was about this. I had my mother write a note and provide me with some document with our address on it. I presented it to the librarian at the counter at the library. I was a worthy citizen that could be trusted. And now I had this powerful object that allowed me to borrow books. As many as I wanted!

The test of memory and imagination for the library, in the first place, is trying to picture what it looked like and how it remained into the late 1970s. The huge wooden doors that face Anapamu St. (and that few even notice these days) were the original entrance for the library. It then opened into a large central room with a check out counter near the door and the reference desk in a corner beneath a partial upper floor, something like a mezzanine that stretched along the wall facing Anacapa St. I got to know this upper floor very well. From A to Z it was all fiction. Below this, at ground level, there was poetry and literary biography. On the opposite side of the room there was shelf after of shelf of history and philosophy and general non-fiction. There was a central patio in those days; a pleasant little sunny place. To the left of the patio was the children's library, a very charming area with its own entrance on that side of the building. To the right of the patio was the art and music section. There were record players and albums and all the big books with reproductions of paintings were there. Beyond that was the Faulkner Gallery, used then as now for public events, though I realize it was more remote, less easy to get to at that time.

In my early years of grade school I was what was once called a "remedial reader." Where did they get that expression? It meant that I didn't read well and it took me a long time to get better at it. I went to what the other kids referred to as "dumbbell reading class." I took this all rather passively, though with some embarrassment. I can't say when my reading improved or when I got interested in books. It just happened with time.

I developed the habit of curiosity. That was the main thing; I remember. I started making lists that came from bits of conversation with adults or things I heard on television. I took the lists to the Public Library and used the *Encyclopedia Britannica*. And as everyone knows, you can't look up just one thing in an encyclopedia. There is always a reference to something else and something else and suddenly you realize you have been following a chain association for hours and can barely remember where it started. In my case, I would sometimes get a tap on the shoulder. It was my mother who had come looking for me and wanted to take me home for dinner. I guess I was easy to find.

Movies frequently preceded books in those days, and there is nothing wrong with that. There were the old movies I saw on television: the Mickey Rooney version of "Huckleberry Finn," Jackie Cooper in "Treasure Island," Dean

Stockwell in "Kim." The movies encouraged me to go to the library where I became a reader of Mark Twain, Robert Louis Stevenson and Rudyard Kipling. "Journey to The Center of The Earth" was a movie from my childhood, and so I read Jules Verne. "Lust For Life" about Vincent van Gogh and "The Agony and The Ecstasy" about Michelangelo were biographical movies made from novels by Irving Stone. I got the novels at the public library, read them, and also spent hours looking at picture books that showed the work of these two artists. If I had a favorite author in these days, however, it was Arthur Conan Doyle. The old movies with Basil Rathbone sent me looking for the adventures of Sherlock Holmes. I have spent my whole life loving Doyle and Sherlock Holmes.

The pleasures of the public library were not all indoors. My boyhood friends and I also discovered the library garbage dumpster in back of the building. We dug through it often and found books and magazine we took home. And we always hoped to find discarded records, but not because we wanted something to listen to. Throwing an old vinyl record is pure pleasure; they cut through the air with remarkable velocity and when they hit an immovable object, shatter to smithereens. So we looked for records and piled them up, then threw them with great delight against the back wall of the art museum. In those days this was all obscured with oak trees; there was no walkway there.

About this time, one day, there was a rummage sale in a little shop on State Street about a block from the public library. I went in, browsed about and, pushing through a pile of books on a table, came across a paperback called, *Existentialism from Dostoevsky to Sartre*. I remember laughing at this. I understood two words in the title, "from" and "to." I guess I had some vague idea of an "ism" but not very clearly. I read enough on the back cover of the book to get interested, but at fifty cents this cut pretty deeply into my ready cash. So I hid the book in part of the shop where I didn't think it would be noticed and went over to the public library, concentrating extra hard to remember the words I intended to look up. My interest was increased from what I discovered and so I went back and bought the book.

There is a famous essay in this Walter Kaufmann anthology (a book which I believe is still in print) titled, "Existentialism is a Humanism" by Jean-Paul Sartre. The author says a few simple things: there is no God and there is no ready-made morality, you are alone and you are going to have to figure it all out for yourself. I think I was sixteen when I read this and I knew something had happened to me. Childhood and the better part of adolescence simply dropped away. I now had to engage the world as an adult.

What followed were more experiences and more books and more libraries. The Sherlockian sense of inquiry, I believe, had prepared me for the rigors of Sartre. The pleasures and demands of Fyodor Dostoevsky's, *Notes from Underground* and *The Brothers Karamazov* were ahead. And the Santa Barbara Public Library was simply waiting for me, ready to help.

If you live in a community, as I have, for most of your life, memories get piled up in layers. You can look at something right in front of you and see it many different ways, through many different ages of experience. I live within a few blocks of the public library. I go there nearly every day. I can see it as it is and I can picture it as I have known it in the past. But the reality of the place hasn't changed. It is there to give something to me permanently, even if it is just loaning me something temporarily.

Elizabeth Stewart
Library Scents

A career appraiser of fine art and antiques, Stewart has a baccalaureate in Architectural Hstory, a masters in Historic Preservation, and a doctorate in Mythological Studies. Her first book, Collect, Value, Divest: The Savvy Appraiser, *was published in 2016. She is also a docent and guest lecturer at the Santa Barbara Historical Society and travels nationwide with her own "Antiques Roadshow" that she presents for non-profit organizations as fundraising events. Her website is www.elizabethappraisals.com.*

IN THE winter of 1983, the Mill Valley Public Library seemed small, dim, underfunded; a repository for, amongst other mundane literature, donated Dick Francis paperbacks and the like. I often hung out mid-mornings there with a local ex-logger living in the hills above Stinson Beach who came to search for lite porn. Those were the aging old hippie days in Mill Valley. Jerry the logger and I met to flirt in the custom 1966 redwood furniture designed by the aptly named Art Carpenter of Mill Valley; Art's matching custom library shelving appeared as cramped as the library's 1966-sized 'open' plan. Jerry (aging at 30 but still handsome as heck) and I met at the library before my afternoon work at Dowd's, the Mill Valley household storage facility. Back then, I was newly married to an artist, living, as one did in those days in Mill Valley, with another artist-couple, thinking art was my future, but I was no artist, making no money. Thirty-four years ago, directionless, careerwise, I only knew I was happiest around books and things I could study. I needed a night job so I signed on as the midnight-shift public library re-shelver, starting work at 8PM.

My boss Gabrielle was a new Ph.D. grad in Library Science and therefore had one of the first library computer programs in Marin County. She was determined to modernize the Mill Valley Public Library (Dewey be damned!), working long hours on that huge computer monitor, perusing hundreds of yellowed cards culled from the light maplewood card catalogues that ranged high around the reference desk. As the graveyard-shift shelver and newbie computer-illiterate laborer, I was perhaps destined to become a thorn in the sides of both library modernization and Miss Gabrielle.

My job was to heave returned books from the red-rusted metal-hinged drop box station in the front wall, heaving them again to my rolling cart with its double shelves. After riding the books around the darkened library in the late evenings to collect other book-stragglers, I was supposed to pair books with circulation cards, to repocket the cards in the front flyleaf of the books, to re-stock the shelves. Matching circulation cards with returned books entailed a good re-shuffle of those cards on Gabby's desk, stacked, (unbeknownst to me) for her systematic modern computer entries. Pulling cards, I no doubt set modernization back a few weeks each evening of my shift.

Though I remember the reprimands by Gabby, how tired I was, how my feet ached, the primary memory of that time remains the scents of a midnight-deserted public library. The cards, when I repocketed them, sometimes smelled like a breakfast table with a toaster or, other times, like a public pool when kids are at rough, splashing play. Or they suggested a lonely Italian dinner for one, redolent with red wine stains. Corners of cards could be turned down, having been deployed as toothpicks. Random phone numbers written in pencil were often paired with the stench of public bathrooms. Only the bird-watching guides' cards smelled fresh and clean.

Around 10pm, when I had a good stack of semi-damaged books amassed on that cart, the matching aroma of glues from the glue pots on the reference desk mingled with the smell of the snowflake-fine crusts of the backsides of torn or loosened pockets. They needed to be re-glued: my job. My hands were often sticky, adhesive to stray shreds of paper. The stately and venerable yellow-varnished card catalogues in the shadows suggested buttery maple, the kind of nice hardwood smell of a well-handled old dinghy in late-night waters. Their patinated brass bail-handles smelled of the aging sculpture in Union Square, that verdigris green fragrance of bronze turning historic. The small brass window-squares containing tiny remnants of the alphabet on the face of each drawer had an odor like a kindergarten in the 1960s, weathering a dry summer vacation.

Each section of the little dark library had its distinctive scent. I didn't need to turn on the hanging tin ceiling lights to know that I was in the kid's book section. The fragrance of pink gum hiding under miniature oak chairs, and spilt milk and cookies from treats at daytime Golden Treasury hour, gave it away. Likewise, the bologna-sandwich smell of the new releases at the front door spoke of lunchtime brown-bag browsers. The Dick Francis shelf, always the fullest, smelled of martinis and money, and was my favorite. Damon Runyon, close by, emanated the same odor, only seedier. In the broom closet were stacked, haphazardly, the soon to be deaccessioned paperbacks with their smell of yellow cellophane tape, aged and peeling off oft-repaired covers. That essence of Scotch Tape couldn't hide the dusty fine sweet smell of wood shavings that janitors used to push around, which were piled in the closet corner, mixed with gray dust bunnies and Doublemint wrappers, partially hidden by a four-foot wide industrial rag broom. Cleaning solvents in big tentatively bulging bleach bottles smelled of fake oranges or lemons through the plastic.

The scent of the hardcover-fiction aisle reminded me of modern chemicals: laminated see-through dust jackets smelled hot and dangerous, threatening to crack and stab as they aged. The saddle-stitching of the oldest, driest, somber-colored fiction was evocative of antique Yankee Stadium baseballs mixed with a Victorian darning sock. Contrasting, the fragrance of the not-so-old fiction, the colorful lucid paper dust-jacketed murder mysteries from the 1950s and 1960s brought me into the twentieth century; the glue of the end-sheets of school rubber cement, which could have been rolled into green snot-looking balls when I was a second grader in the 1960s.

Nonfiction, too, had a distinctive reek: in the automotive aisle, aromas of old oiled machinery subtly perfumed the air; in the craft aisle, a bouquet of old ladies drifted by; in the sewing aisle, a whiff of chalk and tissue paper patterns clung to my nose like a dangling thread. The adhesive case-bindings of those really big manuals devoted to home repair and deck building and major gardening were fingers smelling of garage workshops, amateur florist tables, and long, deep, chalky and serious bonsai ceramic pots.

At midnight, I used to take a break from shelving to sit down at Gabby's desk, opening my brown lunch bag. Mayonnaise and Wonder Bread spun around sweet pickles and a Kit-Kat; the midnight lunch smell stayed with me and the books till 2 AM when it was sucked out with a swing of the exit door onto the cold loading dock in the back of the library. In the clean damp Mill Valley pre-morning air, I breathed, and fished for a flashlight for home.

Linda Stewart-Oaten
My Life in Libraries

Based in Santa Barbara, Stewart-Oaten is a writer of short fiction and nonfiction. She lives with her Aussie husband and a Cairn terrier who flunked out of obedience school. Some of her work can be found at www.lindastewart-oaten.com.

I COULD describe some of the characters who used to haunt the stacks of the UC Berkeley library late at night in the 70s or I could tell you how my first husband used to blow off the stresses of writing his astrophysics thesis by getting stoned and going to the music library, to zone out on Locatelli for hours. Or I could share what I've learned about prison libraries: the ones where my oldest son goes to research some arcane point of law that I don't have the heart to tell him will not shorten his life sentence. Instead, I'm going to tell you about the public libraries I've loved since I was a kid.

In every town, city, state or country where I've lived, one of the first things I do is find the nearest library and apply for a card. Until that happens, I never feel like I'm home.

My first library was a bookmobile, converted from an old school bus, with a repurposed interior, finished in shellacked knotty pine. I was just a first grader, one who'd already plowed through every Dick and Jane book at my school in Bountiful, Utah. An older fourth grade friend in our neighborhood took me with her that day and helped me apply for my own library card, vouching for me to the bookmobile driver. The book I took home was called *Bippy Rides Again*. Although I read it over and over, I have no memory of the plot or even what kind of creature Bippy might have been. What I do remember is that it was only a few days later that my mother announced that she, my two brothers and I were moving to California and that our stepfather was not. After we got to my grandparents' house and had been there for weeks, some battered boxes arrived. My brothers and I ripped them open, with the kind of animalistic joy usually seen only on Christmas morning. Our old toys and clothes were mixed with pots, pans, and bedding. In one box containing bath towels I found *Bippy Rides Again*. My mother didn't seem worried about it not really belonging to me or that it was dreadfully overdue. But her cavalier attitude changed when we got a letter from the Bountiful Library demanding the surrender of the book. There must have been some dire consequence mentioned, because my mother sprang into action and mailed Bippy back to Utah the next day.

During my marriage to the astrophysicist, I occasionally found an hour or so to sit in the elegant North Berkeley Public Library, where I read art magazines. That was where I first saw Judy Chicago's ground breaking work, *The Dinner Party*. That was also the library where I first started seeking out books on such diverse topics as organic gardening, depression, feminism, and eventually divorce.

Although the hours, the rules and the physical structure may vary, a library in Melbourne, Australia, is not very different from a library in Santa Barbara, or one in Seattle, or in Honolulu, or in Glasgow, Scotland. Some libraries (like some librarians) are cold and orderly. Others—my favorites—are slightly untidy with mysterious dark spaces. The other thing I've noticed is that everyone seems to have a unique way of using a library and making it their own. We all have a favorite place to sit, a favorite section to browse. Computers are wonderfully efficient, but I still lament the demise of card catalogues. There was something very satisfying about pulling open one of those long skinny drawers and physically thumbing through the dog-eared cache of possibilities. I also grieve the loss of the due-date slip that used to be glued in the front of every book. It was a way to know how long it had been since someone last checked out the book and felt like a link to all the previous readers.

With each of my three sons, I made a point of introducing them to the pleasures of libraries from the time they were babies. I began this practice with my oldest son, Chris, taking him to the tiny library not far from Berkeley Married Student Housing. As he grew older we began attending some of the special events the library offered. For his fourth birthday party, I took him and three friends to the library for a puppet show. Unfortunately, when Chris attempted to lead a faction against the Big Bad Wolf, we were asked to leave. But we were back the very next week.

From an early age, my middle son, Nicky, was in love with books and would listen until I grew hoarse from reading to him. At the Goleta Library, kids were supposed to be two years old to qualify to sit inside the special space built for story hour. But I knew Nicky could sit and listen to the children's librarian read a few stories from the time he was 18 months. My youngest son, Josh, was more of a squirmy live-wire, but even he loved to be read to. It's just that he couldn't be trusted not to clamber over the reader and interrupt with questions and story embellishments of his own. So I usually just sat and read a stack of books with him in my lap. Often when I looked up, there were four or five other toddlers sitting on the floor near us, listening too.

Nicky and Josh were eleven and nine when we went to Glasgow with their father (my current husband) on his sabbatical. Although Glasgow was named Cultural Capital of Europe that year, it just seemed cold and gray to our California sensibilities. Not to mention wet, inasmuch as it was experiencing four hundred percent of its normal rainfall that year. But the little Kirkintilloch library, just a short walk from our house, turned out to be a saving grace. The boys were invited to enter a contest to design a new bookmark and Josh won first prize with his rendering of "Nessie." Teresa Breslin, the librarian, was friendly and quickly figured out what each of us liked to read and always seemed to have a stack ready for us to check out, whenever we dropped by. She was, and still is, a successful writer of children's books and we've given many of those books to our grandchildren.

Santa Barbara's libraries continue to play a huge part in my life. Each week I replenish my elderly father's stock of mystery novels. I can't always remember which ones he's read, but luckily he can't either.

I've been in a book group with seven other friends for over thirty years. Our group has sometimes been so taken with a book, as we were with Lisa See's non-fiction family saga, *On Gold Mountain*, that we've taken follow-up field trips to savor the experience. After reading See's book, our group went to Los Angeles to attend an opera based on her story and to some Asian museums and eventually to the store, once owned by Fong See, the founding immigrant patriarch of See's family, who'd gotten his start selling crotchless underwear to Gold Rush era prostitutes.

Santa Barbara libraries understand the role they play in our cultural lives, hosting poetry readings, artistic displays, informational events and political discussions. It's an exquisite symbiosis and long may it continue.

Joan Tapper
The Unexpected?
You'll find it under L, for "library"

Santa Barbara-based Joan Tapper was a longtime magazine editor and continues to write frequently about people, places, and the arts. She is the author of eight books about travel, crafts, and popular history, founding editor of National Geographic Traveler *and editor of* Islands *magazine for thirteen years. Her many credits are detailed at www.joantapper.com.*

I RECENTLY met an artist who had devised a project that involved the Santa Barbara library. Intrigued by monographs she'd taken out on other artists she admired, she painted new jackets for those books, put them on the volumes—being careful to keep the text on the flaps and the identifying bar codes—and simply returned the books to the shelves, where other readers might stumble on her work by chance. It was a kind of stealth art project with an important element of surprise.

The enterprise made me laugh, but finding something unexpected is intrinsic to the library. You can experience that simply by walking past the shelves and picking out an intriguing-sounding title or inspecting the volume next to the one you've been looking for and taking it home to find a literary gem.

The whole evolution of the library in my lifetime has been something of a surprise. How far things have come from the days when I watched the librarian hand-stamp the book's due date to today, when I can check my choices out by myself with a touch-screen computer. I do rather miss the tactile experience of fingering the index cards in the wooden catalog, but oh, how convenient to search for a book on my laptop at home, get the needed information, and either locate it on the shelf or have it waiting for me.

Silence has always been golden among the bookshelves, and I still like to take a quiet seat in front of the fireplace in Santa Barbara's Central Library, but it's wonderful to see the place enlivened with tots at a children's reading hour or filled with tweens in the makerspace. The library has interpreted its mission in all kinds of imaginative ways, inviting the community to see art, watch movies, do crafts, listen to music, learn new skills, and, yes, be surprised.

I don't know the names of all the books that my artist friend "painted," so I'm not sure exactly where or when I'll come upon them. I'll simply look forward, as always, to finding the unexpected within the library walls.

Reading Room, 1932

Jervey Tervalon
How the Jefferson Branch Library
Made me a Novelist

After spending his boyhood in the Jefferson Park/Crenshaw area of Los Angeles, Tervalon attended UC Santa Barbara where he graduated with a B.A. in Literature. After earning a MFA from UC Irvine he has devoted himself to writing and teaching. He's had six novels, and a collection of stories and two anthologies and numerous short stories, essays, and articles published. He is the literary director and founder of both Literature for Life and LitFest Pasadena.

I GREW up in the Jefferson Park neighborhood, a largely African American area in Los Angeles, though a rapidly disappearing Japan-American community still had a presence and influence there. Jefferson Park wasn't an impoverished community though there were those who didn't have much; and there were those who had beautiful houses and cars.

My family was smack in the middle—we had more than we needed to be happy, and what I needed to be happy were books and when I ran out of books at home I went to the library. I spent my time at the Jefferson Branch library discovering Andre Norton, Isaac Asimov and Los Angeles's own Ray Bradbury. When the head librarian, a light skinned African American woman, suggested I enter the black history contest they were offering I demurred until she told me that the contest offered a ten dollar prize. Besides books my passions were comic books and hamburgers. The promise of ten dollars was tempting enough for me to even study.

I discovered African American History because I wanted those ten dollars and I whipped through the work and profiles of writers such a Gwendolyn Brooks, Ralph Ellison and Ishmael Reed to get it. I read about the Harlem Renaissance and the black consciousness movement; I became an elementary school expert and I won the contest and the dollars! It didn't take long for the writing bug to bite. Soon, I was writing stories in my head and then they found their way onto the page. I started to win writing contests and had my first poem published in *Scholastic* magazine when I was in junior high. Much later it was a great honor to find *Understand This*, my first novel, at the Jefferson Branch Library just as it was to see my novel *All the Trouble You Need*, set in Santa Barbara, at the Santa Barbara Public Library on Anapamu.

I love libraries and I support them with the passion of a young boy burning to get to the library to lose himself in books.

Jinny Webber
Serendipity in the Stacks

A professor emerita of English from Santa Barbara City College, with a PhD in Religious Studies from UC Santa Barbara, Webber has written plays and historical fiction. Her novel Dark Venus *features Amelia Bassano Lanyer (the spelling used today). For more information about the author and her works visit www.jinnywebber.com.*

LIBRARIES HAVE been places of magical potential since I was a child, a source of delightful surprises. For magic to work one must be receptive, and nowhere am I more so than among stacks of long-ago purchased and much-thumbed volumes.

Once upon a time we entered the downtown Santa Barbara library through the grand door under sculptures of Plato and Aristotle, near the corner of Anacapa Street. I thought of it as the door to enchantment: who knew what treasure would come into my hands?

One memorable day some 30 years ago, that was *Sex and Society in Shakespeare's Age:* Simon Forman the Astrologer, by A. L. Rowse. An interest in that era had drawn me to the literature stacks, and with the combination of "Sex" and "Shakespeare," the book jumped into my hands. I had no idea who Simon Forman was, beyond being the astrologer of the title, but it turns out he was a contemporary of William Shakespeare who kept a notorious diary of women who consulted him. My library card allowed me to take the book home, which eventually I did, but that aimless Sunday afternoon I carried Rowse's study to an unoccupied table and began reading. There I stayed till closing time.

What caught my attention was a minor character in Forman's story: a woman called Emilia Bassano Lanier, whom, remarkably, Rowse identifies as the Dark Lady of Shakespeare's sonnets! Forman has nothing good to say about her, characterizing her as a tease and a harlot. What caught my imagination was that she wrote a book of poetry herself. That discovery introduced me to a woman I'd never heard of who's figured in my writing and study ever since.

What I remember from that extraordinary autumn afternoon is the sense of excitement I felt reading *Sex and Society*, the unforeseen inspiration one finds in the library.

Today the entrance is a convenient wide corridor, with the art in the Faulkner Gallery temptingly to one side. The handsomely remodeled library has lost none of its enchantment. When going in search of one book—for example a travel guide—adjoining shelves offer unexpected nonfiction works set in that destination. Books arranged face-out offer surprise treats. And among the shelves of books on CD we can find forgotten or previously unknown novelists who become new favorites to keep us company behind the wheel.

This is one of the precious gifts our library offers: the randomness of discovery.

No algorithm could have predicted *Sex and Society* for me, nor even that, published in 1974, it existed; so too with the charming *House on Corfu* by Emma Tennant or an audiobook revisiting Dickens' *A Tale of Two Cities* or introducing B.A. Shapiro's novels about art. *Unsought*; they've enriched my life. Algorithm-driven recommendations are limited by what's currently available and endorsed: "since you liked X, you're sure to like Y."

Libraries, however, hold riches for our pleasure and enlightenment, books we'd never imagine we would be interested in until they jump into our hands. Serendipity and magic!

Paul Willis
Library

A professor of English at Westmont College and a former poet laureate of Santa Barbara, Willis was born in Fullerton, California, and grew up in Corvallis, Oregon. Paul earned a BA in biblical studies from Wheaton College in Illinois and a PhD in English from Washington State University. He has published four critically-acclaimed collections of poetry. More about the poet and his poetry can be found at www.pauljwillis.com.

FROM THE blank hush of my cubicle, I listen
to the library. Someone is coughing,
someone confiding plans to a phone.
In the cloistered cell next to mine,
the sweet sound of a page turning.

As a child, on summer afternoons,
I sometimes rode with my father
down the hill to his laboratory.
He would dissect his newts and frogs,
and I would walk under big leaf maples
and dark sequoias to a library of seven floors,
in the coolness of the basement and its many books,
a permanent prospect of borrowed joy.

Those were the days when people
did not think to talk in libraries,
and the air kept a silence I could taste
inside my spine. I would rejoin my father
at the appointed hour, profoundly pleased

with where I had been, carrying with me
sacred space, a way of dwelling.

After college, living at home a month or two,
I took a job in the public library
next to the Sixth Street railroad tracks,
where the clatter of trains and the quiet
of words negotiated a broken truce.

Shelving each book, I paused to consider
chance details about the author, a rundown
on the plot. Then I might see how
the first chapter began, and how the second.
I am there in the aisle when the locomotive
thrums down the street, its whistle calling
to get on with the real work,
the book still resting in my hands,
the hopeless pleasure of chapter three.

Jeff Wing
The Bewildered Public Library

After working as a journalist for the Arizona Republic, *Wing moved to Santa Barbara in 1986 as a singer in a band and shortly thereafter followed his heart to Holland. Returning to the city in 1988, he worked as a marketing writer at UCSB and as a journalist for the former nonprofit news website Mission & State. Since 2012 he has been chronicling the lesser-known face of the city in the State Street Scribe column for outlier news and arts journal the* Santa Barbara Sentinel.

THE PUBLIC Library: what are we to make of it? Its story is many-splendored and covers a crazy spectrum, from torch-bearing Mongol hordes to the Dewey Decimal System. The messages are mixed and frankly unhelpful. There seem to be two Public Libraries slugging it out for primacy in the public imagination. One of them is pure Cecil B. DeMille—the Ancient and Besieged Citadel of Progress Clad in a Mantle of Fire and Thronged by Hollering Extras®. The other, more familiar incarnation is today's Norman Rockwell Temple of Civic Quietude™.

The Bipolar Reading Room

Incredibly, there was a time when "cloud" meant a puff of buoyant steam, "tweeting" was what birds did at sunrise, and "document backup" meant a sighing scribe with forearm tendonitis and a bowl cut. In that day, the laborious process of producing copies often meant that a written bit of knowledge, once lost to the ages, was truly Lost to the Ages. Progress-averse barbarians and politically motivated ne'er-do-wells understood this, and regularly assaulted the overstuffed and grandly designed Public Library with real vigor.

To make matters worse, the Public Library in that time was, again, a Hollywood set designer's fever dream; gigantic, lavishly ornamented, with a reading room the size of a NASA hangar. Outside could be seen exactingly landscaped gardens, sparkling fountains, and angry mobs charging around and yelling. These structurally grandiose loudmouths practically invited attack. And they were attacked without mercy through the turbulent centuries. The libraries of Antioch, Carthage, Banu Ammar, and Constantinople, the wholly destroyed written record of the conquered Mayans, the looting of the Madrassah Library at Granada—the list goes on and on. The tactical trashing of irreplaceable texts was a commonplace once upon a time, and there have been many such bookish Final Stands throughout history, armed citizens beating back attackers bent on destruction.

Today's Whispering Institution

The Other Library, the one not consumed by fire, is your natty little downtown symbol of steadfastness and calm and quietude, its lone sentry a lady in cat glasses. Her hair is pinned up with a #2 pencil, and she is pressing a remonstrative finger to her lips.

"Ssshhh!"

No Barbarians here, and if there are they'd better maraud in a whisper or they will be given the bum's rush by a stern-faced Head Librarian. Contrary to certain Rock 'n' Roll interpretations, the Head Librarian typically wears a sensible cardigan and slacks, or a modest printskirt and practical shoes. This dedicated sentinel is only rarely seen gyrating ecstatically among the stacks. Very rarely, let's say.

This is today's Pubic Library: a buttoned-down civic totem. It features inevitably in your fourth grader's social studies "My Town" diorama, the hastily-scissored, asymmetric cardboard profile adorably glued alongside that of the Bank and the Post Office, the School, and the Fire Station; the Butcher, the Baker, the Candlestick Maker. The contemporary Public Library is demure and even bashful compared to her ancient and politically tormented ancestor, and is to the village square what the laundry room is to the family home: necessary and unglamorous—a workaday civic appurtenance that nevertheless completes and exults the community.

We've imagined the ancient defender, the citizen-swordsman lit by terrible fires, wounded, crying out, spending his last dregs of life and strength to protect his city's civilization-anchoring library. Imagine, too, his heir some centuries later. He is slumped in a comfy chair and pleasantly flipping through a coffee-table book on the subject of The Art Deco Bow Tie. The modern library's purring, climate-controlled reading room enfolds and embraces, is the very picture of a clean, well-lighted refuge. There is fire, yes. It is the reflux caused by our library patron's recently quaffed decaf soy latte with an extra shot. And cream.

Take Up Your Book

And here's that full circle. Yeah, the Public Library; a traditional emblem of order and reason. The besieged Citadel and the Temple of Quietude are one. The annoyingly alliterative might even describe the Public Library as a Bipolar Bastion of Balzacian Beauty—its nutty history fueled by the combustible Human Comedy itself: the touching headlong stumble of our earnest race. From ancient attack magnet to downtown gathering place of whispered repose, the Public Library is what we wish it to be, and this is not just a rhetorical nicety. At this writing, the cruelly named Smart Device is completing its ubiquitous roll-out, the Distractosphere's endless parade of flapdoodle supplanting both reading and interiority. The Public Library is once again assuming the role of Barbarian catnip. The attackers are hefting their spiky clubs and, when not absently scrolling pictures of squirrels on water skis, preparing for a renewed assault.

So here's the advice part—plant your feet at about shoulder width, take up your broadsword and be careful not to spring the binding. You don't need to swing it at the advancing enemy this time. You just need to turn its pages, drink in the language. We'll get through this. We always do.

Josef Woodard
My Life in the Library . . .
or Confessions of a Library Geek

Josef Woodard is a long-time, Santa Barbara-raised arts journalist/critic, a contributor to the Santa Barbara Independent, Santa Barbara News-Press, The Los Angeles Times, DownBeat, Rolling Stone, Entertainment Weekly, Opera Now, *and many other publications. He has published two books, on jazz heroes Charles Lloyd and Charlie Haden, for Silman-James Press.*

I WAS a teenage biliotequephile. Pre-teen, even.

Long before I grew to appreciate with an ever-expanding intensity, the profound virtues of our libraries—pragmatic and symbolic—and understand their value as repositories of wisdom and info, as beacons of civility and public gathering points, I just knew them as magical hang zones with potential for discovery. That value system is global and hyper-local, given the strengths of Santa Barbara Public Library System with its many fine branches in a constellation around the warming and historically rich epicenter of the Central Library.

I know. I've been there, done that, still doing that until the mortal doing's done. For decades, I have worked/written in them regularly, and still do. The Central Library lords over the rest, but a work visit to Montecito, Carpinteria, Goleta, Solvang, and others can also be rewarding and productive.

But this library-love dates back decades. As a six-year-old already being lured into the world o' words, I remember becoming entranced by the Carpinteria Library and its incentivized summer reading program. More importantly, as a 13-year-old with a deepening, near-religious devotion to music of all stripes, I remember being magnetized by not only books, but the Central Library's healthy collection of LPs, and discovering Miles Davis' *Nefertiti* (an acoustic gem, of a different kind than the electric voodoo Miles I had already heard on *Bitches Brew* and *In a Silent Way*).

248

Life beyond the commercial, pop-cultural, or established educational agendas of info-and-values distribution systems can be found at the library, sometimes in the form of accidental discoveries. My *Nefertiti* moment, for instance, was a little epiphany, which I see as the real spark for a lifelong engagement with jazz, almost as reason for being, not to mention a source of work/income as a journalist-critic.

Years later, my passion and obsession for libraries has clung to me like an addiction I have no interest in shedding. In my travels (often on assignment to cover jazz festivals around the world, for *DownBeat* magazine and other publications—a jazz obsession more or less born in the Santa Barbara Central Library), I make a point of finding the main library in a city. Many of these destinations are emblazoned in my memory and natural GPS list, with special fondness going to the impressive, sanctuary-like libraries in Montreal, Copenhagen (the "black diamond," perched on the canal), an especially warming spirit of the library in Helsinki, and—just last summer—coming across a fabulous, architecturally stylish new library in Aarhus, Denmark.

In America, the New York Public Library is something of a national sanctuary, of course, but California boasts many a fine example of the form—the vast structure of the LA Public Library, the comforting antiquity of Pasadena, and San Francisco's looming haven on Market. Up north, a visit to Seattle is incomplete without a stop at the post-modern majesty of that city's relatively new library.

I may be biased by nostalgia and other civic pride, but also I submit that the SB Central Library is a prized model of an American library, of the mid-size city category, and worthy of a pilgrimage for tourists in the area—including the flocks of visitors stopping at the grand Courthouse across the street. Radical changes have occurred here in recent years, including a dazzling new children's library downstairs and, for better or worse (jury's still out in my case), a shift from maximum book shelves to much more open space and computer-centric resources around the compound. For history's sake, the murals by Channing Peake and Howard Warshaw, dating back to the '50s, still grace the entrance from the lobby, and the Faulkner Gallery's schedule of events, exhibitions, concerts and meetings still serves as a community gathering place.

Personally, my full-circle experience came about within the last year-and-change, when my own books were picked up by the library where a fair share of my word-brain development took place.

In an age when basic necessities of modern life and hallmarks of civilization are being challenged, and libraries are no doubt in line for some governmental battering, we mustn't take for granted the sanctity of the library, as concept and reality—in the known world, and on Anapamu Street.

See you at a library branch near you. I'll be the harried character, probably under deadline, with head buried in laptop, occasionally coming up for air, water and an admiring stroll around the place.

Chryss Yost
Mind Striving to Be Library

Since 1997, Yost's poems have appeared in selected poetry anthologies, jour-nals and magazines. She has edited a number of poetry books, including California Poetry: From the Gold Rush to the Present, *with Dana Gioia and Jack Hicks. She served as Santa Barbara Poet Laureate from 2013-2015. She is the co-editor of Gunpowder Press and founder of the Shoreline Voices Project. Her first full-length book,* Mouth & Fruit, *was published in 2014. For more information, visit www.chryssyost.net.*

When I architect a space
for scattered thoughts,
I envision shelves
like these, parallel and high.

I categorize my selves,
my confusions, my hungers,
and sort them
by numerical ritual.

Oh, fierce ambition,
here is a space for you,
and fury, and history.
All thought of. Tended.

Covers and spines align.
From the wet maze of brain,
ordered spaces.
Chaos, converted.

Church of pages,
behold your congregants:
you who hold all
our wisdom
make sense of us.

Afterword
Katie Szopa
President, Friends of the Santa Barbara Public Library

ON BEHALF of the Friends of the Santa Barbara Public Library, I would like to extend my greatest thanks and appreciation to fellow Friends of the Library board member Steve Gilbar who conceptualized this book idea, made the connections, gathered the pieces. and produced this touching anthology of library stories. Complementing his work is Anna Lafferty, another board member, whose expertise in book design gave this anthology the artistic and professional look it deserved.

I am honored to be part of a board that cares so deeply about their local library and to be a card-carrying member of a library whose staff cares so deeply about their patrons. When I reflect on all the hours I have spent in a library since I was a wee one, I am reminded that whatever mood I entered the library in, I left in a happier and more curious state, armed with new information about the world! I know my kids feel the same way today when we leave the Central Library, and I hope that our community will always support this great institution.

Acknowledgments

"The Public Library" used by permission of the Babel estate. From *The Collected Stories of Isaac Babel*, translated by Peter Constantine (W.W. Norton, 2002) Copyright 2002 Nathalie Babel. Translation copyright 2002 Peter Constantine. All rights reserved.

"Exchange" reprinted by permission of Ray Bradbury Literary Works LLC and Don Congdon Associates, Inc. From *Quicker Than the Eye* (Avon Books, 1996) (c) 1996 by Ray Bradbury.

"Why Our Future Depends on Libraries" from "Why Our Future Depends on Libraries, Reading and Daydreaming: The Reading Agency Lecture, 2013" (c) copyright 2013 by Neil Gaiman. First published on Reading Agency.org.uk.

Excerpt(s) from LIFE SENTENCES: LITERARY JUDGMENTS AND ACCOUNTS by William H. Gass, copyright © 2012 by William H. Gass. Used by permission of Alfred A. Knopf, an imprint of the Knopf Doubleday Publishing Group, a division of Penguin Random House LLC. All rights reserved.

"A Poem for My Librarian, Mrs. Long" by Nikki Giovanni, from *Acolytes* (2007), William Morrow. (c) Nikkki Giovanni. Used by permission of author.

"Library in Paradise" by Eva Hoffman, from *Lost in Translation: A Life in a New Language*. Penguin Books (c) by Eva Hoffman, 1989. Used by permission of the author.

"My Libraries" by Ursula K. Leguin. Copyright (c) by Ursula K. LeGuin. First appeared in *The Wave in the Mind: Talks and Essays on the Writer, the Reader, and the Imagination*, published by Shambhala in 2004. Reprinted by permission of Curtis Brown, Ltd.

of Santa Barbara
PUBLIC LIBRARY

The Friends of the Santa Barbara Public Library is a non-profit organization dedicated to the growth and development of the Santa Barbara Public Library, ensuring free access to information and resources to all members of the community. It raises funds for materials, programs and services that would otherwise not be provided, and endeavors to preserve and strengthen the importance of our Library in the community as a vital, irreplaceable source of information, education and culture—thereby providing everyone with opportunities and resources for lifelong learning.

All Santa Barbarans who value our library are encouraged to join the Friends. For details on how, go to:

www.friends-sblibrary.org.

48755523R00150

Made in the USA
Columbia, SC
11 January 2019